W9-AGD-529

INFORMATION ECONOMY REPORT 2011

ICTs as an Enabler for Private Sector Development

DÉPÔT
DEPOSIT

UNITED NATIONS
New York and Geneva, 2011

NOTE

Within the UNCTAD Division on Technology and Logistics, the ICT Analysis Section carries out policy-oriented analytical work on the development implications of information and communication technologies (ICTs). It is responsible for the preparation of the *Information Economy Report*. The ICT Analysis Section promotes international dialogue on issues related to ICTs for development, and contributes to building developing countries' capacities to measure the information economy and to design and implement relevant policies and legal frameworks.

In this Report, the terms country/economy refer, as appropriate, to territories or areas. The designations employed and the presentation of the material do not imply the expression of any opinion whatsoever on the part of the Secretariat of the United Nations concerning the legal status of any country, territory, city or area or of its authorities, or concerning the delimitation of its frontiers or boundaries. In addition, the designations of country groups are intended solely for statistical or analytical convenience and do not necessarily express a judgement about the stage of development reached by a particular country or area in the development process. The major country groupings used in this Report follow the classification of the United Nations Statistical Office. These are:

Developed countries: the member countries of the Organization for Economic Cooperation and Development (OECD) (other than Mexico, the Republic of Korea and Turkey), plus the new European Union member countries that are not OECD members (Bulgaria, Cyprus, Latvia, Lithuania, Malta and Romania), plus Andorra, Israel, Liechtenstein, Monaco and San Marino. Countries with economies in transition: South-East Europe and the Commonwealth of Independent States. Developing economies: in general, all the economies that are not specified above. For statistical purposes, the data for China do not include those for Hong Kong Special Administrative Region (Hong Kong, China), Macao Special Administrative Region (Macao, China), or Taiwan Province of China.

Reference to companies and their activities should not be construed as an endorsement by UNCTAD of those companies or their activities.

The following symbols have been used in the tables:

Two dots (..) indicate that data are not available or are not separately reported. Rows in tables have been omitted in those cases where no data are available for any of the elements in the row;

A dash (–) indicates that the item is equal to zero or its value is negligible;

A blank in a table indicates that the item is not applicable, unless otherwise indicated;

A slash (/) between dates representing years, e.g. 1994/95, indicates a financial year;

Use of an en dash (–) between dates representing years, e.g. 1994–1995, signifies the full period involved, including the beginning and end years;

Reference to "dollars" ($) means United States dollars, unless otherwise indicated;

Annual rates of growth or change, unless otherwise stated, refer to annual compound rates;

Details and percentages in tables do not necessarily add up to the totals because of rounding.

The material contained in this study may be freely quoted with appropriate acknowledgement.

UNITED NATIONS PUBLICATION

UNCTAD/IER/2011

Sales No. E.11.II.D.6

ISSN 2075-4396

ISBN 978-92-1-112833-8

e-ISBN 978-92-1-055120-5

PREFACE

This year's *Information Economy Report* highlights the role of information and communication technologies (ICTs) in enabling private-sector development (PSD), and seeks to establish a bridge between ICT and PSD policymakers.

The United Nations attaches great importance to the role of a vibrant and socially responsible private sector in achieving sustainable development and the Millennium Development Goals. Private-sector development is essential for inclusive and equitable economic growth, and Member States are actively engaged in promoting enterprises capable of creating jobs, raising incomes and productivity, diversifying the economy and generating government revenue. Our challenge is to accelerate progress and ensure that our efforts reach the poorest and most vulnerable in particular.

The *Information Economy Report 2011* identifies four areas in which the ICT-PSD interface is especially promising: strengthening the private sector's role in extending ICT infrastructure and services; enhancing ICT use in enterprises; promoting the ICT sector itself; and making more efficient use of ICTs in various public interventions aimed at promoting PSD. Although some countries are already taking advantage of the close links between ICTs and PSD, much more can be done to make ICTs a powerful force for improving the competitiveness of the private sector.

These policy challenges should be addressed urgently. The information, analysis and recommendations in this report point the way towards fully exploiting the great potential of ICTs for private-sector development.

BAN Ki-moon
Secretary-General
United Nations

ACKNOWLEDGEMENTS

The *Information Economy Report 2011* was prepared by a team comprising Torbjörn Fredriksson (team leader), Cécile Barayre, Scarlett Fondeur Gil, Diana Korka, Rémi Lang, Thao Nguyen, Marta Pérez Cusó and Smita Barbattini, under the direct supervision of Mongi Hamdi and overall guidance by Anne Miroux.

The *Information Economy Report 2011* benefited from major substantive inputs provided by Christopher Foster, Michael Minges, Raja Mitra and Simon White.

Additional inputs were contributed by Tiziana Bonapace, Stephania Bonilla, Julia Burchell, Giuseppe Di Capua, Fulvia Farinelli, Richard L. Field, Frank Grozel, Dylan Higgins, Henriette Kolb, Martin Labbe, Reema Nanavaty, Ali Ndiwalana, Geoffroy Raymond, Michael Riggs, Roxanna Samii, and by various experts at the United Nations Economic Commission for Africa, the United Nations Economic and Social Commission for Asia and the Pacific, and the United Nations Conference on International Trade Law. A contribution by the research team of Professor You Jianxin at Tongji University, China, is also gratefully acknowledged.

Useful comments on various parts of the text were given by experts attending a regional seminar organized in Geneva in April 2011, including Angel González Sanz, Johan Hellström, Neo Matsau, Fiorina Mugione, Antti Piispanen, David Souter, Susan Teltscher and Stijn van der Krogt. Valuable comments were also received at various stages of the production of the report from Frédéric Bourassa, Ineke Buskens, Jillian Convey, Ben Cramer, Daniel Einfeld, Xavier Faz, Marije Geldolf, Richard Heeks, Renata Henriques, Claire Hunsaker, Dorothea Kleine, Mark Levy, Julius Okello, Pranav Prashad, Joni Simpson, Michael Tarazi and Tim Unwin.

UNCTAD is grateful for the sharing of data by national statistical offices, and for the responses received to UNCTAD's annual survey on the ICT sector and ICT usage by enterprises. The sharing of data for this report by Eurostat, ITU, Nokia, OECD and the World Bank is also highly appreciated.

The cover and other graphics were designed by Sophie Combette and Nathalie Loriot. Desktop publishing was carried out by Nathalie Loriot, and the Report was edited by Daniel Sanderson, Lucy Deleze-Black and Mike Gibson.

Financial support from the Government of Finland is gratefully acknowledged.

UNITED NATIONS CONFERENCE ON TRADE AND DEVELOPMENT

UNCTAD

INFORMATION ECONOMY REPORT 2011

ICTs as an Enabler for Private Sector Development

UNITED NATIONS

CONTENTS

Boxes

Tables

Box Tables

Figures

Annex tables

LIST OF ABBREVIATIONS

ADB	Asian Development Bank
AfDB	African Development Bank
AOPEB	Asociación de Organizaciones de Productores Ecológicos de Bolivia
APPM	average price per minute
ARPU	average revenue per user
ASYCUDA	Automated System for Customs Data
B2B	business-to-business
B2C	business-to-consumer
BASIS	Bangladeshi Software and Information Services Association
BDS	business development services
BoP	balance of payments
BPLS	Business Permit and Licence System
BPO	business process outsourcing
BSM	Business Sophistication Modelling
CELAC	Collecting and Exchange of Local Agricultural Content
CGAP	Consultative Group to Assist the Poor
CESO	Canadian Executive Service Organization
CIS	Commonwealth of Independent States
CNBV	Comisión Nacional Bancaria y de Valores
DCED	Donor Committee for Enterprise Development
DPI	United Nations Department of Public Information
EAC	East African Community
ECOWAS	Economic Community of West African States
ECX	Ethiopia Commodity Exchange
EDI	electronic data interchange
eGov4MD	e-Governance for Municipal Development
FAO	Food and Agricultural Organization of the United Nations
FATF	Financial Action Task Force
FOSS	free and open source software
GDP	gross domestic product
GenARDIS	Gender, Agriculture and Rural Development in the Information Society
GIZ	Gesellschaft für Internationale Zusammenarbeit
GNI	gross national income
GPRS	general packet radio service
GSB	Growing Small Businesses
GSMA	GSM Association
IADB	Inter-American Development Bank
ICIP	Inveneo Certified ICT Partner
ICT	information and communication technology
ICT4D	ICT for Development
IFAD	International Fund for Agricultural Development
IFC	International Finance Corporation
IICD	International Institute for Communication and Development
ILO	International Labour Organization
IMF	International Monetary Fund
IT	information technology
ITC	International Trade Centre UNCTAD/WTO
ITU	International Telecommunication Union

IVR   Interactive Voice Receiver
KACE   Kenya Agricultural Commodity Exchange
KADET   Kenya Agency for the Development of Enterprise and Technology
KPO   knowledge process outsourcing
KYC   know your customer
LAC   Latin America and the Caribbean
LDC   least developed country
MDG   Millennium Development Goal
MEST   Meltwater Entrepreneurial School of Technology
MFA   Ministry for Foreign Affairs (Finland)
MFI   microfinance institution
mLab   mobile applications laboratory
MNO   mobile network operator
MoU   minutes of use
MSEs   micro- and small enterprises
NGO   non-governmental organization
NICI   National Information and Communication Infrastructure
NZAID   New Zealand Aid Programme
OECD   Organization for Economic Cooperation and Development
OPPAZ   Organic Producers and Processors Association of Zambia
PC   personal computer
POS   point of sale
PSD   private sector development
R&D   research and development
RFID   radio frequency identification technology
RIA   Research ICT Africa
RPTS   Real Property Tax System
SaaS   Software as a Service
SACCOs   savings and cooperative credit organizations
SEWA   SEWA Self-Employed Women's Association
SMEs   small and medium-sized enterprises
SMEP   Small and Micro Enterprise Programme
SMS   short message service
SOE   state-owned enterprise
TNC   transnational corporation
UCC   Uganda Communications Commission
UNCITRAL   United Nations Commission on International Trade Law
UNCTAD   United Nations Conference on Trade and Development
UNDESA   United Nations Department of Economic and Social Affairs
UNDP   United Nations Development Programme
UNECA   United Nations Economic Commission for Africa
UNECLAC   United Nations Economic Commission for Latin America and the Caribbean
UNESCAP   United Nations Economic and Social Commission for Asia and the Pacific
UNIDO   United Nations Industrial Development Organization
UNWTO   World Tourism Organization
VAT   value added tax
VoIP   voice over Internet protocol
WOUGNET   Women of Uganda Network
WSIS   World Summit on the Information Society
WTO   World Trade Organization
ZNFU   Zambia National Farmers' Union

EXECUTIVE SUMMARY

The *Information Economy Report 2011* demonstrates that effective use of information and communication technologies (ICTs) in both the private and the public sector can significantly contribute to and accelerate progress in private sector development (PSD).

Governments and their development partners should take a holistic and comprehensive approach to leveraging ICTs in PSD, although a review of PSD strategies indicates that this is often not the practice. Similarly, donor strategies often refer to the use of ICTs in PSD in a peripheral manner only, if at all. On its own, new technology will have limited effects on PSD. However, when carefully integrated into policies and processes, ICTs can reduce business costs, promote transparent, rules-based systems, and improve communication between the public and private sector. Governments need to work with the private sector to create an investment climate and a business environment that encourage the use of ICTs within private firms as well as in government. The potential of ICTs can then be realized, through adequate infrastructure and skills, and a commitment by governments to making markets work effectively. In some areas, there is already considerable experience and evidence to guide policy initiatives. In other areas, where opportunities for ICTs to contribute to PSD have emerged only in the past few years (as in the case of mobile money services), more analysis and testing of different business models is needed to assess potential and identify best practices.

Enterprises face many challenges which reflect the need to make markets work better, to make internal management and production systems more efficient, to facilitate improved access to information, knowledge, financial services and other resources, and to make business environments more transparent and enabling. The effective use of ICTs can help to improve all of these areas and thereby pave the way for more enterprise creation and expansion. The *Information Economy Report 2011* identifies four facets of the ICT–PSD interface, which serve as a basis for its policy recommendations.

Firstly, the quality of the ICT infrastructure is an increasingly vital determinant of the overall investment climate of a country. Governments and their development partners need to ensure that the ICT infrastructure meets the needs of different kinds of enterprises, from micro- and small enterprises (MSEs) to larger, transnational corporations. Leveraging the opportunities created by mobile telephony and its related services and applications is particularly important for smaller enterprises in low-income countries. Mobile broadband will require more attention in the coming years as a new way for the private sector in developing countries to leverage the Internet. In order to speed up the roll-out of mobile broadband, Governments need to allocate spectrum, and license operators to provide the service. Indeed, at the end of 2010, some 50 developing and transition economies were yet to launch mobile broadband services.

Secondly, enterprises must be able to make the best use possible of ICTs, as they positively affect productivity in both large and small enterprises. Different kinds of ICTs help enterprises to manage their resources more efficiently, access the information needed for better business decision-making, reduce transaction costs, and enhance their ability to bring products and services to customers. Governments should play a key role in enhancing business use of ICTs in PSD by – for example – ensuring that relevant ICT tools and services are available and affordable, and providing a legal and regulatory framework that supports the uptake and productive use of ICTs.

Thirdly, supporting the ICT sector itself is important. The production of ICT goods and services is providing new opportunities for private firms to start up and grow, create jobs, and spur innovation, thereby contributing to overall economic growth. Governments can create an enabling framework for the ICT sector to expand by liberalizing the sector, enhancing competition in all segments, providing adequate regulations, increasing trust in the use of ICT services, providing training in ICT skills, nurturing ICT enterprises through incubation and by establishing technology parks, and using public procurement to create demand among local ICT enterprises.

Fourthly, Governments and other institutions can apply ICTs to make PSD interventions more effective – both in business environment reforms, and in the provision of business development, business information and financial services. ICTs can reduce the cost of delivering such services, extend their reach, and improve the functioning of markets. The *Information Economy Report 2011* gives some examples: agricultural extension services, providing business development training material online, establishing business helplines, crowd-sourcing to detect and fight pests and diseases, and ICT-related initiatives aimed at helping small-scale producers to meet certification standards and acquire the skills needed to boost exports. To be successful, ICT–PSD solutions need to factor in both user needs (in terms of what information and other inputs are needed), and possible constraints (e.g. illiteracy, aversion to using new tools, scarce electricity, and unaffordable user charges and prices). Involving the private sector in designing and providing training and advisory services can help ensure that the services offered are demand-driven. At the same time, more research and rigorous impact assessments are needed in order to identify best practices in this area.

The introduction of new mobile money systems is one of the most promising opportunities for leveraging ICTs for PSD. Mobile money systems have provided increased access to finance for MSEs, which have traditionally had greater difficulty than larger enterprises in benefiting from existing financial services. The systems allow for real-time transfer and receipt of small amounts of funds at low cost, and can also reduce the costs of processing and administering small loans, thereby alleviating a significant disincentive for lenders to extend credit to micro- and small enterprises. At the same time, they raise important policy issues and challenges for Governments, and deserve attention from policymakers and the research community in order to ensure positive outcomes.

It is still too soon to fully assess the impact of mobile money solutions on access by MSEs to financial services. Uptake will accelerate as more enterprises become active users of the systems, and when services are well adapted to their needs. Key policy areas requiring consideration are the institutional and regulatory framework, user issues, crime and security considerations, and infrastructure. Many Governments will have to pioneer new legislation and regulations, and the international community should actively support the development of sound regulatory frameworks and relevant institutions, as well as supporting the exchange of practice and expertise.

Another distinct area of PSD that can be better addressed by the use of ICTs is women's entrepreneurship. While ICTs do little to redress underlying societal structures and economic systems that hamper opportunities for women entrepreneurs, they may be used to overcome some of the challenges that women face, including access to finance, limited skills and training, lack of time due to family commitments, and limited physical mobility. Initiatives and training programmes must be developed bearing in mind these constraints, and with the active participation of the women entrepreneurs that they are to assist.

Finally, the *Information Economy Report 2011* makes a series of policy recommendations:

(a) *Promote affordable access to relevant ICTs*, taking into consideration what improvements in the ICT infrastructure are required to support private sector activities.

(b) *Enhance investment in, and the use of ICTs by, private firms* to reduce the costs of business transactions, improve business management, and enhance the capacity to get goods and services to the market.

(c) *Include ICT modules in business skills training programmes.* Such training may range from providing advice on using mobile phones as a business tool to more advanced training in using technologies and applications to improve operational management, customer relationship management or resource planning.

(d) *Adopt regulatory frameworks that help to enhance confidence in the use of new technology or new applications of known technology.* In many countries, adequate legal and regulatory frameworks are still needed in order to fully realize the potential of electronic transactions.

(e) *Facilitate the expansion of the ICT sector.* Governments should consider how best to tap into new opportunities presented by the production of ICT goods and services. Governments could facilitate ICT growth and employment creation through policy that is aimed at improving the availability of skills, stimulating demand for ICT uptake among local firms, providing appropriate ICT infrastructure and regulatory frameworks, promoting and clustering entrepreneurship and innovations through incubation and ICT parks, and using government procurement.

(f) *Make ICT use an integral part of business environment reforms.* When applied effectively, ICT-based solutions have reduced the time and cost of registering companies and obtaining licences, and have increased government revenue and transparency. A simplified company registration process may also encourage informal enterprises to formalize – another key PSD objective. ICTs have been able to connect formal and informal businesses to market opportunities, and it should also be possible to connect them to government programmes and services.

(g) *Leverage different ICT tools in the delivery of business development and information services.* Better use of ICTs could extend the reach of BDS to new and growing enterprises, by overcoming the tyranny of distance and reducing the cost of service delivery.

(h) *Leverage mobile money services to create more inclusive financial markets.* Mobile money services hold great promise in reducing the costs of providing financial services, especially to MSEs. The international community should support the development of regulatory frameworks and institutions.

(i) *Recognize the ICT potential in existing or new initiatives to support women entrepreneurs.* More programme and policy attention should be given to the use of ICTs in addressing the specific needs of women entrepreneurs.

(j) *Better reflect ICTs in donor PSD strategies.* Strategies should address the ICT–PSD interface in a comprehensive way and explicitly recognize the importance of multi-level use of ICTs.

(k) *Develop guidelines for donors.* In collaboration with UNCTAD and other relevant organizations, the Donor Committee for Enterprise Development could develop guidelines for donor and development agencies, and their programmatic partners, on how to best integrate ICTs into PSD strategies. Such guidelines would help to establish a bridge between donor assistance related to PSD and donor assistance related to ICT for development.

(l) *Make interventions more demand-driven, and leverage partnerships.* To enhance ICTs' contribution to PSD, policies must be designed and implemented with a solid understanding of the specific needs and situation of diverse enterprises. The input and engagement of enterprises in programme design and implementation should be sought. Such a demand-driven approach will require effective

partnerships between Governments, donors, the private sector and civil society.

(m) *Devote adequate resources to the measurement of ICT use and impact assessments.* There is an absence of systematic, evidence-based impact evaluation regarding the use of ICTs to promote PSD, resulting in reliance on anecdotal evidence. There is a need for reliable and internationally comparable statistics related to both enterprise and government use of ICTs, and for more comprehensive project and policy evaluations based on empirical evidence conducted through independent research.

A vibrant private sector contributes to building the foundations in an economy to generate the resources needed to address the Millennium Development Goals. It is time for Governments and their development partners to start integrating ICT solutions in a systematic and comprehensive way when designing and implementing interventions aimed at nurturing the private sector. It is hoped that the analysis and recommendations presented in the *Information Economy Report 2011* will provide valuable input into this process.

Supachai Panitchpakdi
Secretary-General, UNCTAD

PRIVATE SECTOR DEVELOPMENT AND THE ROLE OF ICTs

1

There is growing potential for information and communication technologies (ICTs) to contribute to the social and economic progress of developing countries. The *Information Economy Report 2010* showed how ICT use by micro- and small enterprises (MSEs) has often improved not only business performance but also livelihoods (UNCTAD, 2010). Thanks to the mobile revolution, many entrepreneurs in developing countries now have – for the first time – a real possibility of benefiting from ICTs in their activities, with enhanced productivity as a result. By improving communication along the value chain, both domestically and internationally, the application of relevant ICTs can greatly enhance the competitiveness of the enterprise sector as a whole.

At the same time, in their efforts towards promoting an expansion and upgrading of the private sector, Governments and their various partners are far from taking full advantage of the opportunities that are emerging in the new ICT landscape. This is evident from the relatively limited attention that has been given to ICTs in strategies aimed at promoting private sector development (PSD). Against this background, the *Information Economy Report 2011* is devoted to exploring areas in which a more effective use of ICTs – by different stakeholders – would facilitate the creation of new and expanding enterprises in developing countries.

This first chapter introduces the relevant issues. It emphasizes the importance of developing the private sector, identifies the various facets of the ICT–PSD interface, and reviews the state of play with regard to how the ICT dimension is captured in current PSD strategies. The chapter concludes with a roadmap to the rest of the Report.

A. DEVELOPING THE PRIVATE SECTOR – A KEY DEVELOPMENT OBJECTIVE

> *A dynamic, broadly based, well-functioning and socially responsible private sector is a valuable instrument for increasing investment and trade, employment and innovation, thereby generating economic growth and eradicating poverty and serving as an engine for industrialization and structural transformation. The private sector therefore is a key to sustained, inclusive and equitable economic growth and sustainable development in LDCs.*
>
> Programme of Action for the Least Developed Countries for the Decade 2011–2020, para. 54

1. Why an expanding private sector matters

The private sector (defined in box I.1) plays a central role in achieving sustained and equitable economic growth and development. The countries that have been the most successful in creating wealth and reducing poverty are those that have managed to sustain high economic growth over prolonged periods, typically by increasing agricultural productivity and then by dynamic growth of modern industry and services sectors.[1] The creation of private sector jobs is both a source of income – and often empowerment – for entrepreneurs as well as for workers, and a source of taxation for Governments. Thus, a vibrant private sector also contributes to building the foundation in an economy to generate the resources needed to finance investments in social welfare.

Most developing countries, as well as their development partners, recognize the relevance of developing the private sector. In Africa, for example, the private sector is seen as the most important agent for the realization of growth objectives and poverty reduction targets (UNECA, 2009: 2). For some time now, support for PSD has been an important ingredient in development and donor agencies' strategies to boost economic growth and achieve a "more equitable diffusion of the benefits of growth" (OECD, 1995: 6). Indeed, development of the private sector is essential for the attainment of most of the Millennium Development Goals (MDGs).

Foreign and domestic flows of private investment complement other sources of financing for development, including official development assistance and remittances, and boost the capacity of developing economies to grow and create new productive and decent work opportunities and to reduce poverty (DPI, 2003). Private investment in infrastructure projects can relieve pressure on public budgets and enable Governments to redirect more resources to social spending. It can also improve the delivery efficiency of essential services and extend these to the poor (ADB, 2000; IADB et al., 2004; UNECA, 2009). In addition, PSD can empower poor people by providing them with services and consumer products, increasing choices and reducing prices (UNDP, 2004).

2. Barriers to enterprise creation and expansion

Various internal and external factors impede the competitiveness and profitability of private enterprises in developing countries. Some of the main *internal* factors are the limited levels of organizational and financial management skill, business experience, financial resources, and technical or production skill. Many MSEs also face serious limitations in their access to information and knowledge, although their needs vary considerably, between different kinds of enterprises and depending on their market orientation (UNCTAD, 2010).

For *subsistence-based enterprises* (i.e. those that provide the most direct livelihood support for the poor), accessing client markets (especially distant markets) presents a particular challenge, requiring interaction with market intermediaries. Enterprises serving local markets often rely on information delivered informally through local networks of communication. Lack of timeliness of information is a serious failure of the information delivery system currently used, and a significant aspect of the vulnerability of subsistence-based enterprises to changes in the surrounding environment (Duncombe and Heeks, 2002). The quantity and range of information received through traditional channels is an issue too, with barriers including literacy and language. Weaknesses in informal information-sourcing should similarly be recognized.[2]

Growth-oriented enterprises frequently seek to extend their market reach. Their sectoral value chains often reach beyond the local area to main centres of

Box I.1. Defining the private sector

The *Information Economy Report 2011* uses the term "private sector" to refer to the sector of the economy that is privately owned, either by an individual or by a group of individuals, in any sector, including agriculture. This includes micro-, small, medium-sized and large enterprises, as well as transnational corporations (TNCs). It encompasses unregistered firms, family-owned enterprises, sole proprietors, incorporated companies, and cooperatives. Private enterprises are the entities that are used to mobilize available resources and to direct them towards the provision of the goods and services that the market demands.

The composition of the private sector varies greatly across countries. This Report focuses on MSEs, which are often the main focus of Governments' PSD strategies. At the same time, much interaction takes place between companies of different sizes and from different sectors. Symbiotic relationships between small and large enterprises may appear, in industries ranging from subsistence farming to sophisticated economic activities such as research and development (R&D) in high-technology areas. In describing the full range of activities that are required to bring a good or service from its initial conception to its end use, the value chain concept provides a useful basis for systematic analysis of the linkages and interactions required for an enterprise to operate and trade in a market (Gereffi, 1999; Humphrey, 2003; Porter, 1985).

Source: UNCTAD.

population, and sometimes across national boundaries. A higher degree of integration of enterprises into market systems requires more formalization of information systems (Gelb et al., 2009; Duncombe and Molla, 2009; Murphy, 2002). Particular characteristics of the transition towards greater formalization include (a) demand for an increased volume and complexity of information, as the value of information is better recognized; (b) reduced information needs gaps, as internal capacity to meet information needs rises; and (c) greater emphasis on external communication.

Linking into global value chains is one potential way for enterprises in developing countries to access high-volume markets for a broad range of primary and manufactured products. But in order to participate in such value chains, enterprises need to have the capacity to handle large-scale production for exports, and they need to conform with strict quality standards (UNCTAD, 2007). This often requires a far higher degree of formalization of information systems (Parikh et al., 2007). Those who lack the capacity and opportunity to comply tend to be marginalized and excluded from global value chains (Kaplinsky and Morris, 2001; McCormick, 1999).

There are also various *external* factors that need to be addressed in order to help MSEs become more productive and competitive. As noted in the Programme of Action for the Least Developed Countries for the Decade 2011–2020 (para. 55): "structural constraints, particularly infrastructural bottlenecks, and institutional constraints have limited the growth of the private sector". External limitations include the markets in which MSEs operate, and the policies, laws and regulations that Governments put in place to regulate and promote business activities, as well as the organizational arrangements, skills availability and quality of infrastructure that surround the enterprise. Thus, an "enabling" external environment is an important element in the promotion of MSEs, as well as other enterprises. The cost of a poor business environment can amount to over 25 per cent of sales, or more than three times what firms pay in taxes (World Bank, 2004). In addition, barriers to competition caused by poor policies, laws and regulations have been found to benefit some firms, while denying opportunities and increasing costs to others, as well as to consumers. These barriers weaken incentives for private firms to innovate and improve their productivity.[3]

Taken together, internal and external constraints often place smaller firms at a disadvantage vis-à-vis larger enterprises, in terms of accessing critical input, reaching out to markets, and coping with government regulations. The World Bank has identified barriers that impact on existing enterprise activities, based on interviews with firms of different sizes from around the world. The most significant constraints were found to be related to tax rates, corruption and electricity (fig. I.1). Depending on the situation, some barriers and constraints are more or less pronounced. Boxes I.2 and I.3 provide insights into the experiences from Latin America and Africa, respectively.

Figure I.1.   Enterprises identifying various factors as major constraint, world average, 2010 (as percentages)

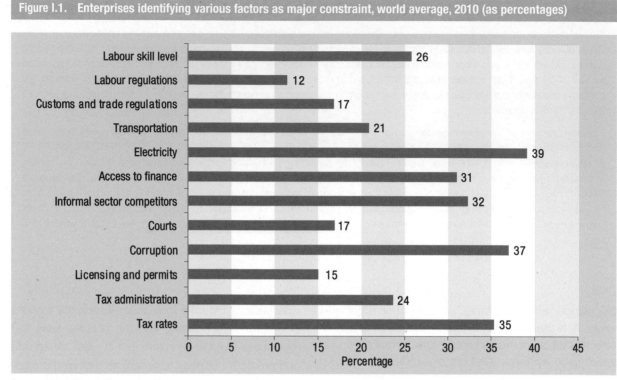

Source: World Bank Enterprise Surveys.

Box I.2.   Factors explaining low productivity in Latin America and the Caribbean

As part of the process of developing a new strategy for the promotion of PSD, the Inter-American Development Bank (IADB) has sought to identify the key barriers to increased productivity among private enterprises in Latin America and the Caribbean (LAC). Some of the most important barriers are highlighted below.

Among the *barriers that are facing the private sector and are impeding investment, expansion of firms, job creation and sustainable growth*, the IADB has highlighted (a) basic infrastructure deficits; (b) institutional failures, such as unclear rules, poorly defined property rights, unreliable enforcement mechanisms and inequitable tax and customs regimes; and (c) market failures related to financing gaps and information asymmetries.

Limited access to financial services and capital markets was another area of concern. In many LAC countries, finance is viewed as a binding constraint on firms' growth and productivity improvements. The situation is the most precarious for micro-enterprises, of which fewer than 8 per cent have access to credit from financial institutions.

High levels of informality also reduce productivity. This is a persistent feature in the region. Informality limits access to productivity-enhancing services, particularly finance and access to legal recourse. Also, the activities of informal firms sometimes undercut the profitability of enterprises in the formal sector.

Limited innovation activity similarly keeps productivity growth low (Griliches, 1979). In terms of adoption of new ICTs, LAC enterprises tend to lag behind other regions for several reasons, including limited quality and coverage of telecommunications infrastructure, regulatory issues that raise connectivity costs, a lack of ICT literacy, and the absence of financial instruments to make technology adoption attractive to smaller firms.

Other barriers noted include low skill levels on the part of workers and management, inadequate infrastructure for competitiveness and trade (especially with regard to transport and electricity), and high volatility and risk.

Source: IADB (2011a).

Box I.3. Barriers to private sector development in Africa

Across the African continent, the private sector is seen as the most important agent of growth, and hence of poverty reduction. A review undertaken by the United Nations Economic Commission for Africa (UNECA) has concluded that African firms face various external challenges in areas such as starting a business, getting the requisite licences, legal regimes for hiring and firing workers, registering property, obtaining credit, protecting investments and enforcing contracts.

The top constraint for the African continent as a whole was related to *access to finance*. This reflects high demand from lenders for collateral, the perceived high risk of loan default, and high transaction costs. African managers ranked *corruption* as the second most serious problem, meaning that enhanced transparency in the regulatory environment would be a welcome improvement.

Related to this, *inefficient government bureaucracy* was the third most cited problem. This translates into more time consumed and higher costs for starting up a business, registering property, or expanding an already existing activity. In sub-Saharan Africa, complying with tax laws takes 321 hours per year on average, but it may take up to 1,400 hours in some countries. In the case of customs management, Africa performs weakly. For instance, customs clearance time ranges from 1 day in Ethiopia to 25 days in Nigeria, with an average for the continent of 12.7 days. *Inadequate supply of infrastructure* was the fourth constraint identified. While major private sector investments in telecommunications infrastructure have contributed greatly to improving the situation, remaining weaknesses in this area are holding back Africa's development.

Thus, priority interventions were primarily called for within the financial markets, in institutional transformation (translated into fighting corruption and bureaucracy), and for the improvement of infrastructure – including with regard to ICTs.

Source: UNECA (2009).

3. Promoting private sector development

Private sector development aims to increase the number of private enterprises that start up, survive, upgrade and expand. This can be achieved by addressing the internal and external constraints that affect enterprises. Improvements in these areas allow private enterprises to become more productive and more competitive, and, as a result, more profitable – which can lead to greater levels of investment.

PSD typically takes a broad approach to the achievement of national development goals, but within this broad approach, the role of MSEs requires specific attention, not least to reach the poor and to reduce poverty (Chen, 2005).[4] Moreover, MSEs often account for up to 99 per cent of all enterprises in low-income countries. Whereas they may enjoy certain advantages compared with larger firms (e.g. in terms of flexibility), they also face particular challenges, with potential negative effects on their productivity and their ability to survive and compete (UNCTAD, 2005b). Compared with large enterprises, they have fewer internal resources, and they often have to operate in volatile niche markets.

Micro-enterprises, as well as small and medium-sized enterprises (SMEs), are often given particular attention within PSD work. Many developing countries are familiar with the problem of the "missing middle", where a high number of informal sector micro-enterprises are found alongside a few large firms, creating a gap left by the absence of formal SMEs (UNCTAD, 2006b).[5] The contribution of the informal sector to gross domestic product (GDP) is estimated at 30 per cent in Latin America, 31 per cent in Asia, and 64 per cent in sub-Saharan Africa (OECD, 2009).

It is similarly important to recognize the gender dimension of PSD, not least to "make better use of untapped economic potential".[6] While women are active in the private enterprise sector in most developing economies, their representation in the MSE sector and in the informal sector is, in general, disproportionately high. Many women support themselves and their families through the income they receive from their entrepreneurial activities, making supporting women's entrepreneurship important to family well-being (Kantor, 2001). Moreover, some constraints on the growth of MSEs "do not affect men's and women's businesses in the same way, since men-owned and women-owned businesses do not operate in the same sectors or locations, or have equal access, control, and use of the same resources and marketing outlets" (Esim 2001: 9; see also Chapter V).

Various kinds of intervention can be used to promote PSD in developing economies. Governments and their development partners – including civil society and business organizations, and international donor and development agencies – can support the development of the private sector. PSD promotion can be organized into three levels: macro-, meso- and micro-level interventions.[7]

Macro-level interventions focus on making the broader investment climate more attractive to private sector activities. Key concerns here include the development of an open, competitive economy, macroeconomic stability, provision of the infrastructure and education system necessary to stimulate economic growth, and the establishment of rule of law. Specific interventions may aim at improving governance and strengthening state institutions, liberalizing the economy, privatizing state-owned enterprises (SOEs), establishing competition laws and institutions, reforming financial institutions, and mobilizing private investment for infrastructure development.

Improvements at the meso level seek to create a more enabling environment for enterprise growth – i.e. an environment that displays well-designed, sensibly enforced regulations (avoiding unnecessary red tape) and is consistent with an open, innovative and growing business community and with a competitive economy. Interventions at this level are geared towards strengthening the institutions that affect the performance of the private sector. This includes government institutions that regulate and support private enterprises, as well as the mechanisms through which private enterprises organize and participate in public–private dialogue. Close interaction with the private sector is of essence, in order to allow the Government to understand the needs and opportunities of businesses in specific sectors and activities.

Micro-level interventions target private enterprises, either directly, or through intermediary organizations such as government agencies, private service providers, community-based organizations, business associations, or chambers of commerce. These interventions attempt to address enterprises' internal constraints, by providing training and information, facilitating business linkages, and improving access to finance to enhance the capacity of private enterprises to start up and grow. In recent years, increased attention has been paid to the functioning of the markets in which enterprises operate, and to developing systemic responses to the needs and capacities of targeted firms. The role of enterprises within specific sectors and value chains has also become a critical area of focus.

Whereas Governments and donor agencies have increasingly shifted the emphasis towards interventions at the meso and macro levels, micro-level interventions still have an important role to play. Improvements to the investment climate and business environment, which help to stimulate markets for PSD and mobilize investment, are "not enough to maximize the investment potential in developing countries" (OECD, 2005: 14). In Latin America and the Caribbean, for example, the removal of barriers to entry, and improved competition, have not been sufficient to stimulate innovation within and among firms. The need for specific policy instruments to promote innovation has been recognized, especially after a process of deregulation and trade liberalization (Lederman, 2009).

B. FACETS OF THE ICT–PSD INTERFACE

ICTs can contribute to a broad range of aspects on the PSD agenda. Many of the challenges and constraints facing enterprises are associated with a need to make markets work better, to make internal management systems more efficient, to facilitate improved access to information and other resources, to enhance transparency, and to make environments more enabling. These are all domains in which the effective application of ICTs can make a significant difference (UNCTAD, 2009a and 2010). ICTs thereby contribute to creating a business environment that is more conducive to PSD, and open new ways of communication among and between enterprises and Governments.

The role of ICTs in the context of PSD can be viewed from at least four perspectives (fig. I.2). The first perspective, which is concerned with the broad investment climate for private firms, includes the provision of affordable access to relevant ICT infrastructure and services. There are two private sector aspects to ICT infrastructure. On the one hand, ICT infrastructure is an increasingly critical input for the development of the private sector. On the other hand, the private sector itself has a leading role in the development of ICT networks and services.

The second perspective is related to business use of ICTs. ICT use can lower transaction costs, help firms obtain information about new market opportunities, improve their communication along the value chain, and broaden the ways in which products and services are provided to the customer. Private firms invest in ICTs to become more productive and more competi-

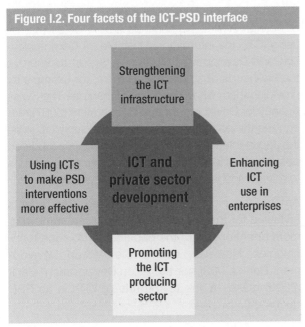

Figure I.2. Four facets of the ICT-PSD interface

Strengthening the ICT infrastructure

Using ICTs to make PSD interventions more effective

ICT and private sector development

Enhancing ICT use in enterprises

Promoting the ICT producing sector

Source: UNCTAD.

tive. Policy efforts to enhance the productivity of the private sector may therefore seek to boost the uptake and productive use of different ICTs.

The third perspective is to promote the ICT sector itself. The production of ICT goods and services represents in itself an important part of the private sector, which can be stimulated in order to create opportunities for private firms to start up and grow. Opportunities are emerging both in manufacturing and in services, and also in business activities that have been enabled by improved access to ICTs. Examples of the latter include various forms of business process outsourcing (BPO), and micro-enterprises in the mobile sector (chapter III). Governments may adopt measures that aim to strengthen the ICT-producing sector.

The fourth perspective relates to the various ways in which Governments and other relevant institutions can make use of ICTs to create an enabling business environment. This involves regulating and promoting private sector activities, including through various e-government and business support programmes. Similarly, Governments have a role to play in developing and implementing a legal and regulatory framework that makes it possible for ICTs to help markets function better. Recent technological developments have created completely new ways of leveraging ICTs in this context to reduce the cost of delivering services, extend the reach of services, and improve the functioning of markets.

All four facets of the ICT–PSD interface are relevant. However, their nature and significance vary, depending on the specific situation and on the policy priorities of Governments. Even with such caveats in mind, it is clear that effective use of ICTs can contribute in several ways to enhancing the performance of the private sector.

C. THE ICT–PSD DIMENSION IN DEVELOPMENT STRATEGIES

An important starting point, in order for policy interventions to generate full benefits from ICT use in support of PSD, is for Governments, donors and other stakeholders to specify in their PSD and other development strategies how ICTs can make a difference. This section reviews the current state of play in that area.

1. The PSD strategies of development partners

In its practical guidance for development agencies on how to support business environment reforms, the Donor Committee for Enterprise Development (DCED) succinctly explained why development partners should pay attention to the role of ICTs (DCED, 2008: 16–17):

"Development agencies are advised to consider the ways in which they can support the introduction or upgrading of information and communications technology (ICT) to improve regulatory processes and provide a more effective communications channel to constituent businesses. The potential benefits arising from the effective use of ICT, as part of a larger regulatory simplification initiative, can include some or all of the following:
  (a) increased efficiency of the reformed regulatory processes;
  (b) reduced scope for official corruption;
  (c) improved information availability and transparency;
  (d) reduced obstacles to formality;
  (e) increased tax compliance and government revenue generation; and
  (f) improved facilitation of new investment projects."

Despite these and other opportunities for ICTs to contribute to PSD, relatively few development partners have so far paid much attention to the ICT dimension in their strategy documents. This section presents the results of a review of available PSD strategies issued during the past few years by selected bilateral and multilateral development agencies. Most of the strategies were formulated in 2007 or later, while some are considerably older. The results from the desk review were complemented by direct interaction with the relevant agencies.

A total of 22 PSD strategies formulated by bilateral development agencies or ministries of foreign affairs were considered (annex table I.1). Out of these, nine (41 per cent) made no reference to the ICT dimension.

In seven documents, ICTs were mentioned as an *important part of a country's infrastructure*. For example, the Aid for Trade Action Plan of Finland notes that "ICT is also a key element of economic infrastructure" (MFA, 2008: 19). The New Zealand Aid Programme (NZAID, 2008: 27) notes that effective "communications and infrastructure, including [...] information and communications technology, provide an essential foundation for economic growth and wider development efforts."

Two PSD strategy documents highlight *promotion of the ICT producing sector*. The first document mentions the growing opportunities for outsourcing of ICT services to developing countries, and the importance of removing related trade barriers (Ministry of Foreign Affairs, Netherlands, 2007: 7). Meanwhile, the Finnish Aid for Trade Action Plan singles out the Information Society as one of its priority targets.

In two donor strategies, the ICT dimension is reflected through the *promotion of greater ICT use in enterprises*. For example, a comprehensive study by Germany's GTZ (now GIZ) on sustainable economic development in Asia notes that Governments "often try to influence the broad direction of structural change without favouring specific industries, for example by [...] fostering the use of ICT" (GTZ, 2008: 136). A Spanish PSD strategy document explicitly stresses the role of ICT use in enhancing enterprise productivity (Ministerio de Asuntos Exteriores y de Cooperación, 2005).

Finally, six strategies recognize the opportunities that ICTs provide for *making PSD interventions more effective*. Australia sees a need to strengthen the market for business development services by, among other things, building the capacity of local trainers to develop in the area of information technology (IT)

(Commonwealth of Australia, 2000: 18). The Ministry of Foreign Affairs, Netherlands (2007) notes that by using ICTs, the International Institute for Communication and Development (IICD) has helped to improve the livelihoods of small-scale farmers, for example by providing them with knowledge of markets. The Swiss Agency for Development and Cooperation (2007) recognizes the potential of mobile money services, while the Japan International Cooperation Agency (undated document) emphasizes the importance of using ICTs to make trade facilitation procedures more effective.

Among the eight multilateral strategy documents reviewed for this report, ICTs were given somewhat more attention; six of the papers refer to such technologies. However, neither the African Development Bank (2008) nor the Asian Development Bank (2006) makes a link to the role of ICTs in its PSD document.

Only one of the eight documents touches upon ICTs in the context of infrastructure development (ILO, 2007). The United Nations Development Programme (UNDP) gives considerable attention to *the ICT sector* within its PSD work. For example, the ICT sector is included among the industries covered by the Growing Small Businesses (GSB) programme (UNDP, 2008a). Moreover, UNDP's Global ICT Skills Building Programme is helping to narrow the digital divide in 10 countries in Africa, Asia, Latin America and Eastern Europe, by expanding ICT access to underprivileged groups.

Two documents note the importance of promoting *greater ICT use in enterprises*. For example, UNIDO (2009: 37) states that "helping businesses in these countries to gain access to business information and ICTs plays an important role in overcoming these development hurdles. The gradual creation of such an information society in developing countries, and particularly in LDCs, is a key prerequisite for stimulating increased innovation, productivity, competitiveness, and market linkages." Similarly, ILO cites access to ICTs as one important determinant of the productivity of firms (ILO, 2007: 12): "To develop international competitiveness, enterprises need to keep pace with international developments in [...ICTs and] knowledge management." In the area of rural development, the same document finds that new advances in ICTs "can help rural agricultural-based and non-farm enterprises respond in a more timely fashion to changing market opportunities and to market niches resulting from their isolation, thereby turning disadvantage into advantage" (ibid.: 146).

The area in which the multilateral agencies most frequently cite opportunities for ICTs to make a difference is related to their application to *make PSD interventions more effective*. The International Finance Corporation (IFC), for example, has developed its SME Toolkit, which uses ICTs to help SMEs in emerging markets learn sustainable business management practices (IFC, 2007b). ILO (2007) recognizes the potential of mobile microfinance to facilitate transactions, of radio programmes to support small businesses, and of the effective use of ICTs to improve access to services provided by business associations.

The PSD strategy of OECD (2006a) notes that ICTs can help simplify administration, improve small business development services with a view to providing targeted assistance to expand existing activities, penetrate new markets, and improve efficiency. There is also reference to ICT applications geared towards women producers. Meanwhile, UNIDO (2009) stresses that building bridges between Government and industry is vital to reducing bureaucratic complexities and facilitating access to key information. Electronic portals that offer access to integrated information on aspects such as regulatory mandates, support institutions and generic business advice are especially helpful for SMEs and entrepreneurs. According to the paper, such e-government solutions can facilitate the delivery of industry-specific

public services, because, firstly, they contribute to increasing the transparency, effectiveness and coverage of such services, and secondly, they set standards for ICT usage, particularly among SMEs.

In summary, despite the DCED recommendation to give due attention to the introduction or upgrading of ICTs, many donor strategies related to PSD do not mention ICT at all. Moreover, among those strategy documents that do recognize the opportunities offered by ICTs, the recognition is often only given in a peripheral way – for example, only highlighting a specific issue. Few strategy papers consider the broad spectrum in which such technologies could make a difference.

2. National PSD and ICT strategies

The potential that ICTs offer for PSD is more often reflected in national strategies, though there is room for improvement in this case too. The findings presented in this section draw on several surveys and reviews conducted by UNCTAD, UNECA, UNECLAC and UN-ESCAP.

a. Africa

The link between ICTs and PSD has been recognized by many African Governments, as demonstrated in their national strategy documents – notably in National

---

Box I.4. Examples of links between ICTs and PSD in national strategies in Africa

In *Ghana's* Second Medium-Term Private Sector Development Strategy, the overriding focus is to develop a private sector that creates jobs and enhances livelihoods for all. To this end, the strategy envisages, among other things, that the Government and the public sector should focus on improving the quality of ICT infrastructure.

In *Mali*, the Strategic Framework for Growth and Poverty Reduction 2007–2011 identifies PSD through SMEs as a priority pillar, and puts an emphasis on ICTs, among other services. It places priority on several ICT-related activities, namely ICT skills, universal access to information through computerization, private investment in cybercentres and multi-purpose community centres, the provision and use of market information, and better telecommunications infrastructure.

In *Nigeria*, the National Economic, Empowerment and Development Strategy emphasizes private sector growth to support the development agenda in all sectors, including ICTs. Meanwhile, the national ICT policy identifies programmes to enhance the role of the private sector in ICT developments, including the establishment of the National ICT Statistical Information Service; the development of e-banking, e-commerce, e-trade, and electronic financial services; the development of a local ICT industry; software development and technology parks; programmes for the utilization and development of ICT in industry; and BPO services.

In its second NICI (2006–2010), the Government of *Rwanda* stated its intention to make Rwanda an information and knowledge-based economy and society. This strategy identified activities that pertain to all four aspects of the ICT–PSD interface. These include the development of a national ICT infrastructure; the creation of an enabling environment to deploy and use ICTs; the development of a local ICT industry and of human resources; the development of e-commerce; and the development of standards, practices and guidelines to deploy ICTs and to contribute to the development of e-government.

Source: Information provided by UNECA.

Information and Communication Infrastructure (NICI) plans, policies and strategies. These aim principally at assisting countries to deploy, harness, and exploit ICTs for development. A review of national strategies, undertaken by UNECA, found that the ICT–PSD interface was visible in most African countries, either in the NICIs or the national PSD strategies, or in both. A few illustrations are provided in box I.4.[8] Although most African countries make clear references to the role that ICTs can play in supporting PSD, there is little information about whether the many goals and activities that are mentioned in the strategy documents have actually been implemented.

b. Latin America and the Caribbean

A review of the national ICT strategies adopted by LAC countries (UNECLAC, 2010: 6) concludes that there is a need for a second generation of digital development and inclusion strategies based on greater coordination between institutions. In addition, the study underlines the importance of stepping up the pace of ICT dissemination towards micro-enterprises and SMEs, and of promoting the software, applications, and content industries (ibid.: 7). According to the report, most of the current digital strategies in the region do not sufficiently stress the need to coordinate the dissemination of ICT use with promotion of the local ICT sector (ibid.: 20). Moreover, production sector issues, such as e-business and the development of the ICT sector, are frequently absent from the relevant policy agendas.

With regard to PSD, the UNECLAC report argues that a second generation of policies should seek to integrate policies through e-government, training, funding, and technical assistance policies, so that micro-enterprises and SMEs would not only have access to ICTs, but would quickly move to advanced uses, especially in the fields of management and e-commerce (ibid.: 24). The presence (or lack) of a sector producing ICT solutions affects the availability of applications and services tailored to the needs of local enterprises and institutions. At the same time, enterprises should enhance their use of ICTs to boost their productivity.

c. Asia-Pacific region

Many countries in the Asia-Pacific region have policies, laws and legislation which pave the way for ICT use and which, albeit to a lesser extent, promote PSD.[9] In some cases, including in the LDCs, ICT policies and laws are relatively extensive. However, as in Africa, implementation and operationalization are lagging. According to a recent review (table I.1), countries in the region can be grouped into three categories – in terms of the level of coverage and implementation of available strategies with regard to ICT infrastructure, ICT use for e-business and e-commerce, and development of the ICT sector.

High level. The ICT policies of these economies are the most comprehensive in the region (table I.1). They generally lay out a platform for PSD and consider forward-looking utilization of new technologies (particularly wireless/mobile broadband, and in some cases, cloud computing) for e-business and e-commerce activities. Policies are typically set out in terms of addressing infrastructure development, and of adapting the legal environment to increased digital convergence.

In *China*, for example, the Eleventh Five-Year Plan 2006–2011 outlines the need for enterprises to use new technologies productively to foster innovation. Drawing, in addition, on the National Informatization Development Strategy 2006–2020, China retains a focus on infrastructure, e-commerce, e-government, information security, government information transparency, and personal data protection. In *Malaysia*, the Third Industrial Master Plan (2006–2020) focuses on bioinformatics, shared services and outsourcing, e-commerce, and digital content development. The

Table I.1.	Extent to which ICT policies cover private sector development in the Asia-Pacific
Relative level of coverage and implementation	**Economies**
High	Australia, China, India, Japan, Malaysia, New Zealand, Republic of Korea, Singapore, Taiwan Province of China
Medium	Brunei Darussalam, Indonesia, Islamic Republic of Iran, Mongolia, Pakistan, Philippines, Sri Lanka, Thailand, Viet Nam
Low	Bangladesh, Bhutan, Lao People's Democratic Republic, Maldives, Myanmar, Nepal, Timor-Leste and Pacific island countries and territories

Source: UNESCAP desk research and literature review, April–May 2011.

Box I.5. ICT policies for private sector development in the Republic of Korea

The Government of the Republic of Korea has designed and implemented various policies to expand ICT infrastructure to rural areas, and to promote competitiveness and new ICT services to bridge the digital divide.

In order to make full use of the expanding ICT infrastructure and to increase productivity, the Government has endeavoured to spread developments in ICT to services industries and SMEs, which are characterized by lower levels of ICT use. In this context, the Ministry of the Knowledge Economy is implementing a comprehensive plan to promote the productivity of the services industries by the use of ICTs. The plan identifies several ways for ICTs to contribute to the services industries, namely by (a) creating new and high value-added businesses; (b) promoting the use of knowledge and innovation; (b) expanding openness and accessibility to services by expanding the use of time and space inputs; (d) improving service quality; and (e) promoting collaboration and networking among enterprises.

For the implementation of the plan, seven action plans, under three strategies, will be enacted from 2008 to 2012, with an investment of 0.12 trillion won ($112 million) from the public and private sectors. In addition, several relevant Acts have been passed:

  (a)   Comprehensive Plan on Cloud Computing (December 2009);

  (b)   Comprehensive Plan on Wireless Internet Development (April 2010);

  (c)   Plan on Enhancing Smart Work Infrastructure and Development of the Private Sector (July 2010);

  (d)   Industry Fusion Promotion Act (April 2011);

  (e)   Comprehensive Plan on Smart Mobile Security (December 2010); and

  (f)   Revised Act on Using and Protecting Location-based Information (June 2010).

Source: Information provided by UNESCAP.

"u-Korea" master plan of 2006 aims, in a comprehensive manner, at enhancing national infrastructure facilities, strengthening the competitiveness of existing industries, creating an enabling environment, and promoting international cooperation. Box I.5 illustrates the ICT policies of the *Republic of Korea* for PSD.

Singapore has taken a number of steps to leverage new developments in ICT for PSD, as outlined in its 10-year master plan entitled *Realising the iN2015 Vision: Singapore: An Intelligent Nation, A Global City, Powered by Infocomm* (iN2015). To make Singapore an "intelligent nation", the Infocomm Development Authority (2010), together with industry, has identified several programmes and initiatives aimed at (a) extending broadband access, through an integrated network of wireless LAN, broadband Internet, and mobile telephony; (b) supporting a globally competitive infocomm industry; (c) ensuring access to the relevant manpower; and (d) sectoral transformation of economic sectors, Government and society. The Eleventh Five-Year Plan (2007–2012) of *India* focuses on infrastructure development and the expansion of broadband. This plan also promotes the development of new e-business applications, m-commerce, and other business models to mainstream e-commerce and thus enhance benefits to SMEs. The plan refers to the promotion of start-up companies, SMEs, women entrepreneurs, IT incubation facilities, and various e-government initiatives.

Middle level. In *Indonesia,* Strategy ICT-315 identifies SMEs as needing special support, and places emphasis on the development of the ICT industry through strategic public–private partnerships. In order to support ICT use, laws on cybersecurity and electronic transactions have been in place since 2008. In the *Philippines*, the National IT Plan for the Twenty-first Century, launched in 1997, outlines the development of ICT infrastructure and competitive IT products, and seeks to position the country as a knowledge centre for Asia. An important aspect of the National ICT Policy Framework 2011–2020 of *Thailand* is the recognition of emerging technologies such as cloud computing, and the societal impacts of the increasing use of social networks. Whereas ICT developments have been vibrant, the level of operationalization of legislative frameworks in *Mongolia, Pakistan* and *Sri Lanka*, for example in relation to e-commerce, has been low. In the *Islamic Republic of Iran*, promotion of the ICT industry, via the empowerment of SMEs, incubation centres, and technology parks, is one of the national ICT agency's seven focus areas with regard to ICT initiatives.

Low level. In this group, there is growing awareness of the potential of ICTs, but implementation of policies and strategies is limited. The Government of *Bhutan* had set a target of creating an enabling framework to promote e-business by the year 2009, and has sought to boost the ICT activities of local companies by outsourcing government ICT work to local private enterprises. However, implementation has been slow. The National ICT Policy 2009 of *Bangladesh* encourages maximum utilization of ICT services nationwide to enhance SME productivity and increase efficiency in the management of the agricultural supply chain, but has not yet been operationalized. The Digital Bangladesh "Vision 2021" promotes the use of ICTs in business as one of its four key components. This component aims to increase market access and promote ICTs as a complementary measure to other key components such as human resource development, people involvement, and civil services.

In *Cambodia*, enterprise development is one of four areas recognized in the National ICT Policy. There are reduced import taxes on ICT equipment and systems. In addition, the Government has pledged to provide special support to SMEs to adopt and use e-commerce systems and to take appropriate measures to ensure the efficiency, privacy, security and reliability of e-commerce systems based on international, interoperable standards. In the *Lao People's Democratic Republic*, the National ICT Policy 2009 focuses, among other things, on creating an enabling environment for investors in the ICT sector to upgrade their knowledge and experience. While a number of cyberlaws have been passed, their implementation and operationalization have been hampered by a lack of a national information infrastructure. In *Afghanistan* and *Maldives,* and in the *Pacific Islands*, current national ICT strategies contain no explicit mention of promoting ICT use in the domestic private sector, and *Timor-Leste* has no ICT policy in place.

* * * * *

Reviews by United Nations regional commissions suggest that many national strategies recognize the important interface between ICTs and PSD. However, as has been illustrated by looking at developments in Asia and the Pacific, there are considerable differences across countries regarding the level of comprehensiveness of the strategies, and regarding the extent to which actions and goals proposed have been implemented in practice. Thus, for a large number of developing countries, there appears to be significant scope for better leveraging of the ICT–PSD interface.

D. SUMMARY AND CONCLUDING REMARKS

This chapter has underlined that PSD is a key objective in most developing countries and among donors. Special attention is often given to MSEs, as these face particular barriers and challenges, some of which can be addressed in part by effective use of ICTs – by enterprises and Governments alike. With recent advances in ICT connectivity, and the emergence of new ICT applications and services (chapter II), including in LDCs, the scope for ICT-enabled solutions to make a difference in the area of PSD has radically improved.

This chapter noted that PSD interventions can be made at the micro, meso or macro level, and it identified four aspects of the ICT–PSD interface:

   (a) An improved ICT infrastructure makes the investment climate more attractive.

   (b) ICT use in enterprises can enhance the productivity of the private sector.

   (c) An expanding ICT producing sector represents an important part of the private sector, and can support the sustainable use of ICTs in other industries.

   (d) ICT use by Governments and other relevant institutions can support the creation and growth of enterprises.

While the potential for ICTs to contribute to business environment reforms is well recognized, many PSD strategies currently do not give this area adequate attention. The review of recent donor strategy documents in this area showed that many of the strategies do not make any reference at all to how ICTs might be leveraged for PSD. Moreover, among those documents that do acknowledge opportunities from ICT use in this context, this acknowledgement is often only given in a peripheral way – for example, highlighting a specific issue rather than the broad spectrum in which such technologies could make a difference.[10]

Many developing countries' national strategies do assign importance to the role of ICTs. This is reflected either in PSD strategies or ICT strategies, or in both. The fact that the ICT–PSD interface is frequently well reflected in national strategies does not mean that all the goals and activities proposed in them are actually implemented. Many countries pay particular attention to the development of ICT infrastructure, to the contributions of the ICT sector, and to the need to boost

ICT use in the enterprise sector. Fewer examples were found with regard to the potential of ICTs to make the delivery of PSD interventions more efficient. However, some countries, such as Rwanda and Singapore, have chosen to view ICTs as a powerful lever towards improving the competitiveness of their private sectors, and have identified concrete actions with regard to improving all four aspects of the ICT–PSD interface.

* * * * *

The four facets of the ICT–PSD interface will serve as the organizing principle for the remainder of this report. Chapter II is devoted to the question of facilitating uptake of relevant ICTs by different kinds of enterprises, taking their varying needs into account. It reviews the extent to which affordable ICT infrastructure and services are available to and used by the private sector, and it discusses policy options to promote uptake. Chapter III focuses attention on the ICT sector itself, to identify key opportunities for a sectoral approach to PSD. Based on a review of available data on the size and composition of the ICT sector in different countries, it explores policy options for nurturing vibrant growth and development in the ICT sector. Chapter IV is devoted to the use of ICTs, by Governments and other relevant institutions, in interventions that aim to address some of the internal and external constraints on enterprise creation and growth. Special emphasis is given to the role of ICTs in business environment reforms, in business development services, and in improving access to finance. Chapter V explores how ICT use can help promote women's entrepreneurship. Finally, Chapter VI presents recommendations to national Governments and their development partners.

NOTES

[1] Keeping the promise: a forward-looking review to promote an agreed action agenda to achieve the Millennium Development Goals by 2015. Report of the Secretary-General. A/64/665. 12 February 2010.

[2] Studies from Kenya (Moyi, 2003) and Botswana (Duncombe and Heeks, 2002) found that many enterprises relied on informal information sourcing, which was largely inadequate for their needs and which resulted in high search costs and in poor-quality information being acquired.

[3] Analysis carried out in 130 countries concluded that higher regulatory costs resulting from poorly conceived laws were associated with more poverty, larger informal sectors, higher unemployment, lower productivity and more corruption (World Bank, 2003).

[4] However, it should also be recognized that while a higher proportion of MSEs in the economy is associated with higher growth, MSEs do not necessarily create higher economic growth or improve pro-poor growth (Bylund, 2005).

[5] In Ghana, for example, the informal private sector accounts for about 81 per cent of the employed workforce, with the formal private sector accounting for only 8 per cent of the employment of the economically active population. See Republic of Ghana (2003).

[6] See *Programme of Action for the Least Developed Countries for the Decade 2011–2020*, para 56.

[7] There are variations in the way agencies define these levels, but in general there is agreement regarding the value of this typology of intervention. See OECD (2005). Some also include interventions at the "meta level", which refers to those that are geared towards changing perceptions and values for the adoption of new and innovative entrepreneurial activities. This concerns the cultural and social norms of society, and the extent to which citizens, including businessmen and businesswomen, exhibit entrepreneurial values and attitudes.

[8] Information provided by UNECA, March 2011.

[9] This section is based on information provided by UNESCAP.

[10] This observation was confirmed in a recent study of policies of international development donors and investors engaged in support for small and growing businesses in developing countries (Barbarasa, 2010).

FACILITATING ENTERPRISE
USE OF ICTs

2

Information and communication technologies (ICTs) are used by private enterprises to improve their productivity and competitiveness in the marketplace. Various kinds of ICTs help firms in all sectors to manage their resources more efficiently, access the information needed for better business decision-making, reduce the costs of business transactions and enhance their ability to bring their products and services to customers. Consequently, it is useful to consider ways to enhance business use of ICTs in the context of private sector development. To promote ICTs within firms, governments need to provide an enabling environment that is conducive to business use of ICTs. Characteristics of such an environment include the availability of affordable and relevant ICT infrastructure – an area which is still characterized by significant divides. There is also a need to ensure access to adequately trained human resources and a legal and regulatory framework that supports the uptake and productive application of ICTs.

A. ICT USE BY ENTERPRISES VARIES

Evidence from both developed and developing countries has shown that effective use of ICTs affects productivity in both large and small enterprises (UNCTAD, 2011a). A firm-level study covering 56 developing countries found that "ICT is playing an important role in allowing businesses to grow faster and become more productive – this alone suggests that creating an appropriate environment to exploit ICT is important" (World Bank, 2006: 72). Developing-country enterprises using ICT had better performance compared with enterprises that did not use ICT, with notable improvements in enterprise growth, profitability, investment and productivity (table II.1).

However, benefits from ICT use are not equally distributed across the private sector. ICTs vary in terms of accessibility, functionality and user requirement. The extent to which an enterprise gains from enhanced access to different ICTs depends on its needs for information, storage and communication, which in turn are affected by its size, industrial sector, location and workforce skills. It also depends on whether its

suppliers and customers are frequent users of ICTs. It is furthermore influenced by the business skills of managers, the availability of personnel trained to use and maintain the equipment, and the availability of additional information sources that enable improved decision-making in procurement and other business processes.

The degree of ICT use has become a proxy for many business development strategies that endeavour to identify those enterprises with the greatest potential for growth. For example, the Business Sophistication Modelling (BSM) applied by FinScope (2006) in South Africa classifies private businesses into seven levels of "sophistication". Firms classified as "BSM1" make no use of ICTs, while the classification criteria for BSM2 firms include among others ownership of a mobile phone. BSM5 firms are home-based with a fixed telephone line, BSM6 businesses have invested in a computer, and BSM7 business use credit card machines.

For micro- and small enterprises (MSEs), the main observed benefits of ICT use are twofold (UNCTAD, 2010): (a) a reduction in information search and transactions costs; and (b) improved communications along the supply chain, with possible beneficial effects for individual enterprises as well as in terms of overall improvements in the functioning of markets. Furthermore, there is evidence that ICT use can help strengthen social and human capital through the enhancement of skills, increased self-confidence, participation of women, empowerment and security against income loss. For growth-oriented enterprises equipped with personal computers (PCs), together with their effective use, ICTs can also strengthen internal information systems and facilitate the participation in international value chains. Firms that are either exporters or foreign owned are typically more frequent ICT users.

ICT use enables enterprises to benefit from diverse forms of information and business support services (see also chapter IV).

- In order to *access information* on market demand and prices in a timely fashion, entrepreneurs may need access to radio, fixed telephony, mobile and SMS services or Internet, depending on the capabilities of the user;

- ICT use can help access *advice and training in business skills*. Basic use of ICT is needed to support skills for internal management such as training, cost calculation, product design and enterprise administration. At this level, both computers and smartphones may serve as a basis. In cases where

Table II.1.	Effects of ICT use on enterprise performance in developing economies		
Performance indicator	Enterprises that do not use ICTs	Enterprises that use ICTs	Improvement
Enterprise growth			
Sales growth (%)	0.4	3.8	3.4
Employment growth (%)	4.5	5.6	1.2
Profitability (%)	4.2	9.3	5.1
Investment			
Investment rate (%)	n.a	n.a	2.5
Re-investment rate (%)	n.a	n.a	6
Productivity			
Labour productivity (value added per worker, $)	5 288	8 712	3 423
Total factor productivity (%)	78.2	79.2	1

n.a.   Not applicable.
Source: World Bank (2006). Based on data from *Investment Climate Surveys 2000–2003*.

marketing and product research is relevant, Internet access grows increasingly relevant;

- The ability to interact with various e-government services will also require different ICT access, depending on the tools used by the government for a given service.

But even if access to ICTs is improved, firms in developing countries may sometimes choose to stay with traditional business processes rather than adopting ICT solutions. This may be because the latter are unsuitable for their business or because expected returns from business re-engineering are small. Any supporting role played by ICTs is crucially dependent on business processes within firms and the broader economic environment. The adoption of new information sources can therefore not be taken for granted. People have established and trusted information sources, many of them within their own communities. New sources need to gain the trust and confidence of users by demonstrating accuracy, reliability and the ability to add value to business performance (Souter *et al.,* 2005; Molony, 2007). In addition, costs and capability requirements remain significant for some MSEs and informal enterprises in developing countries, particularly with regard to computers and the Internet. For example, a 2009 survey of the informal sector in South

Africa found that around one fifth of respondents needed assistance to access technology (figure II.1).

The diversity of business needs as well as capabilities should be kept in mind when assessing the likely impact of enhanced access to different ICTs. The next section reviews the infrastructure and connectivity situation in countries at varying levels of development, and the final section discusses policy implications.

B. CONNECTIVITY AND AFFORDABILITY TRENDS

The extent to which countries are able to leverage ICTs in their efforts to promote private sector development (PSD) is greatly affected by the quality of ICT infrastructure. In order for enterprises to reap efficiency and productivity gains from ICTs, affordable information and communication infrastructure and services must be available. Drawing on a variety of data sources, this section presents information on the variation in the extent to which the private sector has access to and use various ICT tools, applications and services. Special attention is given, where possible, to low-income countries and to developments related to

Figure II.1. Persons with a non-VAT registered business reporting need for assistance in different areas, South Africa, 2009

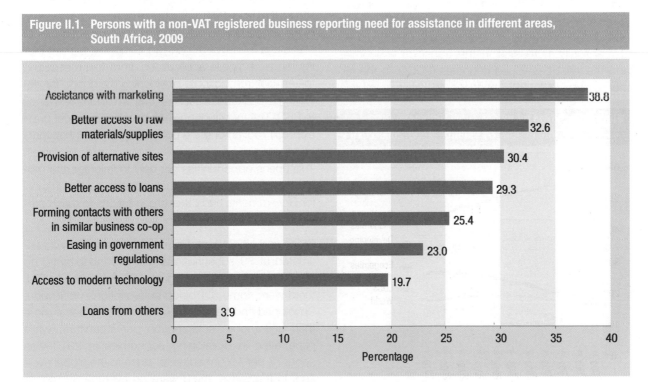

Note: One person may fall in more than one category as the respondents were asked to indicate all forms of assistance they required, so each category is treated separately.
Source: Statistics South Africa (2010).

ICTs that are of particular relevance for PSD, notably mobile telephony, Internet and broadband. While radio remains a crucial tool to reach entrepreneurs in remote areas (UNCTAD, 2010), it is not discussed explicitly below.

1. Fixed telephony

Poor coverage of fixed telephony in many developing countries has become less of a business constraint as a result of the diffusion of mobile phones. Nonetheless, fixed telephones remain important to many enterprises. They may support a line-sharing platform for offices, tariffs are often lower compared with mobiles, and a fixed telephone line can support DSL broadband access. There are also circumstances where there is a need for a telephone to remain tied to a business location so that customers and associates call a common number rather than someone's cell phone. For enterprises in urban areas, fixed telephony is often the main channel to access the Internet for commercial use.

At the end of 2010, there were 1.1 billion fixed telephone lines around the world for an average penetration of some 16 subscriptions per 100 inhabitants (figure II.2). In developed and developing economies, fixed telephone lines continue to decrease as users disconnect conventional fixed line voice telephony subscriptions to switch to mobile and voice over broadband connections. The number of subscribers is marginally increasing in the transition economies and the least developed countries (LDCs). In the former group, low tariffs continue to make traditional

fixed telephone lines an attractive option. In the latter group, most growth is from fixed wireless rather than traditional, copper-based fixed lines.

Average affordability – measured by the International Telecommunication Union's (ITU's) fixed basket as a percentage of gross national income (GNI) per capita – improved from 6.2 per cent in 2008 to 5.8 per cent in 2010.[1] The relevance of current tariff benchmarks for fixed telephone service is increasingly being questioned due to technological shifts and user preferences. This impacts their usefulness for understanding affordability vis-à-vis enterprises and particularly small and medium-sized enterprises (SMEs). For example, when making international calls, SMEs in developing countries are more likely to use public telephones and inexpensive Internet telephony options (see section II.B.4). A more relevant component of fixed telephone tariffs is the monthly rental cost in relation to its potential for broadband use.[2]

2. Mobile telephony

a. Expansion continues

The diffusion of mobile phones continues to transform the ICT landscape with major potential implications for PSD (UNCTAD, 2010). First, it is extending access to those at the bottom of the economic pyramid, i.e. to MSEs and to the self-employed. Secondly, the expanding range of mobile applications, from text messaging to financial transactions, is widening the scope for delivering a multitude of services that are of high relevance to PSD. The mobile phone has become the most prevalent ICT tool among the poor, among rural inhabitants and among micro-enterprises in low-income countries. This opens opportunities not only to leverage the mobile phone as a business tool, but also a new channel for Governments and other organizations to reach previously unconnected parts of the private sector.

At the end of 2010, global mobile penetration was estimated at 79 subscriptions per 100 inhabitants, up from 69 the year before (figure II.3). According to ITU, there were some 5.4 billion subscriptions worldwide. Developed and transition economies now boast more than one mobile subscription per inhabitant, while penetration in developing economies in 2010 was about 77 per 100 inhabitants, close to the global average. In the LDCs, there were on average 33 mobile subscriptions per 100 inhabitants, a remarkable improvement in a very short time.[3] There appears, how-

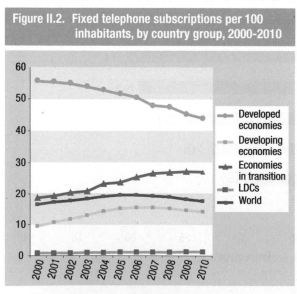

Figure II.2. Fixed telephone subscriptions per 100 inhabitants, by country group, 2000-2010

Legend:
- Developed economies
- Developing economies
- Economies in transition
- LDCs
- World

Source: Adapted from ITU World Telecommunication/ ICT Indicators database.

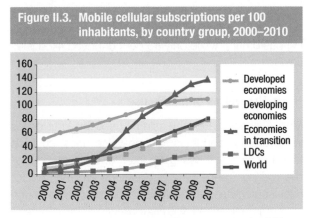

Figure II.3. Mobile cellular subscriptions per 100 inhabitants, by country group, 2000–2010

Source: Adapted from ITU World Telecommunication/ICT Indicators database.

ever, to be a "gender gap" in mobile phone ownership in the developing world, with 300 million fewer women than men owning a mobile phone (GSMA and Cherie Blair Foundation, 2010).

The best performing economies in mobile subscription growth are all developing or transition economies (figure II.4). Transition economies did particularly well, accounting for five countries with the greatest improvement in penetration levels between 2005 and 2010, largely thanks to added competition. In addition,

pan-regional operators, such as Turkcell, Vimpelcom and MTS, operate in these countries and throughout the Commonwealth of Independent States (CIS), enabling them to leverage on expertise and economies of scale. The licensing of second or third operators triggered rapid mobile growth also in countries such as Botswana, the Islamic Republic of Iran, Samoa and Fiji. One quarter of the top-performing countries have now reached the milestone of one subscription per inhabitant and the remainder is expected to reach this in the next few years.

Nevertheless, lack of service availability remains a constraint to mobile uptake. Although mobile signal coverage, the share of the population that is within range of a mobile network base station, continues to increase and stood at 88 per cent in 2010 (figure II.5), there is still some way to go for many LDCs. In these countries, more than 30 per cent of the population still lacked access to a mobile signal on average, with an even higher share in rural regions. Further, the increase in coverage of wireless networks has slowed recently as those areas that are commercially viable have mostly been provided service. Reaching the more remote areas may require some kind of subsidy as well as special solutions to provide electricity.

Figure II.4. Top 20 economies by largest increase in mobile cellular subscriptions per 100 inhabitants, 2005–2010

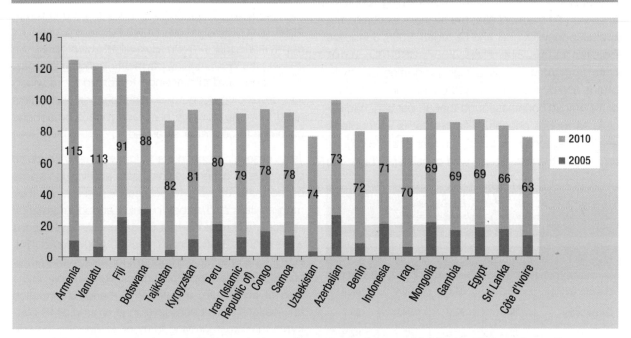

Note: Excludes countries that had already reached more than one subscription per inhabitant in 2009 and those with a population of less than 100,000. Economies ranked in descending order according to the increase in penetration between 2005 and 2010.

Source: Adapted from ITU World Telecommunication/ICT Indicators database.

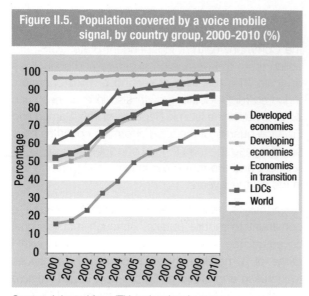

Figure II.5. Population covered by a voice mobile signal, by country group, 2000-2010 (%)

Legend:
- Developed economies
- Developing economies
- Economies in transition
- LDCs
- World

Source: Adapted from ITU and national sources.

There is only limited systematic and up-to-date information on the extent and nature of mobile phone use by enterprises in developed and developing countries.[4] International statistics on ICT use by enterprises generally do not include mobile phones (UNCTAD, 2009a). But like other ICTs, mobile phones can affect the internal processes of a business and the way it relates to clients and suppliers (Donner and Escobari, 2009). Micro-enterprises and SMEs, many of which operate in the informal sector in developing countries, appear to be the most affected by the adoption of mobile telephony (Donner and Escobari, 2009; Junqueira Botelho and da Silva Alves, 2007; UNCTAD, 2010). Data from Africa show a high proportion of mobile phone use by enterprises. A 2005–06 survey of SMEs of 14 African countries found that 83 per cent had access to mobile phones, a figure that is undoubtedly even higher today (table II.2) (Esselar *et al.*, 2007). Interestingly, the level of use was consistently high also

Table II.2. SMEs with access to mobile cellular phones for business purposes, 14 African economies (%)

	Informal	Semi-formal	Formal	All
Manufacturing	80.5	84.5	85.9	82.7
Construction	86.1	92.0	94.0	89.7
Services	83.4	82.6	82.7	82.9
All	82.9	83.3	83.7	83.3

Source: Research ICT Africa (2006): 11.

in informal-sector SMEs. The same study found that 76 per cent of the SMEs used the phones for contacting customers, while only 48 per cent used fixed lines (*ibid.*).

b. New forms of mobile use

Mobile phones are increasingly used by enterprises in developing countries for non-voice uses, such as text and picture messaging, Internet access and mobile money. These new applications are relevant for micro-enterprises and SMEs, supporting areas such as communications with suppliers and customers, market information and business networking. Their use has been found to help raise productivity and reduce information search and communication costs through better price information. Moreover, it reduces the need for travel, and thereby lowers transportation costs (UNCTAD, 2010).

The integration of computer-like processing and features in smaller devices with connectivity via wireless broadband networks could be particularly beneficial for SMEs, because of their frequent mobility and need for a lower cost solution than the traditional computer connected to fixed broadband. However, most mobile Internet subscribers in developing countries are using low-end mobile handsets with minimal features, which limits their functionality, particularly with regard to advanced business applications. For the trend in developed economies, where smartphones are used for applications that previously required a laptop as accessing the Web, making payments, sending invoices, e-mail and word processing,[5] to spread more widely into developing economies, smartphones and tablets need to come down in price and mobile broadband coverage to be further extended.

Text messaging continues to grow. It represents an alternative to expensive voice calls and for users who do not have or want to access the Internet on their mobiles. It is also a tool for value added information services. ITU reckons that 6.1 trillion SMS messages were sent in 2010, three times the 2007 figure (ITU, 2010). The practice is important for micro-enterprises and SMEs in developing countries. For example, in the area of agriculture, a number of market information applications have been developed around SMS platforms that are improving farmers' livelihoods through better knowledge of prices (UNCTAD, 2010: chapter IV). SMS is also used by enterprises as a marketing and communication tool.

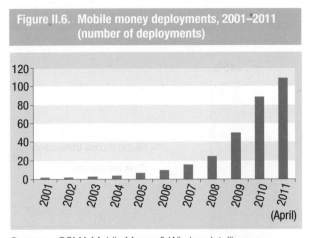

Figure II.6. Mobile money deployments, 2001–2011 (number of deployments)

Source: GSMA Mobile Money & Wireless Intelligence (http://www.wirelessintelligence.com/mobile-money).

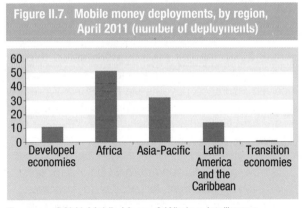

Figure II.7. Mobile money deployments, by region, April 2011 (number of deployments)

Source: GSMA Mobile Money & Wireless Intelligence (http://www.wirelessintelligence.com/mobile-money).

Mobile money deployments have taken off in the past two years (figure II.6). According to data from the GSM Association, some 109 such deployments had been implemented as of April 2011, spanning all developing regions. In fact, only 11 of the 109 deployments were in developed countries (figure II.7). Africa was leading the trend with 51 mobile money systems, followed by 33 in Asia and Oceania, and 14 in Latin America and the Caribbean. As many as 37 deployments were in LDCs. There are now more than 40 million users among providers for which subscription data are available.

The expansion of mobile money deployments is expected to continue. According to the GSMA, another 89 deployments were in the pipeline in April 2011. It is expected that most African countries will have at least one mobile money system in place in the near future. Another study predicted that in Brazil, China, India, Mexico and the Russian Federation, the number of people making use of mobile money services will surge from 32 million in 2010 to 290 million in 2015 (Arthur D Little, 2010). Key challenges include the development of sustainable business models and achieving technical compatibility between payments services operated by mobile companies and services provided by financial institutions (see chapter IV).

A study of 18 mobile money services across ten developing countries found that mobile-based transactions were on average 19 per cent cheaper than traditional bank services, and 38 per cent cheaper in the case of low-value transactions (McKay and Pickens, 2010). For high transaction values, however, mobile money transfers were more expensive (figure II.8). Consequently, these new channels of transferring money are likely to be of particular relevance to MSEs in low-income countries, which have a frequent need for making low-value transactions. One problem is the "walled garden" mobile operators use for their money services where they charge their own users much less. For example, Safaricom (Kenya) charges up to 7.5 times more to send the same amount of money to a user on another mobile network compared to sending it within the Safaricom's M-PESA network.[6]

Mobile money is important for small businesses as it facilitates payments, reduces transaction costs compared to traditional banks and improves security.[7] A recent study on the use of mobile money in the United Republic of Tanzania identified several reasons why many MSEs are embracing this new tool (Bångens and Söderberg 2011). First, it saves time, which can instead be used to develop the business. Secondly, it makes logistics more efficient. One company cited in the study had been able to reduce the time from order to delivery from four to two days, with less strain on liquidity as a result. Thirdly, it is possible to keep better records of payments made or received. Fourthly, safety increases as the need to carry cash was reduced. Fifthly, some entrepreneurs see a value in *storing* money (in addition to transferring money) as airtime. At the same time, a majority of the enterprises interviewed had still not switched from cash-based transactions.

However, the study identified a number of factors that influence the extent to which mobile money practices are adopted for business purposes:
- Only once an entrepreneur gains some experience with the mobile money system is he or she willing to use it for business purposes. In other words, a threshold level of trust between sender and receiver of funds is needed;

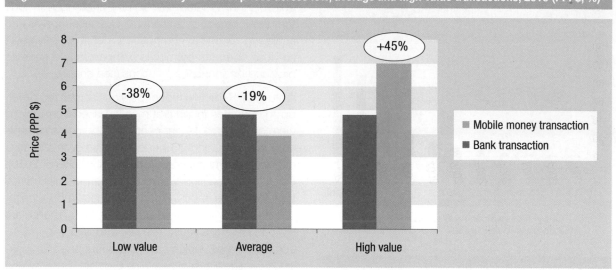

Figure II.8.   Average mobile money and bank prices across low, average and high value transactions, 2010 (PPP$, %)

Source: McKay and Pickens (2010).

- A minimum geographical distance between the two parties is normally required;
- Standardized products are more conducive to the use of mobile payments;
- Government regulations may need to be adapted to business use of mobile money systems. A tiered mobile money service may be relevant, with higher transaction and balance limits as well as higher security measures for small business users. For example, in the United Republic of Tanzania, the use of mobile payments is currently restricted to single transactions of less than about $330. In Kenya and Uganda, however, a dialogue between mobile network operators (MNOs) and the Central Banks has resulted in the approval of new limits, which are yet to become operationalized.[8]

Kenya has been at the centre of the emergence of many new innovations that are pioneering mobile banking and insurance schemes, and creating new job opportunities in the mobile sector (see chapter III). One financial area with large potential is micro-insurance, which is not available in many rural areas in developing nations. If risks can be reduced, rural farmers would be more willing to expand operations by investing in seeds, fertilizers and equipment. Kilimo Salama is an index-based micro-insurance product offered to farmers in Kenya. Farmers can protect their investments in improved seeds and farm inputs against drought and excess rain through their mobiles. The project is a partnership between Syngenta Foundation for Sustainable Agriculture, UAP Insurance and Safaricom, and was launched in March 2010. In Sep-

tember 2010, the first payouts were issued through the M-PESA system. Over 100 farmers in Embu then received insurance payouts via M-PESA.[9] While few similar projects have so far been implemented, the industry recognizes the potential (Zurich Financial Services Group, 2011: 6):

"As low-cost collection/transmission of payments is a key requirement for access to insurance, mobile payments could be the next big enabler for insuring new customers."

c. Pricing of mobile services

Affordability is a key demand side factor for mobile services.[10] Indeed, in a study of African SMEs, the main obstacle to ICT use was cost-related (Esselaar *et al.*, 2007). ITU data suggest that the average price of a prepaid mobile cellular monthly basket around the world in 2010 stood at about 8.6 per cent of per capita income, down from 11 per cent in 2008.[11] However, according to Nokia, which compiles mobile price baskets composed of a prorated handset cost, services charges based on a prepaid user and taxes, the global price average actually rose somewhat in 2009 due to the financial crisis (figure II.9).[12] This was the first increase since it began compiling the basket in 2005. In 2010, prices fell back to almost the level of 2008. Between 2005 and 2010, prices declined by 14 per cent, bringing the global average price for the monthly mobile basket aimed at a low-income user to $11.46.

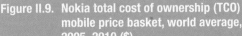

Figure II.9. Nokia total cost of ownership (TCO) mobile price basket, world average, 2005–2010 ($)

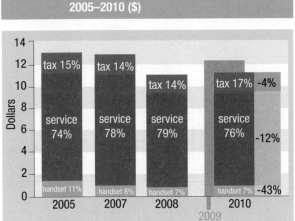

Note: Percentages indicated at the right side of the figure show the change in price in the three components between 2005 and 2010.
Source: Information provided by Nokia.

The biggest decline was related to the price of handsets (figure II.9), which is becoming less of a barrier to service take-up. According to one estimate, the average retail price of Nokia phones declined by 39 per cent between 2005 and 2009, while for Samsung handsets the drop was 33 per cent.[13] The growing replacement ratio (i.e. users replacing phones rather than a new user buying a handset for the first time) has expanded the availability of used handsets on the market, driving down prices for second hand mobile phones. This trend is particularly relevant for the micro-enterprises.

Mobile price baskets do not reflect the actual *usage* among countries. Users adjust their talking according

to pricing and in general, the lower the price, the more they will use the service. This is reflected in indicators such as average revenue per user (ARPU) and minutes of use (MoU). ARPU and MoU can be combined to produce the average price per minute (APPM), which provides another benchmark for mobile pricing (table II.3). India's ARPU is one of the lowest in the world and often used as a benchmark for low-income countries. Table II.3 shows the ARPU for selected telecom operators in India, other large emerging economies and the Africa region. Although Bangladesh had a lower ARPU than India (at $2.3 per month) in 2010, given the higher level of use in India, the average price of a minute of use was about the same in the two countries (approximately $0.01 per minute). In Africa, ARPU is on average much higher and minutes of use are lower. This suggests that prices need to fall further for mobile services to become widely affordable there. Meanwhile, the most expensive country in the table is Brazil, where average revenue per minute was $0.11 in 2010. Even though China has almost the same ARPU as Brazil, usage is more than five times higher, making the average price of a call only $0.02 per minute.

Given the popularity of mobiles and their use beyond voice, it is relevant to compare the prices of text messaging as well. As the marginal cost of an SMS is close to zero, there is potential to significantly expand access and usage of these applications if the price of text-messaging can be driven down. Some operators provide bundles of free SMS with prepaid recharges or as a low-cost tariff option. Text-messaging prices vary widely around the world, ranging from $0.02 in Bangladesh to $0.37 in Turkey (figure II.10).

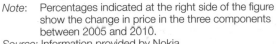

Table II.3. Average mobile revenue and minutes per user, selected economies and regions, 2010

	Average revenue per user (dollars per month)			Minutes of use (per month)		Average price per minute (dollars)		
	2010	2009	% change	2010	2009	2010	2009	% change
Africa	7.3	n.a.	n.a.	120	n.a.	0.06	n.a.	
Bangladesh	2.3	2.5	-8.00%	232	259	0.01	0.01	2.70%
Brazil	10.8	12.6	-14.80%	96	93	0.11	0.14	-17.40%
China	10.6	11.3	-5.90%	520	494	0.02	0.02	-10.60%
India	4.4	4.9	-10.20%	449	446	0.01	0.01	-10.80%
Russian Federation	11.2	10.6	5.70%	222	214	0.05	0.05	1.60%

Note: 2009 data for Africa not available.
Source: Adapted from Airtel, América Móvil, China Mobile, Orascom Telecom and Vimpelcom.

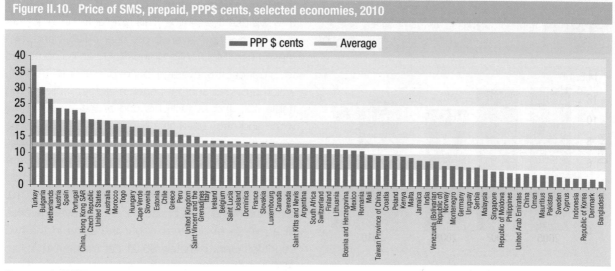

Figure II.10. Price of SMS, prepaid, PPP$ cents, selected economies, 2010

Source: ictDATA.org.

3. Computer use

A PC – desktop, laptop or notebook computer – is an essential tool for information technology software applications. A higher level of computer use in enterprises combined with other technologies has been linked to higher productivity in firms and computers are vital elements of enterprise operational networks (Eurostat, 2008; OECD, 2004; UNCTAD, 2008). Computer use is also an important indicator of the readiness of enterprises to integrate and benefit from the Internet. Despite the increasing popularity of Internet-enabled mobile phones and other devices, PCs remain the principal means of access to the Internet by all enterprises. But while computer use is potentially important to boost efficiency, this does not apply for all enterprises. Knowing how to use a PC is thus an essential ICT skill, while electricity, literacy, language and content are other important prerequisites for enterprises in poor regions to benefit from PCs.

As could be expected, UNCTAD data show that almost all large enterprises, whether in developed or developing economies, are using computers (figure II.11). However, while in many countries, PC use is almost as common in medium-sized enterprises as in large enterprises, the gap typically widens significantly vis-à-vis MSEs.[14] In developing countries, smaller enterprises, in particular micro-enterprises, often have less real or perceived need for a computer. There are no economies of scale that would justify the automation of processes. In addition, many entrepreneurs in low-income countries lack the skills needed to use a computer or the knowledge of how it could be useful.

Expected benefits may then be too small to justify the investment in hardware and software.

With respect to sectoral differences,[15] enterprises in developed economies generally use computers across the board. In developing economies, however, usage patterns vary significantly. Information on computer use is often not available for all industries, but mostly for manufacturing, construction, and wholesale and retail trade (see annex table II.4). There is a significant divide in the extent to which enterprises use computers in the sectors concerned. While the level of use is relatively uniform across sectors in developed and transition economies, real estate, renting and business activities is the industry with the highest incidence of computer use in most developing economies for which data are available. This is primarily an effect of high use among enterprises in computer-related business activities. Retail trade, hotels and restaurants have the lowest levels of computer use. This may reflect the large number of micro- and small enterprises in these two sectors.

4. Internet and broadband use

a. Connectivity is improving

(i) Internet use

The Internet offers huge potential benefits for enterprises by enhancing access to information, enabling transparent and efficient commerce between customers and suppliers, and improving interaction with government. In order to exploit such possibilities, enter-

Figure II.11. Enterprises using computers, selected economies, by enterprise size, latest year (%)

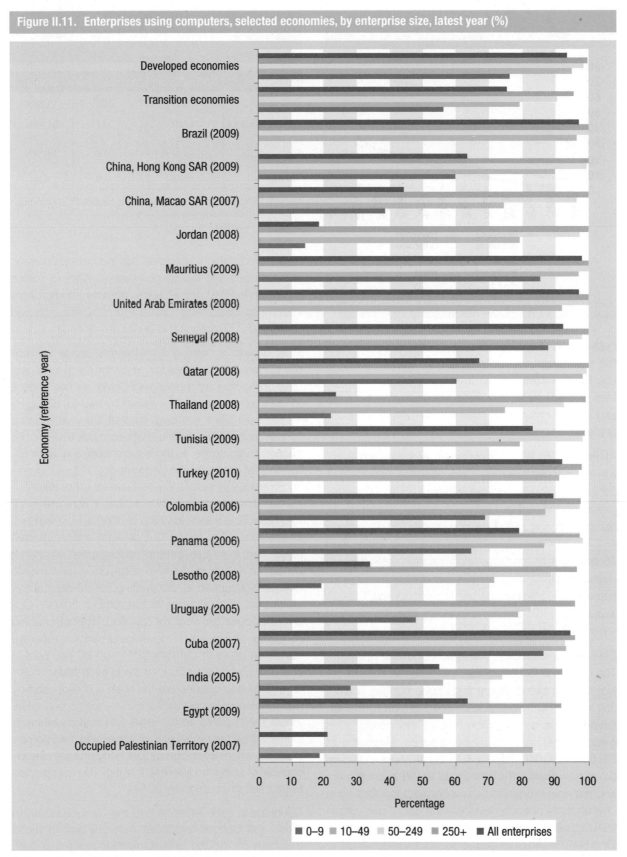

Source: Information Economy Database.

Figure II.12. Internet users per 100 inhabitants, 2000–2010*

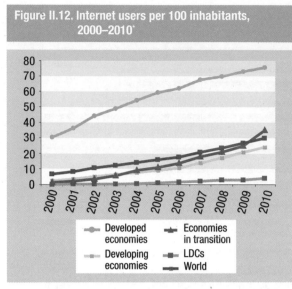

*Estimates.
Source: ITU World Telecommunication /ICT Indicators data
           base.

Table II.4.   Sales of computing devices and mobile handsets, 2009 and 2010 (quantity in millions)

Device	2010 sales (m)	2009 sales (m)	Change
PCs	351	308	13.80%
Mobile handsets	1 597	1 211	31.80%
of which smartphones	297	172	72.10%
Tablets	19.5	0	n.a.

Note: PC includes desk-based PCs, mobile PCs including
          mini-notebooks, but not tablets.
Source: Adapted from Gartner.

prises need affordable Internet connectivity as well as the knowledge and skills to use it. Whereas Internet use remains fairly limited in many low-income countries, this is likely to change as the deployment of fixed and mobile broadband makes faster Internet access available.

At the end of 2010, there were an estimated 2 billion Internet users, which corresponds to about 30 per cent of the world's population (figure II.12).[16] There remains a significant gulf between developed and developing economies and between developing economies and the LDCs. In developed economies, more than 75 per cent of the population was Internet users. In developing countries, only 24 per cent of the population used the Internet; in transition economies, the rate was higher at 35 per cent. In LDCs, the rate was just 4 per cent.

Devices for accessing the Internet have proliferated. The days of a PC being the main Internet access device are numbered. According to one industry source, 351 million PCs were sold in 2010 to add to the estimated base of 1.5 billion around the world.[17] This pales against sales of mobile phones, estimated at 1.6 billion in 2010 (table II.4).[18] "Smartphones" feature processor chips similar to those found in computers and are now produced by a variety of manufacturers. Overall sales of such devices were up 72 per cent in 2010, totaling almost 300 million units and accounting for around a fifth of all mobile handset sales.[19] Another entry into the device world came in April 2010: the

Apple iPad, which straddles the boundary between smartphones and laptop computers. With 15 million units sold in 2010, the iPad has attracted competitors into the so-called tablet arena and sales are expected to exceed 200 million units by 2014.

Most growth is coming from Internet usage via mobile phones, as illustrated by data for the two largest developing-country markets. In China, mobile access to the Internet rose to 277 million by mid-2010, up by 19 per cent since the beginning of the year.[20] Some 12 per cent of Chinese Internet users use their mobile phones to go online. In India there were a quarter billion mobile data users in September 2010.[21] Comprehensive data on mobile Internet use for other developing countries are not readily available. Where provided, they reflect the trends in China and India. For example, in Colombia, five million out of eight million Internet users had a mobile Internet subscription in March 2010.[22] In Kenya, there were some 3.2 million mobile Internet subscriptions, accounting for 99 per cent of all Internet subscriptions in September 2010.[23] Opera, a popular browser for low-end Internet-enabled handsets, particularly in developing nations, reported 90 million users in January 2011, up 80 per cent in one year and data traffic is growing even faster.[24] Given that mobile phones are the main ICT tool used by micro-enterprises and SMEs in low-income countries, these trends reinforce the likelihood that mobile networks will be their main way of accessing the Internet. In Africa, where 84 million mobile handsets are already capable of using the Internet, 7 out of 10 are expected to be Internet-enabled by 2014.[25]

Countries in Latin America and the Caribbean, North Africa and Central and West Asia are among those that have shown the largest increase in Internet penetration over the past five years (figure II.13).[26] In Latin

Figure II.13. Top 20 economies by largest increase in Internet users per 100 inhabitants, 2005-2010

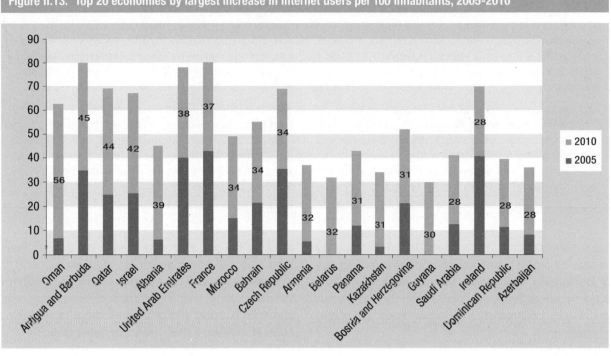

Note: Excluding economies with a population of less than 100,000. Economies ranked according to the increase in penetration between 2005 and 2010.

Source: Adapted from ITU World Telecommunication/ICT Indicators database.

America, the Dominican Republic and Panama have seen increased Internet use, with around two out of five persons now being online. Similarly, in North Africa and West Asia, the top performing countries in terms of increased penetration during 2005–2010 now have more than 30 per cent of their population using the Internet. This strong growth has contributed to social media use.

(ii) Broadband

Broadband is gaining increasing attention by Governments worldwide as a general-purpose technology with important impacts on the economy, employment, education and health (see e.g. Broadband Commission (2010); box II.1). At the end of 2010, there were an estimated 527 million fixed broadband subscriptions around the world. Global penetration rose less than one point between 2009 and 2010 from 7.0 to 7.7 fixed broadband subscriptions per 100 inhabitants (figure II.14). The gap between developed and developing countries remains massive (26 versus 4) and in LDCs there were less than 1 million fixed broadband subscriptions in 2010. An average person in a developed economy was 294 times more likely to have access to fixed broadband than one living in an LDC.

Almost all economies that have seen the largest increases in fixed broadband connectivity in the past few years are developed ones, mainly from Europe (figure II.15). Of the three non-developed economies top performers, Belarus and Croatia are transition economies whereas Dominica is a high-income developing country with relatively small population and land area making it relatively easy to connect with fixed high-speed infrastructure.

The global broadband landscape is characterized by huge gaps not only in basic connectivity but also in terms of download speeds. The world average in 2010 was about 6.4 Mbps. But whereas the highest average download speed was noted for the Republic of Korea at 37.6 Mbps, the situation in developing countries such as Nepal, Lebanon and Bangladesh were below 1 Mbps (figure II.16).

Digital Subscriber Line (DSL) technology over fixed telephone lines accounts for the lion's share of fixed broadband connections followed by cable modem (20 per cent) and fibre optic to the premise (12 per cent) (Point Topic, 2010). The remaining share (2 per cent) includes such technologies as fixed wireless (e.g. WiMAX). At the same time, given the far greater penetration of mobile phones compared with fixed broad-

Box II.1. The Broadband Commission for Digital Development

The Broadband Commission for Digital Development was launched in May 2010 during the *World Summit on the Information Society (WSIS) Forum 2010* in Geneva. It is led by two co-chairs, H.E. Mr. Paul Kagame, President of Rwanda; and Mr. Carlos Slim Helú, Honorary Lifetime Chair of Grupo Carso. The heads of the ITU and the United Nations Educational, Scientific and Cultural Organization (UNESCO) serve as vice-chairs. Other commissioners are from government, the private sector, international agencies (including the Secretary-General of UNCTAD) and civil society and academia.

The Broadband Commission has produced two initial outcome reports and has also created a number of working groups to focus on specific areas of importance. The first, high-level, report is entitled *Broadband: A Leadership Imperative*, and reflects input from the Commissioners and was presented to United Nations Secretary-General Ban Ki-moon in September 2010, ahead of the 2010 Millennium Development Goals (MDGs) Summit. The second report, *Broadband: A Platform for Progress*, is a more comprehensive analytical piece, which looks at financing models, return on investment, technology choices, and strategies for deployment across a range of different types of economies.

Source: The Broadband Commission (www.broadbandcommission.org).

band subscriptions, wireless broadband holds significant potential for boosting high-speed Internet access in developing economies. Many developing nations have mobile subscription penetration rates similar to developed countries but far lower fixed broadband penetration.

Mobile solutions are likely to be the preferred route to extending broadband in many low-income countries with limited fixed line infrastructure. In some developing countries that have launched mobile broadband networks, including in Africa, high-speed wireless subscriptions now surpass fixed broadband. For example, according to data from the GSM Association, in September 2010, there were 2.2 million wireless broadband subscriptions in South Africa but only 1,200 fixed broadband subscriptions, and in Nigeria, there were almost four times as many mobile as fixed broadband subscriptions.[27] Although mobile broadband penetration in low-income countries is still far below the world

average, the gap is smaller than in the case of fixed broadband. ITU estimates that there were about 872 million active mobile broadband subscriptions in 2010. Whereas global mobile broadband penetration was about 65 per cent higher than fixed broadband penetration, in Africa it was 1,400 per cent higher.[28]

In order to speed up the roll-out of mobile broadband, countries need to allocate spectrum and license operators to provide the service. At the end of 2010, almost 50 developing and transition economies had yet to launch mobile broadband services (table II.5). But licensing mobile broadband services is insufficient for guaranteeing access throughout a country. Only around 2 billion people out of the entire world's population are covered by high-speed data networks, and even in developed regions such as Europe it is estimated that around 20 per cent of the population is not yet covered by mobile broadband.[29] The mobile industry expects to see rapid growth in the coming years. According to Ericsson, the number of mobile broadband subscriptions is predicted to grow from about 1 billion in 2011 to almost 5 billion by 2016.[30]

(iii) International bandwidth

International bandwidth – i.e the total capacity available for accessing websites and other Internet applications located outside of a country – is another important aspect of connectivity for the private sector. Due to a lack of local content, most Internet traffic in developing countries is often to overseas locations. If international bandwidth is constrained, the broadband experience will be poor, limiting the types of applications users can access and discouraging them from using the full potential of the Internet. Although international connectivity can be provided by satellite and other transmission mediums, the most cost-effective

Figure II.14. Fixed broadband subscriptions per 100 inhabitants, by country group, 2000-2010

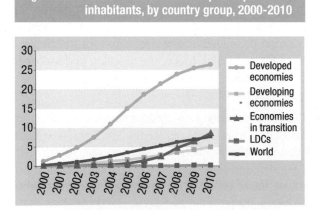

Source: ITU World Telecommunication/ICT Indicators data base.

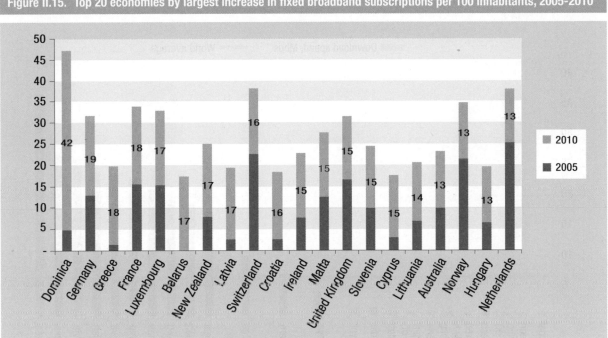

Figure II.15. Top 20 economies by largest increase in fixed broadband subscriptions per 100 inhabitants, 2005-2010

Note: Excluding economies with a population of less than 100,000. Economies ranked according to the increase in penetration.

Source: Adapted from ITU World Telecommunication/ICT Indicators database.

Table II.5. Economies in which no mobile broadband services had been launched by December 2010

Region	Economy
East Asia and Oceania	Bangladesh, Democratic People's Republic of Korea, Federated States of Micronesia, Islamic Republic of Iran, Kiribati, Lebanon, Marshall Islands, Myanmar, Occupied Palestinian Territory, Samoa, Solomon Islands, Timor-Leste, Tonga, Tuvalu, Vanuatu, Yemen
Latin America and the Caribbean	Antigua and Barbuda, Bahamas, Costa Rica, Cuba, Dominica, Grenada, Guyana, Saint Kitts and Nevis, Saint Lucia, Saint Vincent and the Grenadines, Suriname
Africa	Algeria, Benin, Burundi, Cape Verde, Central African Republic, Comoros, Congo, Djibouti, Eritrea, Gabon, Guinea, Guinea-Bissau, Niger, Sao Tome and Principe, Seychelles, Somalia, Swaziland, Togo, Tunisia, Zambia
Transition economies	Albania

Source: UNCTAD, adapted from CDG and GSMA.
Note: The countries and territories that the CDMA Development Group (CDG) and the GSM Association (GSMA) reported had no EV-DO or HSPA mobile broadband networks in commercial operation as at May 2011.

solution is through fiber-optic cable. This is a challenge for landlocked countries that lack direct access to undersea cable systems and must ensure national fibre-optic backbones connect to neighboring countries for high-speed international bandwidth. Competitive limitations restraining the number of upstream suppliers are another issue in a number of countries. Without regulatory relief, wholesale prices are often above costs with consequent negative implications for retail prices. Reduced affordability limits access to the Internet for the poor and for small enterprises.

International Internet bandwidth grew by 55 per cent in 2010 and stood at almost 40 terabits per second (Tbps) (figure II.17). The growth in capacity is helping to drive down prices but the impact is constrained due to skyrocketing demand for bandwidth intensive video applications. Operators are having trouble keeping up with this demand and are increasingly resorting to tactics such as capped volume plans and throttling of bandwidth heavy applications (TeleGeography, 2010). One region that has long had constrained international bandwidth is sub-Saharan Africa, where

Figure II.16. Average download speeds, selected economies, 2010, (Mbps)

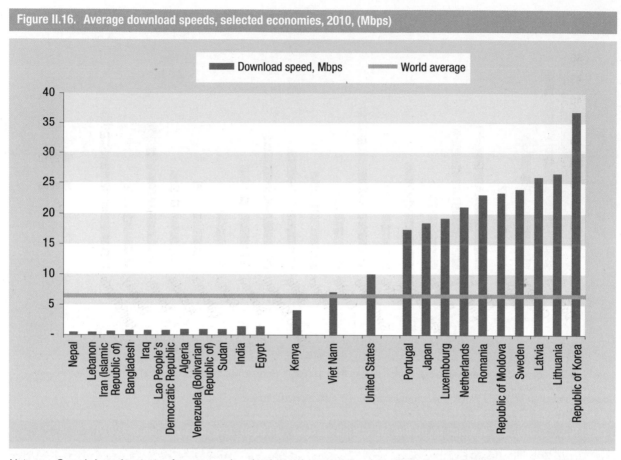

Note: Speeds based on tests of consumer download speeds around the globe. The value is the rolling mean throughput in Mbps over the past 30 days where the mean distance between the client and the server is less than 300 miles. Data were downloaded on 9 March 2010.

Source: OOKLA (www.ookla.com/).

there was only one major interregional undersea cable until 2009. Since then, five new systems have been launched and another two are scheduled to go operational over the next few years.[31] These new cable systems have already helped prices come down in some countries and will raise the total capacity delivered by fibre-optic cable in the region from 3 Tbps to 21 Tbps.[32] It will also provide direct access for practically every sub-Saharan African country bordering the sea, and could begin to integrate the region into the global information economy. For this to happen, regulators need to ensure that supply bottlenecks are minimized through effective price pressure such as extensive competition and controls on operators with significant market power.

b. Business use of the Internet

Developing economies lag behind significantly compared to developed ones and world average in terms of enterprise use of the Internet. For example, less than one in five enterprises in sub-Saharan Africa has a web site, compared to four out of five in the Organization for Economic Cooperation and Development (OECD) countries and about 30 per cent for the world as a whole (figure II.18).

While Internet use by enterprises continues to grow in developing countries, large differences still remain in the type of use according to enterprise size and economic sector. As with computers, there is a clear difference in the level of Internet use between medium-sized and large enterprises, on the one hand, and of small and (especially) micro-enterprises on the other (see figure II.19). Take Jordan, where virtually all enterprises with more than 250 employees but just 6 per cent of the micro-enterprises use the Internet.

Low levels of Internet adoption by the smallest firms tend to pull down overall levels of ICT use in developing economies, as evidenced by the data regarding Internet use by sectors. In terms of the economic sector, available data for developing countries do not

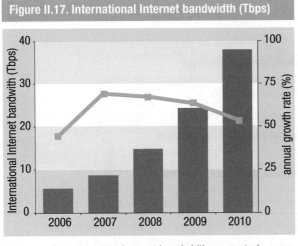

Figure II.17. International Internet bandwidth (Tbps)

Note: Data represent Internet bandwidth connected across
           international borders as of mid-year.
Source: TeleGeography, Inc.

show a consistent pattern across countries.[33] To illustrate, in the wholesale and retail trade industry, which has the largest number of countries with available information on enterprise use of the Internet, the level of Internet use varies from 5 per cent in Jordan to almost 92 per cent in Brazil. In developed countries, however, the level of Internet use is high across all sectors (see annex table II.5). When sectors are compared, financial intermediation enterprises show the highest levels of use, while the lowest are found for community, social and personal services. However, international comparability is hampered by differences in survey characteristics of different countries. For example, the share of manufacturing enterprises using the Internet varies from 9 per cent in Thailand to 64 per cent in Tunisia, and in the wholesale and retail trade industry between 5 per cent in Jordan and almost 92 per cent in Brazil. One explanation is that Thailand and Jordan include micro-enterprises in their survey, while Tunisia and Brazil do not.

In addition to the industry, Internet use is also influenced by the market-orientation of the enterprise. One survey of ICT use in developing countries found that exporters and foreign-owned firms relied significantly on e-mail and the Internet, and that this applied regardless of their size. In contrast, the size of a firm became a critical factor when the firm was both a non-exporter and domestically owned. Among the non-exporting micro-enterprises surveyed, only 27 per cent used e-mail and 22 per cent used the Internet to interact with clients and suppliers (Qiang et al., 2006).

PSD strategies should promote Internet use that goes beyond the practice of sending and receiving e-mails. The Internet potentially enables enterprises to engage in electronic commerce, for example, to facilitate their transactions. UNCTAD data show that more firms are using the Internet to place than to receive orders, a pattern that appears to apply to countries at different levels of development (figure II.20, annex table II.6). It might be inferred that with adequate connectivity, enterprises are able to purchase almost immediately,

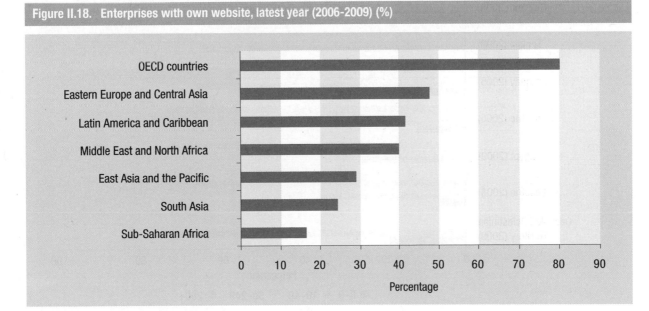

Figure II.18. Enterprises with own website, latest year (2006-2009) (%)

Source: World Bank Enterprise Surveys.

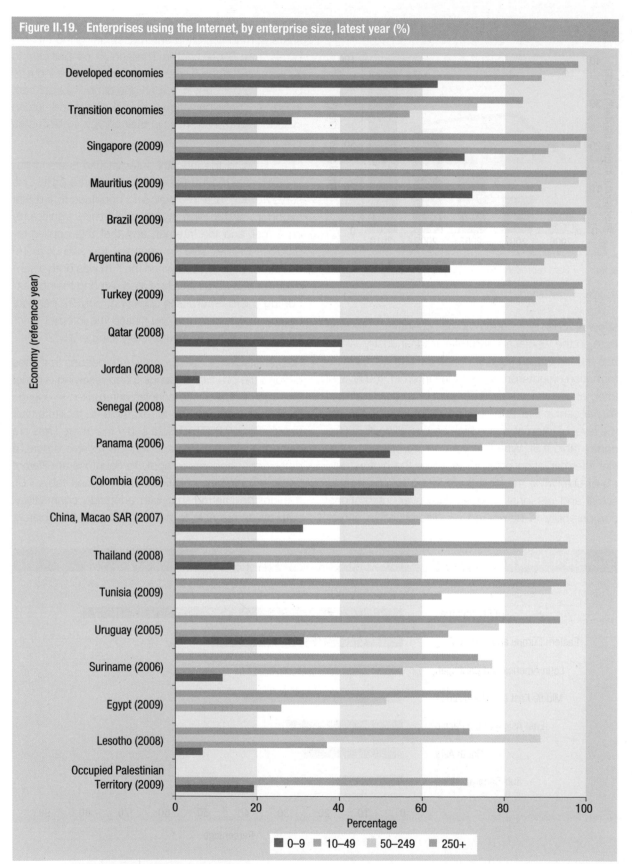

Figure II.19. Enterprises using the Internet, by enterprise size, latest year (%)

Source: UNCTAD Information Economy Database.

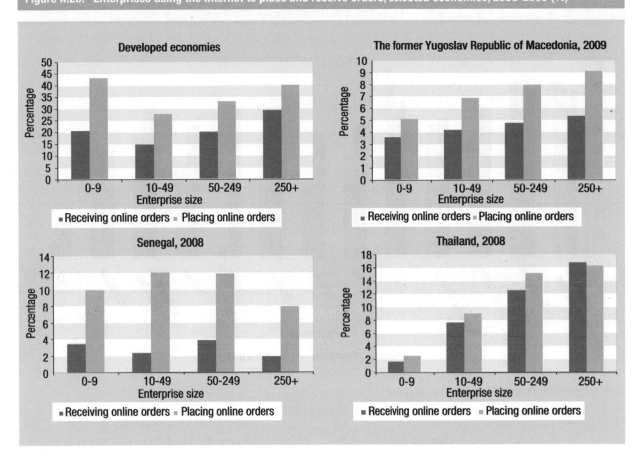

Figure II.20. Enterprises using the Internet to place and receive orders, selected economies, 2008-2009 (%)

Source: UNCTAD Information Economy Database.

but setting up systems that will allow them to sell online, in particular if it involves creating or upgrading a Web presence and restructuring sales and inventory processes, requires more time and resources. Large and medium-sized enterprises may be better placed to engage in e-commerce more quickly, and may also have a greater need for such systems.[34]

The Internet is an important channel for enterprises to engage online with Governments. The provision of e-government services is a way for Governments to apply ICTs in support of PSD (see chapter IV). Better access to relevant information from the government can reduce information search costs, and the ability to make transactions with government organizations carries even greater potential for improved efficiency and cost reduction. E-government-to-business transaction services include the declaration and payment of taxes online, payment of utilities and other fees, automated customs systems, job banks matching employers with potential employees or application for government assistance.[35]

UNCTAD data suggest that developing-country enterprises use the Internet more for obtaining information from governments than for conducting transactions with them (figure II.21). This may be due partly to the limited range of e-government services on offer. According to the United Nations *E-Government Survey 2010,* "only a few countries are able to offer many secure transactions online... although the trend is toward more e-forms and e-payments" (UNDESA, 2010: 77). Even in cases where enterprises report that they use the Internet more for interaction than for getting information, such as in Brazil, this interaction does not necessarily reflect online transactions.[36] For example, a recent study of the "gov.br" domain found that approximately 80 per cent of documents published in Brazilian Government websites were in ".pdf" format, and only 5 per cent were in ".xml" format, used for data interoperation.[37] When integrating ICT in their PSD strategies, countries might envisage not only facilitating the provision of government services for enterprises online, but also building trust in the online environment so as to promote uptake by enterprises.

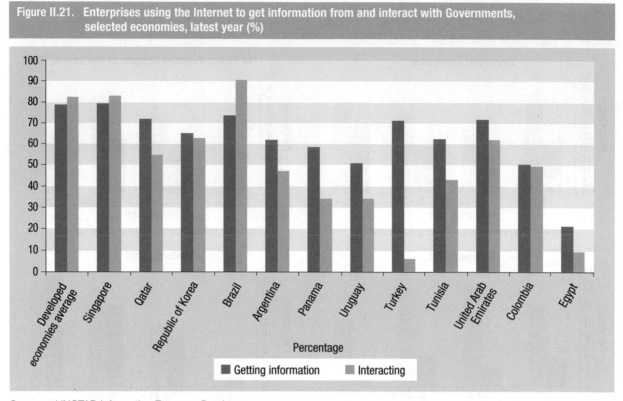

Figure II.21. Enterprises using the Internet to get information from and interact with Governments, selected economies, latest year (%)

Source: UNCTAD Information Economy Database.

High-speed connections are essential to make full use of today's multimedia-rich Internet and to enable powerful business applications. Studies in developed countries show that broadband is essential to enable enterprises to make full use of Internet-based services and applications (UNCTAD, 2009a). As can be seen from figure II.22, fixed broadband use is almost ubiquitous in developed economies, with around 90 per cent of enterprises benefiting from high-speed Internet access. In developing countries for which data are available, the pattern is more diverse. For example, while more than three quarters of medium and large enterprises in Brazil, Colombia, Qatar, Republic of Korea, Singapore, Turkey and the United Arab Emirates have broadband Internet access, the corresponding share is much lower in other economies, especially in the case of MSEs.[38]

One advantage of having broadband access is the possibility to use Voice over Internet Protocol (VoIP), which is rapidly expanding (figure II.23). This is of particular relevance for micro-enterprises and SMEs in developing countries, given its lower cost structure compared to traditional telephone services.[39] A 2008 survey in Fiji found that 21 per cent of SMEs used the VoIP application Skype to communicate and

negotiate with their foreign-based suppliers (Devi, 2008). Over one fifth of fixed broadband subscriptions around the world include voice over broadband service.[40] This amounted to some 110 million in mid 2010 (figure II.23) or around 10 per cent of conventional fixed telephone lines. It should be noted that several countries reportedly either ban VoIP services (as in Ethiopia, Kuwait and Oman) or have restrictions that make it almost impossible for such services to be provided by competitive providers (as in Armenia, Bangladesh, Egypt, Philippines, Saudi Arabia, Thailand and the United Arab Emirates) (Voice on the Net Coalition, 2010).[41]

The wholesale pricing legacy of traditional telephone networks has impacted on VoIP services. Fixed telephone operators charge a wholesale "termination" rate to complete calls within their networks. This applies to calls coming from an IP-based service and terminating on a telephone line. This explains why a VoIP service, such as Skype, offers free computer-to-computer calls but charges for computer-to-telephone calls. The lowest price Skype charges for a call to conventional telephone numbers around the world is $0.023 per minute. However, Skype offers that rate only for calls to fixed lines in three dozen primarily developed

Figure II.22. Enterprises using the Internet via fixed broadband, selected economies, latest year (%)

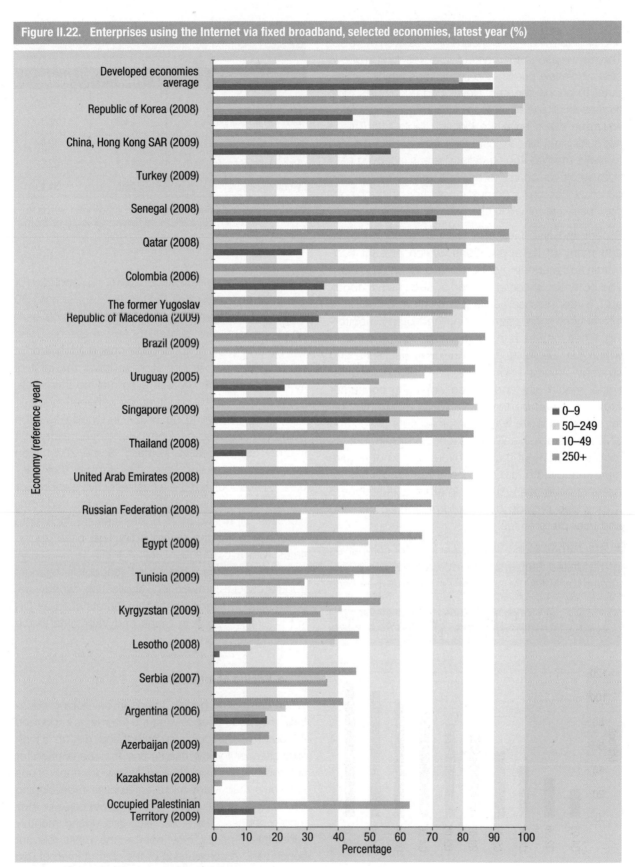

Source: UNCTAD Information Economy Database.

countries. Calls to other fixed lines are more expensive and calls terminating on mobile phones even more so. The main reasons are market failure, resulting in above cost wholesale prices, and regulations banning computer to phone services. Developed economies have the lowest Skype "Out" (computer to telephone) rates while the LDCs have the highest (table II.6). This is not surprising, since most LDC citizens cannot afford to make many outgoing calls whereas incoming calls from wealthier countries are less price-sensitive and generate income for domestic operators through non-cost-based termination charges.

Broadband also facilitates the use of social media and many of its applications, which present economic and marketing opportunities for enterprises.[42] The potential of social networks, such as Facebook and Twitter, lies particularly in relation to customer interaction, such as marketing and brand monitoring. Their nature encourages customer feedback, which can serve to guide business decisions and strategy. Young people are particularly adept at social media use and are an emerging consumer group that can be targeted. Social media may offer a cost-effective way for informal enterprises and SMEs to establish a Web presence. Furthermore, as mobile versions of social networking do not require much bandwidth, they can be attractive options for users in countries with slow Internet connections.[43] It may also provide better information on demand and user preferences.

A 2010 study found that 20 per cent of companies in the United States and Europe already use blogs, forums or wikis for internal or external purposes

Table II.6.	Skype out rates, US cents per minute, March 2011	
Group	Fixed	Mobile
Developed economies	4.5	22.5
Developing economies	24.3	26.1
LDCs	41.6	42.8
Transition economies	15.2	22.6
World	23.5	31.2

Note: Average (mean) rates for calls made from Skype to fixed or mobile telephone numbers in each economic group.
Source: Adapted from Skype.

(Deutsche Bank Research, 2010). In April 2010, some 37 per cent of all Twitter users (or around 40 million people) were "tweeting" from their mobiles.[44] Short "tweets" are similar to text messages and therefore a good fit for mobile phones.[45] Twitter is working with mobile operators to lower the cost of sending tweets via SMS or even making them free. Most of the top 10 countries by penetration are in the developing world. In Brazil, Indonesia and the Bolivarian Republic of Venezuela, around every fifth Internet user accesses Twitter.[46] Some 200 million people are accessing Facebook through their mobiles.[47] Facebook can be a cost-effective platform for micro-enterprises and SMEs compared to traditional websites. More and more businesses are flocking to Facebook to tap into its expanding user base, sometimes with a consequent fall in traffic to traditional company websites.[48] But while Facebook is the most popular social networking application worldwide, others lead in specific national markets such as Orkut in Brazil, Qzone in China and Vkontakte in the Russian Federation.[49]

c. Pricing of Internet use

When comparing pricing trends in developing countries, the mode of accessing the Internet is important. Although much focus is on broadband, dial-up is typically cheaper for low usage, and may be enough for enterprises using simple, low bandwidth applications such as e-mail. Many micro-enterprises in developing countries go online only through Internet cafés or their mobile phones. Therefore, fixed broadband monthly subscription prices may not be the most relevant benchmark. A comparison of the cost of Internet use at public facilities or mobile Internet prices would be

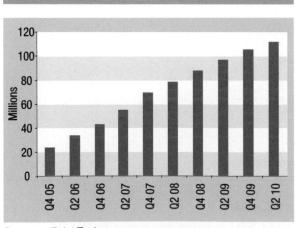

Figure II.23. Global subscriptions of voice over Internet Protocol, Q4 2005–Q2 2010, (millions)

Source: Point Topic.

more useful. In addition, broadband price benchmarks are complicated by the variety of speeds on offer and data cap policies. Even assuming the arguably low but internationally agreed minimum speed definition of 256 Kbps for broadband poses problems, since entry-level speeds are much higher than this in many developed countries.[50] Moreover, a device such as a PC or an Internet-enabled mobile handset is necessary to use the Internet. The device price is included in some mobile price basket methodologies. In the case of fixed broadband, however, few price comparisons do factor in the cost of the telephone line rental (for DSL) or the device.

The ITU Internet price basket, which is based on fixed broadband, suggests that affordability improved between 2008 and 2010, with the world average price falling from 165 per cent to 79 per cent of world per capita income.[51] Other data confirm this trend. Between the first quarter of 2008 and the fourth quarter of 2010, the price per Mbps of broadband packages around the world fell by half (figure II.24).[52] One reason is increased competition as operators look to move into untapped lower income market segments. Reductions are more pronounced for DSL and cable modem, possibly reflecting that many new users are looking for the cheapest connection rather than the one that provides the best value.

Despite the prevalent use of mobile phones to access the Internet, particularly in developing economies, there are no regularly updated or official sources of international price benchmarks. According to Nokia's "Internet premium" price comparison, which reflects the impact of additional mobile Internet usage (2 Mb per month) on a mobile voice basket, the average monthly mobile data price was $3.58 in 2010 with significant variation across countries (figure II.25).

Table II.7 contrasts entry-level fixed and mobile broadband prices for a group of developing countries from different regions. In almost every case, mobile broadband seems a more affordable option than fixed broadband, with less expensive plans as well as lower prices per Mbps. Although mobile broadband generally has usage caps, it is often available on a pay-per-use basis whereas fixed broadband generally requires monthly payment (in addition to the cost of telephone line rental). Advertised speeds of mobile broadband also tend to be higher than fixed broadband packages. Lower cost of mobile broadband, the fact that it does not require a fixed line and that it can be purchased in pre-paid increments make it an attractive

proposition for small firms. Coverage of high-speed mobile networks needs to be extended so that more small enterprises can take advantage of them.

C. POLICY IMPLICATIONS

Enhanced business use of relevant ICTs is important in the context of PSD, and governments can play a key role in this context. When considering what strategies and actions to take, the diversity of both ICTs and enterprises needs to be borne in mind. As noted in the preceding subsections, ICTs vary greatly in terms of accessibility, functionality and user requirements. Certain technological applications may be either out of reach for small enterprises or of little relevance, depending on their specific needs and capabilities.

A 2007 review of barriers preventing SMEs in Asia–Pacific from capitalizing on ICT developments identified a number of factors which are relevant also in other parts of the developing world (UNDP, 2007).[53] The first was limited availability of reliable Internet and broadband connectivity at competitive prices. For rural enterprises in low-income countries, a lack of other kinds of infrastructure (mobile networks, electricity) may also hamper uptake.[54] Secondly, SMEs continued to be plagued by a lack of human as well as financial resources needed to keep up with rapidly evolving technologies and services. Intense competition and low profit margins made SMEs reluctant to allocate the necessary costs of maintaining and upgrading IT systems.[55] Thirdly, weak privacy and legal protection for

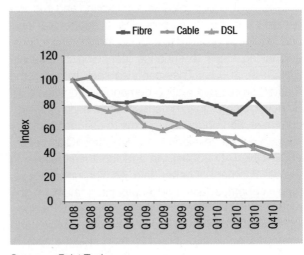

Figure II.24. Fixed broadband price index ($/Mbps)

Source: Point Topic.

Figure II.25.   Price of monthly mobile data usage (2 MB per month), 2010 ($)

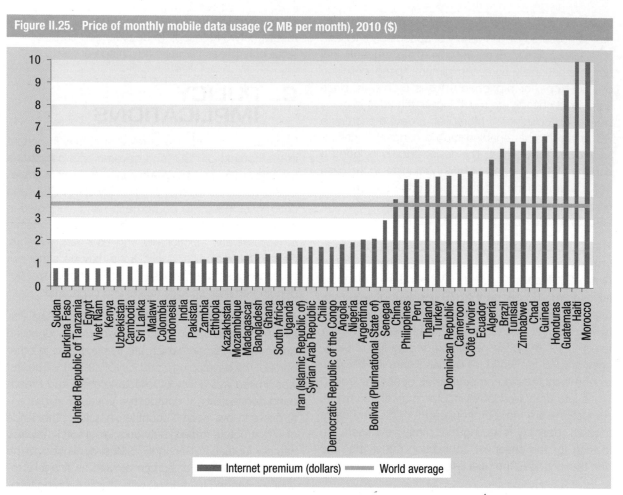

Legend: Internet premium (dollars) — World average

Source: Nokia.

electronic transactions was an issue in many countries in Asia Pacific, especially LDCs. Moreover, the special needs of SMEs seldom feature in regulatory systems addressing security, privacy and consumer protection.

Governments can create environments for greater ICT uptake, by liberalizing markets to expand and improve network infrastructure, providing a supportive legal and regulatory environment for electronic transactions, and taking steps to enhance technological diffusion (UNCTAD, 2009a). They can also seek to overcome market failures by creating demand aggregation (e.g. by developing e-government services, such as e-procurement, and encouraging firms to use them) and by supporting the development of ICT skills (Qiang *et al.,* 2006; UNCTAD 2009a). An additional area relates to the development of better data. As highlighted above, many countries lack up-to-date information on the nature of ICT use among their enterprises, hampering their ability to formulate and monitor policies and strategies in this area (box II.2). As part of the work of the Partnership on Measuring ICT for Development,

UNCTAD and several regional commissions of the United Nations are actively supporting the production of statistics related to ICT use in enterprises.[56] However, the need for capacity-building and training in this area remains huge.

In terms of enhancing access to different ICTs, Governments can contribute by opening up ICT markets and improving competition. This involves macro-level reforms of the investment climate and business environment. Competition increases the likelihood that private sector investment – whether with a partnership of the public sector or not – will help make relevant (i.e. size and sector-specific) ICTs available to the business community at increasingly affordable rates (see chapter III). Where relevant connectivity is still lacking due to market failures, such as in the case of mobile networks in rural areas of LDCs, Governments and their development partners need to explore approaches to extending both network access and local access (UNCTAD, 2010).

Table II.7. Mobile versus fixed broadband pricing, selected economies, March 2011 (dollars)								
	Brazil	**Kenya**	**Morocco**	**Saint Kitts and Nevis**	**Sri Lanka**	**Turkey**	**Viet Nam**	**AVERAGE**
Fixed broadband basket unlimited, 2011	$31.31	$39.36	$11.86	$37.34	$14.18	$30.09	$8.72	$24.69
Speed (Mbps)	0.512	0.256	1	2	0.512	1	1.536	0.97
$/Mbps	$61	$154	$12	$19	$28	$30	$6	$25
% income	3.60%	53.20%	5.00%	4.40%	7.20%	3.50%	9.10%	12.30%
Mobile broadband basket 1 GB, 2011	$51.27	$26.24	$11.86	na	$4.34	$19.93	$6.34	$19.99
Speed (Mbps)	1	7.2	1.8	na	7.2	7.2	3.6	4.67
$/Mbps	$51	$4	$7	na	$1	$3	$2	$4
% income	5.90%	35.50%	5.00%	na	2.20%	2.30%	6.60%	9.60%

Source: UNCTAD, based on information from operator tariff schedules.

As noted above, prices of ICT services are on their way down in most markets, largely as a result of intensified competition and improved connectivity. However, the pace and scope of price reductions vary by service and country. So while micro-enterprises and SMEs in some countries are benefiting from lower prices, others are not. Price obstructions include market failures resulting in higher wholesale prices, a lack of market entry in some segments and bans or regulatory restrictions on certain services. Another factor in some countries is high taxes on ICT devices and services. These barriers impede ICT uptake since high communications prices elevate operating costs. Usage is also constrained by high prices, limiting the potential for micro-enterprises and SMEs to explore new business opportunities offered by the Internet. UNECLAC (2010) emphasized the need to develop broadband strategies in Latin America and the Caribbean to reduce access costs.

For micro-enterprises, lower prices for various mobile services are particularly important. Meanwhile, more affordable broadband connectivity is crucial for certain economic activities, such as ICT-enabled services. It also contributes to linking up with global value chains. Keeping costs down will encourage not only enterprises but also governments and consumers to make use of ICT-based solutions, e.g. for e-government, m-government, e-commerce and m-commerce. Governments can do more to achieve lower costs for the poor and MSEs through encouraging greater competition together with foresight over high wholesale costs. Their role in demand facilitation through affordability programmes is critical to match the traditional emphasis placed on infrastructure investment. Indeed, it is likely to assume greater importance as supply side bottlenecks are alleviated in countries.

Making sure enterprises possess the required set of skills and capabilities to use relevant technologies productively is very important to secure economic benefits from enhanced ICT access. Many entrepreneurs in developing countries, and especially in LDCs, lack the necessary capacity or awareness to take full advantage of ICTs. Thus, even if they have access to mobile phones or the Internet, they may not know how best to leverage them for their business operations. They may in fact fail to see how investments required to use technology could be valuable and relevant to their business. One way to address this issue is to integrate ICT skills development in general business management training curricula (box II.3). In Malaysia, the Government has rolled out a series of "SME Business Success with ICT" seminars nationwide to encourage SMEs to adopt ICT and e-commerce with a view to enhancing their efficiency and widen their market reach.[57] For more advanced ICT use, initiatives may be required to promote operational management tools, such as customer relationship management, enterprise resource planning and e-billing systems, as well as advanced e-commerce applications (for business-to-business (B2B), business-to-consumer (B2C) and Web 2.0). Training of professionals, technical assistance and credit support to help enterprises adapt their business models are also important (UNECLAC, 2010).

Box II.2. The challenge of leveraging ICTs for PSD in Peru

A recent UNCTAD review of the innovation system of the ICT sector and related policies in Peru observed that the country enjoys several strengths but also important weaknesses. Among the former, the country benefits from a sound legal framework, a relatively well-developed infrastructure (at least in the main economic centres) and a certain level of domestic productive capacity.

The study also highlighted certain challenges for the Government to leverage ICTs in their efforts to support PSD. The first was related to the level and nature of ICT use in the private sector. The Government has limited knowledge of the extent to which SMEs access and use ICTs. Enterprise surveys of ICT use are currently not covered by the National Statistical Office (INEI). However, it is likely that ICT use remains limited among the SMEs. Household surveys suggest that most (71 per cent) Internet users access the Internet through public cyber cafés; in 2008 only 12.5 per cent stated that they used the Internet at work (INEI, 2009). Very few users go on-line to undertake banking transactions (4.5 per cent) or to interact with government organizations and public authorities (3.4 per cent) (INEI 2009).

The second challenge was linked to the limited extent to which ICTs are reflected in government strategies. In addition to collecting better data on enterprise use of ICTs, Peru would also benefit from designing a specific policy to promote ICT access and use among SMEs. Similarly, it should consider implementing a strategy for the strengthening of the ICT producing sector, including a national software industry that could support the use of ICTs in the private sector. The UNCTAD review proposed that such a strategy should among other things address the need for accreditation of IT training and use of certification systems in the IT industry.

Source: UNCTAD (2011b).

Governments – at the national and subnational levels – may also set an example in terms of ICT use, by taking the lead and providing online information and services, including e-procurement services. Such initiatives can help raise awareness about ICTs as a tool to support business operations. For example, the Shanghai Municipal Economic and Informatization Commission, which is in charge of promoting ICT in enterprises in Shanghai, China, publishes all policies, news and other valuable information for enterprises to use ICT on a dedicated website. In addition, it has organized various awards and programmes, including the "Top ten excellent enterprise ICT solutions", the "Top ten best practices of enterprise ICT applications" and a detailed list of "recommended enterprise ICT solutions". These are publicized on the website with a view to helping enterprise access information of relevant solutions.[58] UNECLAC (2010) called for e-government strategies to increase online transactions and open government procurement systems to small enterprises, provide facilities and security for e-billing and e-commerce, and promote standards and quality certifications.

Indeed, a prerequisite for more widespread uptake of ICTs for commercial purposes is that enterprises and consumers trust the systems. Some Governments still need to adopt and enforce adequate legal frameworks to unleash the full potential of electronic transactions, in particular, by improving consumer and business confidence. In addition, rapid technological progress in business practice over the past few years has raised new legal challenges. For instance, the use of mobile devices for commercial transactions creates specific issues with respect to security of the transmission, secure identification of the parties, structure of contracts, options for payment, privacy and data retention, and consumer protection (chapter IV).[59] The existing legal framework for e-commerce might not suffice to address those issues (UNCITRAL, 2011). This is particularly relevant for low-income countries where the mobile platforms are critical as an enabler of electronic transactions for businesses, governments and consumers.

The international community provides guidance to developing countries wishing to implement legal reforms related to e-commerce and m-commerce and promotes regional and global harmonization in order to facilitate online international trade.[60] UNCITRAL texts on electronic commerce, including the United Nations Convention on the Use of Electronic Communications in International Contracts (2005),[61] may serve as a model in this context.

Developing countries are increasingly aware of the need to harmonize their cyberlegislation with neighbouring countries and other significant commercial partners. Regional cyberlaw initiatives are underway to support regional integration or foster countries' par-

---

Box II.3. Training entrepreneurs to use mobile phones as a business tool

In collaboration with the Government of Panama and four partner United Nations agencies (the United Nations Industrial Development Organization (UNIDO), the Food and Agriculture Organization of the United Nations (FAO), the World Tourism Organization (UNWTO) and the United Nations Development Programme (UNDP)), UNCTAD is implementing a Joint Programme on "Entrepreneurship Network Opportunities for Poor Families" in Panama.[a] In 2010, specific mobile exercises were integrated for the first time into UNCTAD's Empretec entrepreneurship training for micro-entrepreneurs in that country. Although most of the entrepreneurs had their own cell phones, the majority used them only to communicate with friends and relatives. The Empretec workshop helped them treat the phone as a business tool. As a result, participants subsequently started using them to store clients' contact details, to calculate costings and sending texts for marketing purposes. Notably, many of the entrepreneurs that participated in the training now seek out more information about prices, competition and potential clients through their cell phones.

The need to train entrepreneurs in using ICTs has been observed in other countries as well. In collaboration with the International Institute for Communication and Development (IICD), the SEND Foundation in Ghana and the Federation of Agricultural producers in Burkina Faso both started in 2009 to use the West African ESOKO market information system delivered via mobile services to access relevant market information. Despite improved access to information, however, the results did not match expectations. The intended beneficiaries – small-scale farmers (especially women) – generally lacked the technical and marketing skills needed to use the information and the mobile services effectively. To address this situation, the organizations focused on building the capacities of underprivileged women to use mobile phones and product codes to request information from the platform. Participants learned how to interpret the information provided, relate it to their own production plans, and to make better marketing and sales decisions. As explained by one of the women, "I learned how to use the mobile phone to find a market for my own goods. Accessibility to markets has enabled me to pay school fees, purchase animal draft power and construction of a house."

Source: UNCTAD, based on information provided by Empretec and IICD.
[a]   The project is financed by the Government for Spain.

---

ticipation in international trade. In Asia, for instance, 8 of the 10 members of the Association of Southeast Asian Nations (ASEAN) have adopted harmonized e-commerce laws based on UNCITRAL models. The remaining two, Cambodia and the Lao People's Democratic Republic, are intending to adopt similar legislation by 2012. In Africa, several regional groupings are in the process of developing guidelines in view of the development of e-commerce and m-commerce. The East African Community (EAC), for example, has already made significant advances by preparing a regional Framework for Cyberlaws. EAC member countries have taken a number of steps to adopt cyberlaws based on the recommendations contained in the Framework prepared by the EAC and UNCTAD. In Latin America and the Caribbean, the adoption of cyberlaws is given attention at the supra-national as well as the national level.[62] A number of Central American countries have *de facto* harmonized their e-commerce legislation on the basis of UNCITRAL texts. Similarly, the ITU HIPCAR project is promoting the adoption of uniform texts for cyberlegislation in the Caribbean.

To be effective and reach intended beneficiaries, policy interventions to promote greater ICT uptake and use in the private sector must be tailored to specific contexts and based upon a clear understanding of the real experience and requirements of different enterprises (UNCTAD, 2010). Policymakers should in this context actively seek the input and engagement of enterprises in programme design and implementation. Their direct involvement brings relevant experience – of the constraints faced by enterprises and of ways in which they can make use of technology – to the fore and helps to focus interventions on outcomes of higher value to end-users.

NOTES

[1]   The fixed telephone price basket published by ITU is based on the monthly line rental plus 15 peak and 15 off-peak three-minute local calls. It does not include calls to mobile phones, which are much more expensive than local calls to fixed lines. See "ICT services getting more affordable worldwide", Press Release. 16 May 2011, http://www.itu.int/net/pressoffice/press_releases/2011/15.aspx.

[2]   In some countries, operators have waived this additional fee and bundle the telephone line with a broadband DSL subscription or so-called "naked DSL". This can be particularly relevant for SMEs in developing countries where fixed broadband tends to be expensive and the additional cost of paying for the telephone lines can make or break the decision to have broadband.

[3]   While these penetration rates are based on subscription data and therefore do not necessarily reflect actual mobile ownership, the data indicate growth of the sector in general terms.

[4]   A survey of small businesses in the United States confirms that use of mobile applications is also of high relevance in developed markets. Nearly three quarters of the enterprises surveyed were using mobile applications in their businesses. Their primary reasons were to save time, increase productivity and reduce costs. See "AT&T Survey Shows Mobile Apps Integral to Small Business Operations, Remote Workers on the Rise, Facebook Use Growing Rapidly", AT&T Press Release, 15 March 2011, available at http://www.att.com/gen/press-room?pid=19326&cdvn=news&newsarticleid=31689&mapcode=enterprise.

[5]   Almost half of the SMEs in the United Kingdom have already adopted smartphones because of their ease of use, decreasing costs and increase in power. Barclays Plc. "Mobile businesses rush to embrace smartphones." Press Release, 3 September 2010. http://www.newsroom.barclays.com/content/Detail.aspx?ReleaseID=1807&NewsAreaID=2.

[6]   "Africa's Mobile Money Pricing Systems Need Fixing". *The East African*, 21 March 2011. http://allafrica.com/stories/201103211297.html.

[7]   Entrepreneurs in Uganda have been found to benefit by saving on transport costs and time waiting in banks. "MTN MobileMoney and Zain Zap boosting SMEs In Uganda". *Mobile Money Africa*, 13 August 2009. http://mobilemoneyafrica.com/?p=427.

[8]   Information by MNOs and confirmed by discussions with Central Bank representatives during field trips in June 2011.

[9]   See http://kilimosalama.wordpress.com/.

[10] See the *Information Economy Report 2010* (UNCTAD, 2010) for an extensive review of ICT service affordability issues and methodologies.

[11] See "Newly released data from ITU's ICT Price Basket (IPB) show that ICT services are getting more affordable worldwide" at: http://www.itu.int/ITU-D/ict/ipb/index.html.

[12] Information provided by Nokia from its Total Cost of Ownership study 2011.

[13] "Global average retail prices for 70 per cent of mobile phones to fall under USD 100 by 2015". Press Release, 1 March 2011. http://www.evalueserve.com/EVSRecentPressReleases/tabid/181/Default.aspx.

[14] For this and all other indicators, there are issues of comparability due to the use of different methodology and different population or sample characteristics. For example, micro-enterprises in Senegal appear to have a higher level of computer use than the average, even for developed economies. This is partly explained by the fact that the Senegalese survey covered only the formal sector, while most micro-enterprises are in the informal sector (Granström, 2009). Considering that household PC penetration in Senegal was merely 5.7 per cent in 2010 (ITU data), there is a distorted image of the actual adoption of computers by the business sector as a whole (including informal enterprises).

[15] As reflected by data on computer use disaggregated by industrial classification ISIC rev. 3.1.

[16] Based on the percentage reported for each country times the total population. This may cause some overestimation for countries in which the reported share refers to specific age groups and not the entire population.

[17] UNCTAD estimation based on Gartner shipment data and assuming PCs are replaced every five years. "Gartner Says Worldwide PC Shipments in Fourth Quarter of 2010 Grew 3.1 Percent; Year-End Shipments Increased 13.8 Percent." *Press Release*, January 12, 2011. http://www.gartner.com/it/page.jsp?id=1519417.

[18] "Gartner Says Worldwide Mobile Device Sales to End Users Reached 1.6 Billion Units in 2010; Smartphone Sales Grew 72 Percent in 2010." *Press Release*, 9 February 2011. http://www.gartner.com/it/page.jsp?id=1543014.

[19] Ibid.

[20] China Internet Network Information Center. July 2010. *Statistical Report on Internet Development in China*. http://www.cnnic.net.cn/en/index/index.htm.

21   Telecom Regulatory Authority of India. 2011. *The Indian Telecom Services Performance Indicators, July – September 2010*. http://www.trai.gov.in/reports_list_year.asp.

22   Ministerio de Tecnologías de la Información y las Comunicaciones. August 2010. *Informe Trimestral de Conectividad – Marzo 2010*. http://www.mintic.gov.co/.

23   Communications Commission of Kenya. 2011. *Quarterly Sector Statistics Report*. http://www.cck.go.ke/.

24   Opera. January 2011. *State of the Mobile Web*. http://www.opera.com/smw/2011/01/.

25   Ledgard, J. M. "Digital Africa." *Intelligent Life*. Spring 2011. http://moreintelligentlife.com/content/ideas/jm-ledgard/digital-africa.

26   A number of central and southern European economies are also included in the top 20 list, closing the gap on more developed countries in the region.

27   See "Mobile Broadband Success Story, Challenges and Opportunities", http://www.gsmamobilebroadband.com/upload/resources/files/GSMA%20-%20SMC%20Tunisia%208Nov2010%20MBB.pdf.

28   See http://www.itu.int/ITU-D/ict/statistics/at_glance/KeyTelecom2010.html.

29   See ABI Research. "Two Billion Covered by 3G and 4G Data Services." *Press Release*, 29 November 2010. http://www.abiresearch.com/press/3562-Two+Billion+Covered+by+3G+and+4G+Data+Services.

30   See "Ericsson teams up with Akamai to speed up mobile internet", *Reuters*, 14 February 2011, http://uk.reuters.com/article/2011/02/14/mobile-fair-ericsson-idUKLDE71D0C620110214.

31   The TEAMs, Seacom, EASSy, MainOne and Glo1 undersea fibre-optic cables are in commercial deployment and WACS and ACE are scheduled for launch. See "African Undersea Cables" at http://manypossibilities.net/african-undersea-cables/.

32   In East Africa, mobile data prices have fallen sharply since the introduction of new fibre-optic submarine cables. Prepaid data plans are available for as little as $0.08 per 1 Mb, enough for daily e-mail checking. See http://whiteafrican.com/2010/10/28/snapshot-mobile-data-costs-in-east-africa/.

33   The sectors with the most available data on Internet use are: manufacturing; construction; wholesale and retail trade; hotels and restaurants; transport, storage and communications; financial intermediation; real estate, renting and business activities; and other community, social and personal service activities (annex table II.5).

34   For example, data from European countries show that the presence of automated supply chain management systems increases with enterprise size (Eurostat, 2010).

35   For example, crisis-response websites following the recent economic crisis (UNDESA, 2010).

36   In European countries, 60 per cent of enterprises download government forms, and 50 per cent fill them in and return them electronically (Eurostat, 2010).

37   See "Dimensions and characteristics of the Brazilian Web, a study by the gov.br", at http://www.cgi.br/publicacoes/pesquisas/govbr/cgibr-nicbr-censoweb-govbr-2010-en.pdf.

38   Among countries that report data on mobile broadband, it is still significantly behind fixed broadband use among enterprises. For example, in Senegal and Singapore, less than 10 per cent of enterprises reported using mobile broadband to access the Internet, compared with 82 per cent (Senegal) and 60 per cent (Singapore) using fixed broadband (annex table II.6).

39   Other compelling reasons to use VoIP include the possibility to chat, do videoconferencing and send files.

40   "More Than One in Five Consumer Broadband Lines Now Come with VOIP." *Press Release*, 19 October 2010. http://point-topic.com/press.php.

41   Information provided by Voice on the Net Coalition, June 2011.

42   See Web 2.0 at http://en.wikipedia.org/wiki/Web_2.0.

43   Sid Murlidhar. "Fast and Free Facebook Mobile Access with 0.facebook.com." *The Facebook Blog*. 18 May 2010. http://www.facebook.com/blog.php?post=391295167130.

44   "Just the Facts: Statistics from Twitter Chirp." *ReadWriteWeb*, 14 April 2010, see http://www.readwriteweb.com/archives/just_the_facts_statistics_from_twitter_chirp.php.

45   A "tweet" is 140 characters (compared to 160 characters for an SMS).

46   comScore. "Indonesia, Brazil and Venezuela Lead Global Surge in Twitter Usage." Press Release. August 11, 2010. http://www.comscore.com/Press_Events/Press_Releases/2010/8/Indonesia_Brazil_and_Venezuela_Lead_Global_Surge_in_Twitter_Usage.

47 http://www.facebook.com/press/info.php?statistics.

48 "Facebook becomes the new company website." *Financial Times*, 31 March 2011. http://www.ft.com/cms/s/0/240f19d4-5afc-11e0-a290-00144feab49a.html#axzz1IOOh6o5G.

49 "World Map of Social Networks." *Vincos Blog*. http://www.vincos.it/world-map-of-social-networks/.

50 Although entry-level prices may seem high, it is a better value since users are getting more bandwidth. A related issue is that there can be significant variation between the "advertised" and the actual speed. In some developing countries entry-level packages are even below 256 Kbps and the main criteria for broadband is that the connection is "always on". Upload speeds also vary.

51 See "Newly released data from ITU's ICT Price Basket (IPB) show that ICT services are getting more affordable worldwide" at: http://www.itu.int/ITU-D/ict/ipb/index.html.

52 Point Topic. "Consumers now pay 50 per cent less for bandwidth than in 2008." *Press Release*, 1 February 2011. http://point-topic.com/press.php.

53 See also UNECLAC (2010).

54 An analysis of ICT-related projects implemented by the International Institute for Communication and Development (IICD) noted that, in rural areas, a lack of electricity and ICT connectivity as well as high levels of illiteracy acted as a key constraint on the use of both Internet and mobile-based services. Inhibitive costs associated with SMS-based information services also limited large-scale use of mobile services. Information provided by IICD.

55 UNDP-APDIP e-Primer "e-Commerce and e-Business, 2003," http://www.apdip.net/publications/iespprimers/eprimer-ecom.pdf and http://en.wikibooks.org/wiki/E-Commerce_and_E-Business.

56 See e.g. http://measuring-ict.unctad.org.

57 See http://www.pikom.org.my/cms/General.asp?whichfile=Press+Releases&ProductID=22708&CatID=33.

58 Information provided by the research team of Professor You Jianxin, Tongji University.

59 For consumer protection in online and mobile payments, see OECD (2010).

60 For more information, see e.g. UNCTAD (2006a: chapter 8), UNCTAD (2005a: chapter 6).

61 Relevant UNCITRAL texts included the *Electronic Communications Convention* (2005); the UNCITRAL Model Law on Electronic Signatures (2001) and the *UNCITRAL Model Law on Electronic Commerce* (1996). See: http://www.uncitral.org/uncitral/en/uncitral_texts/electronic_commerce.html.

62 See UNCTAD comparative studies on cyberlaw in Latin America (UNCTAD, 2009b) and Central America (UNCTAD, 2009c).

PROMOTING PRIVATE ICT-SECTOR DEVELOPMENT

3

A dynamic ICT sector contributes to making the private sector more productive and competitive. It creates new jobs, spurs innovation, and – not least – supports sustained use of ICTs throughout the entire economy. Recent studies confirm that even in low-income countries, a thriving ICT sector can make a major contribution to economic growth. Kenya is interesting in this context. Its ICT sector has been the main driver of economic growth over the past decade. Since 2000, this sector has grown annually by more than 20 per cent, and it was responsible for a staggering 24 per cent of Kenya's GDP growth during that period (World Bank, 2010b). Moreover, thanks to technological change and the birth of new business models, many employment opportunities are emerging in the ICT sector in low-income countries. As part of their efforts to promote PSD, Governments and other actors are increasingly considering how best to tap into these opportunities.

A. AN EVOLVING GLOBAL ICT SECTOR

From the perspective of supporting PSD, the competitiveness of the ICT sector is relevant for several reasons. Firstly, it is an important part of the economy in many countries. Secondly, in a number of developing countries, the ICT sector is characterized by relatively high productivity and rapid growth. Thirdly, it is a sector that comprises a wide array of economic activities, ranging from basic tasks that require little formal education, to highly sophisticated functions such as software development and chip design (box III.1). Depending on its characteristics and level of development, an economy may be in a more or less favourable position to develop the various sectoral activities. Fourthly, the documented impact of ICT use on the productivity of enterprises (chapter II) is another reason to facilitate a stronger ICT sector. Without adequate ICT sales, repair services, consultancy, and software development, it is difficult for other businesses to properly integrate ICTs into their operations.

UNCTAD annually collects two statistical indicators on the ICT sector: the share of total business sector employment accounted for by the ICT sector (ICT-1), and the share of the total business sector value added accounted for by the ICT sector (ICT-2).[1] While a growing number of countries collect and report such data, more efforts are needed to further improve coverage (UNCTAD, 2010). As at early 2011, the ICT-1 indicator was reported by 54 economies (of which only 18 were developing economies), and the ICT-2 indicator was available for 47 economies (of which only 13 were developing economies).

The importance of the ICT sector in the national economy varies considerably across developing and transition economies (table III.1). In employment terms, the ICT sector carries particular weight in countries with a sizeable ICT manufacturing sector (e.g. Malaysia, the Republic of Korea, and Singapore), as well as in countries that are significant exporters of IT services and ICT-enabled services (e.g. Egypt and Mauritius). The ICT sector typically accounts for a larger share of value added (ICT-2) than of employment, reflecting its relatively high capital-intensity (UNCTAD, 2010).

Various recent studies suggest that the ICT sector is playing a growing role in a number of developing countries not captured in table III.1. As noted above, Kenya's ICT sector has experienced very high growth in the past decade, outperforming every other sec-

---

Box III.1. What is included in the ICT sector?

The ICT sector encompasses the production of both goods and services. It includes – among other things – the manufacturing of goods such as computers, electronic components and telecommunications equipment. It also covers wholesale and rental services related to ICT equipment, as well as telecommunications, IT consultancy services (e.g. software and hardware, database), and other computer-related activities. The agreed definition only covers activities where production of ICT products is the main activity; it excludes retail activities.

Some ICT-related activities do not fall within the definition of the ICT sector. This applies, for example, to various mobile- and PC-related services provided by ICT micro-enterprises, such as retailing of mobile phones and accessories. Furthermore, such activities often occur in the informal sector and are not properly captured in official statistics. Another example is the ICT-enabled services that have emerged thanks to improved ICT connectivity, such as the business process outsourcing (BPO) of accounting, human resources or payroll services.

According to the definition used in UNCTAD's most recent collection of ICT statistics (based on ISIS Rev. 3.1, OECD, 2002),a the ICT sector comprises activities which result in products that "are primarily intended to fulfil the function of information processing and communication by electronic means, including transmission and display, or must use electronic processing to detect, measure, and/or record physical phenomena or to control a physical process." In the revised definition for the ICT sector (based on ISIC Rev. 4, OECD, 2007),b the scope is limited to products that "are primarily intended to fulfil the function of information processing and communication by electronic means, including transmission and display." The new definition is expected to be gradually applied when developing countries report data on the ICT sector. See also UNCTAD (2010) for a further discussion on the definition of the ICT sector.

Source: UNCTAD.
a   OECD (2002). Reviewing the ICT sector definition: Issues for discussion. DSTI/ICCP/IIS(2002)2.
b   OECD (2007). Information economy – Sector definitions based on the International Standard Industry Classification (ISIC Rev. 4). DSTI/ICCP/IIS(2006)2.

Table III.1. UNCTAD core indicators for the ICT sector, selected developing and transition economies, latest year

Economy	Reference year	Proportion of total business sector workforce involved in the ICT sector (ICT-1) (%)	Value added in the ICT sector, as a percentage of total business (ICT-2) (%)
Malaysia	2007	7.1	12.1
Republic of Korea	2008	6.1	..
Egypt	2009	5.6	..
Mauritius	2008	5.6	6.9
Russian Federation	2008	4.6	4.9
Singapore	2009	4.6	..
Jordan	2008	3.6	..
Thailand	2007	3.2	..
China, Hong Kong SAR	2008	3.1	4.7
Brazil	2007	3.8	5
Uruguay	2007	2.9	10.5
Panama	2006	2.7	..
Cuba	2007	2.6	4.1
Mexico	2008	2.2	4
Kazakhstan	2000	1.9	..
Croatia	2007	1.9	3
Azerbaijan	2009	1.6	..
Chile	2004	1	3
India	2008	..	7.4
Mongolia	2007	..	0.9

Source: UNCTAD Information Economy Database (http://unctadstat.unctad.org); OECD; Porcaro and Jorge (2011); Malik and Mundhe (2011).

tor (World Bank, 2010b). Similarly, five recent country studies (on Brazil, Cameroon, Egypt, India and Malaysia), which measure statistically the size and composition of the ICT sector, suggest that the sector has grown in importance in recent years in most cases.

(a) In Brazil, the evolution of the ICT sector over the last decade fluctuated, with a contraction at the beginning of the decade followed by rapid growth. On average, it grew at an average rate of 2.1 per cent between 2000 and 2007. At the end of that period, the ICT sector accounted for approximately 5 per cent of total business sector value added (Porcaro and Jorge, 2011).

(b) In Cameroon, the ICT sector has made a vital contribution to an otherwise relatively stagnant economy. Between 2000 and 2008, it grew annually at rates of between 15 and 46 per cent (Nzépa et al., 2011).

(c) In Egypt, the ICT sector's value added reached $5.6 billion in 2009, corresponding to 3.8 per cent of GDP. Moreover, in 2009, it recorded the highest growth rate of all industries in the country (El-Shenawy, 2011).

(d) In India, the growth of the ICT sector has been nothing short of spectacular. Its share of GDP rose from 3.4 per cent in 2000/01 to 5.9 per cent in 2007/08. During that period, the Indian ICT sector grew consistently at over 20 per cent annually (Malik and Mundhe, 2011).

(e) In Malaysia – a country with a very large ICT sector – the sector accounted for about 9 per cent of GDP in 2007, however this represented a decline from the 11.4 per cent recorded at the beginning of the decade (Ramasamy and Ponnudurai, 2011).

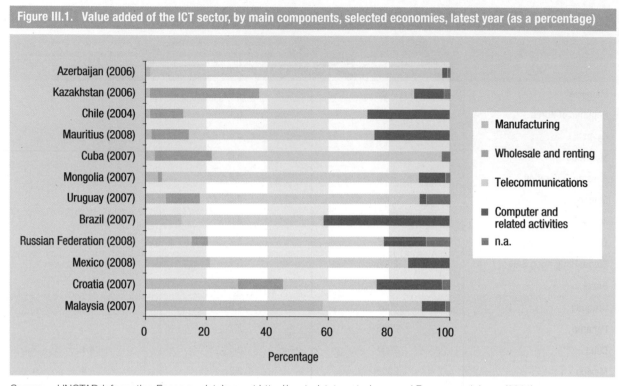

Figure III.1. Value added of the ICT sector, by main components, selected economies, latest year (as a percentage)

Source: UNCTAD *Information Economy* database at http://unctadstat.unctad.org, and Porcaro and Jorge (2011).

Traditionally, the ICT sector has been dominated by large public corporations or transnational corporations (TNCs). Previously, the need for upfront capital meant that progress in the ICT market was driven by larger firms. Indeed, most of the related business technology services such as data storage, cloud computing and software development are dominated by large entities. However, there are also important roles for smaller businesses. Many new job opportunities have emerged among ICT MSEs (UNCTAD, 2010).

Millions of people in developing countries have found new income-generating opportunities in the ICT sector – in formal or informal enterprises. For example, while some 60,000 people are employed in the formal ICT sector in Cameroon, it is estimated that another 200,000 are working in the informal ICT sector (Nzépa et al., 2011). In Egypt, the ICT sector, and enterprises in ICT-enabled services, together employed approximately 182,000 people in 2009 (El-Shenawy, 2011), while in India, formal ICT-sector employment stood at some 2.5 million in 2004/05 (Malik and Mundhe, 2011). Despite a decline since 2000, formal ICT-sector employment in Malaysia was about 479,000 in 2007 (Ramasamy and Ponnudurai, 2011). In Brazil, in 2006, approximately 1 million people, or 3.8 per cent of the business-sector workforce, were employed in the ICT

sector – about 80 per cent of which were in the formal sector and 20 per cent in the informal sector (Porcaro and Jorge, 2011).

Jobs in the ICT sector have proved to be more productive than in other sectors. Among the OECD countries, labour productivity growth rates during the period 1995–2008 were, with few exceptions, generally higher in the ICT sector than for all industries.[2] The data reported in table III.1 confirm that the ICT sector's share is typically higher in value added than in employment terms, suggesting relatively high labour productivity in developing economies too. Moreover, ICT-sector employees tend to have an above-average level of education, and to be younger than the employees in other sectors. Furthermore, jobs in the ICT sector are often perceived as desirable, because of upward mobility, job security, and the availability of training opportunities.[3]

Although the economic role of the ICT sector is expanding in a number of developing economies, the underlying factors for this trend differ, reflecting the varying composition of the sector across countries (fig. III.1). In order to understand the scope for PSD opportunities in the ICT sector, it is important to look into trends and developments at disaggregated levels.

B. PSD OPPORTUNITIES IN ICT AND ICT-ENABLED SERVICES

ICT services and ICT-enabled services offer growing PSD opportunities. Not only do they provide business and employment opportunities in their own right, but they are also essential for diffusing ICT use throughout the economy, and facilitating the adoption, adaptation and maintenance of ICTs by local companies – thereby contributing to their productivity and competitiveness. The availability of relevant skills locally is therefore important. ICT services encompass telecommunications, activities related to commerce (e.g. wholesale, renting) and computer-related services (box III.1). Services enabled by improved ICT connectivity are also relevant to consider, including those related to business process outsourcing (BPO) and knowledge process outsourcing (KPO). While export-oriented activities in this area remain relatively concentrated geographically, new opportunities to tap into this market are emerging, including for low-income countries.

1. Telecommunications

The telecommunications sector is large and vibrant, and accounts for a significant proportion of the economy in most countries. Worldwide telecom revenues were $1,381 billion in 2009.[1] The sector was impacted by the global financial crisis, but nonetheless managed to register positive growth (table III.2).

As indicated in figure III.1, telecommunications services account for a significant share of ICT sector value added in many developing countries. They constitute a basic infrastructure, and are important even if other parts of the ICT sector are relatively modestly

developed. The relative importance of this subsector is most pronounced in countries in which the ICT sector is relatively small (UNCTAD, 2010). For most low-income countries, telecommunications services offer the greatest opportunities for employment creation within the ICT sector – in both formal and informal enterprises. In Cameroon and Kenya, for example, this subsector dominates the ICT sector (World Bank, 2010b; Nzépa et al., 2011). In Egypt, telecommunications account for 70 per cent of total sector revenues, most of which were related to the mobile sector (El-Shenawy, 2011). In Brazil, telecommunications account for almost half of all ICT-sector value added (Porcaro and Jorge, 2011).

a. Private-sector investment in telecommunications

Since liberalization and the removal of barriers to foreign market entry began, the private sector has been the driving force in the development of ICT infrastructure, with tangible results. Arguably, no other infrastructure area has evolved as positively in low-income countries. Between 1990 and 2009, more countries reported private participation in telecommunications projects than in any other infrastructure sector, and the investment value was the highest in telecoms, too (table III.3). The private sector has been especially important in rolling out mobile telecommunications – the predominant ICT technology used by MSEs in developing countries. During the same period, out of some 800 telecom projects with private-sector participation in developing countries, almost three quarters involved greenfield operations primarily in mobile telephony.[5] As indicated in figure III.2, all parts of the developing world have been affected by the investment surge since 2003. For example, between 2003 and 2009, sub-Saharan Africa saw projects with pri-

Table III.2. Global telecommunications services market, 2006–2010 (billions of dollars)					
	2006	2007	2008	2009[a]	2010[a]
Fixed telephony	403.7	392.1	375.3	348.6	326.0
Mobile services	604.7	670.9	714.3	738.7	775.8
Data and Internet	214.2	232.4	250.7	262.8	279.6
Total	1 222.7	1 295.3	1 340.3	1 350.2	1 381.3
Annual growth rate	5.5%	5.9%	3.5%	0.7%	2.3%

[a]   Forecast.

Source: IDATE (2010). World Telecom Services Market 2010: Global market worth 1,348.9 billion USD in 2009. 25 August. http://blog.idate.fr/?p=133.

Table III.3. Infrastructure participation in developing regions, 1990–2009 (number of economies; millions of dollars)				
	Telecommunications	Energy	Transport	Water and sewage
Number of economies with private participation	133	107	82	61
Investment in projects (millions of dollars)	719 645	481 695	253 197	60 280

Source: World Bank. *Private Participation in Infrastructure Projects* database.

vate participation worth more than $50 billion, and the corresponding value in South Asia was $68 billion. Despite the improvements, the remaining weaknesses are among the most important economic issues holding back Africa's development (box I.3).

In 2009, 241 infrastructure projects with private participation reached financial or contractual closing in 42 low- and middle-income countries. These projects involved a total investment of $153 billion – a drop of

7 per cent from the levels reported in 2008. In telecommunications, investment fell by 23 per cent to $61 billion, driven by the slowdown in network expansion across most regions. This was the first time since 2003 that investment in telecommunications had declined (fig. III.2). In the coming few years, the need to roll out fixed and mobile broadband is expected to sustain investments in telecommunications networks.[6]

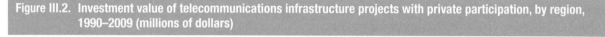

Figure III.2. Investment value of telecommunications infrastructure projects with private participation, by region, 1990–2009 (millions of dollars)

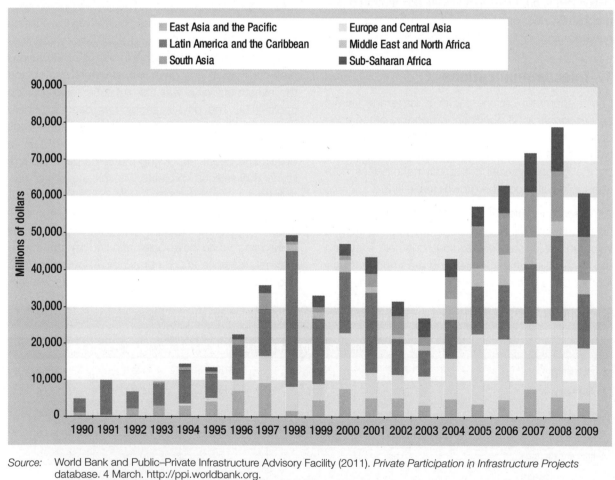

Source: World Bank and Public–Private Infrastructure Advisory Facility (2011). *Private Participation in Infrastructure Projects* database. 4 March. http://ppi.worldbank.org.

Note: Data include projects in low- and middle-income countries. Projects include management or lease contracts, concessions, greenfield projects, and divestitures.

b. Opportunities for PSD in the mobile sector

Mobile communications have been a success story, enjoying phenomenal growth over the past decade. The mobile sector has contributed to economic growth and many new jobs across the value chain. This is opening new business opportunities among poor segments of the population, and is also helping to disseminate telephony services to sections of society that have traditionally been poorly catered for by formal-sector enterprises (UNCTAD, 2010).

Many of the new jobs in the mobile sector in developing countries are informal, and indirect employment is many times higher than direct employment in the sector. For example, in Latin America, some 107,000 people were directly employed by mobile carriers in 2006, compared with about 370,000 in downstream jobs (GSMA, 2008). In the Asia-Pacific region, some 2.6 million people were employed by mobile operators, compared with 10 million indirect jobs generated (GSMA, 2009a). And in East Africa, the mobile sector is estimated to be responsible for the creation of over 400,000 jobs for airtime sales by streetside and official vendors (GSMA, 2009b).

The accuracy and comparability of data on mobile-sector employment is debated. However, the infor-

mation available suggests that the mobile sector[7] has emerged as a significant private-sector employer in many low-income countries, and that related employment is continuing to grow.[8] Mobile-sector employment in developing countries probably now exceeds 10 million. In addition, new opportunities arising from the deployment of mobile broadband networks are expected to continue to boost job creation. It is anticipated that something in the range of 120,000 to 140,000 jobs will be generated in India from the deployment of high-speed mobile networks, with some 28,000 jobs in South Africa (Analysys Mason, 2010a and 2010b).

Figure III.3 depicts the relative distribution of total mobile-sector employment along the supply chain in four developing countries. Although formal roles such as internal management and telecoms equipment maintenance account for substantial proportions, the majority of the employment has been created in roles which interact with more marginal customers. This involves handset retailers, and airtime and SIM card distributors. In addition, a number of additional activities that are linked to the mobile sector may not be officially recorded, even though they represent important growth areas in low-income countries (M-PESA, 2010; Sivapragasam, 2009). These activities include

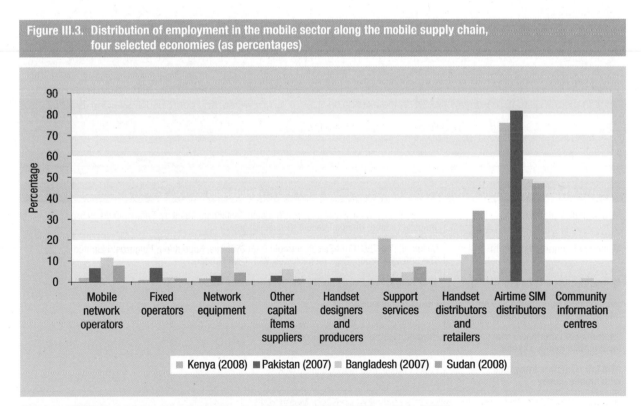

Figure III.3. Distribution of employment in the mobile sector along the mobile supply chain, four selected economies (as percentages)

Legend: Kenya (2008) · Pakistan (2007) · Bangladesh (2007) · Sudan (2008)

Source: UNCTAD, based on information from Deloitte (2008), GSMA (2008) and Zain (2009).

mobile money retailing, selling second-hand phones, and repairing mobile phones, as well as the activities of payphone operators and people selling mobile top-ups. Thus, not only does the mobile sector employ millions of people in the developing world, but the majority of the jobs engage people who are in marginal positions, or who interact with people in marginal positions, close to poverty.

Surveys of the informal ICT sector in Burkina Faso and Senegal confirm the prominent role of the informal sector in mobile-sector employment (85 per cent in Burkina Faso and 75 per cent in Senegal) (Bayala et al., 2010; Ndiaye et al., 2009).[9] In Senegal, there is a large discrepancy between urban and rural areas in terms of access to telecommunications, making the role of the informal sector in providing services particularly important. At the same time, many of those working in the informal mobile sector need to leverage other income-generating activities as well (UNCTAD, 2010). A minority of the micro-entrepreneurs surveyed reported increases in their profit margins in the 12 months before the surveys were carried out (25 per cent in Burkina Faso and 34 per cent in Senegal). In both countries, entrepreneurs faced difficulties in expanding their businesses due to intense levels of competition and limited purchasing power among clients (Yam Pukri, 2010). Generally, entrepreneurs based in rural areas experienced more volatility in their businesses than entrepreneurs in urban areas.

The activity of informal-sector mobile entrepreneurs is having a positive impact on other private enterprises, not least in the informal sector. Mobile-sector micro-enterprises are often in a better position to understand the needs of other informal-sector entrepreneurs, and

---

Box III.2. The emerging mobile ecosystem in Kenya

Partly thanks to a buoyant ICT sector, Kenya's GDP growth during the past decade surpassed its population growth. The Kenyan ICT sector has flourished since the liberalization of the telecommunications sector, providing economic opportunities for large and small business alike, both in the formal and informal sectors. The introduction of competition and the increase in the volume of traffic enabled costs to fall from $0.20 per minute to $0.04 per minute between 2002 and 2010. With a 23 per cent average annual growth rate since 2000, the ICT sector has outperformed the rest of the economy by far.

This success has also spurred innovations and employment opportunities related to ICT use – particularly mobile phones. Foreign and local enterprises in Kenya are today spearheading the development of new applications in areas such as mobile money and mobile insurance and are thereby providing services that are essential to PSD, in view of the fact that large parts of the population are unbanked and uninsured. Kenya is quickly becoming a global leader in financial and payment-technology innovation. Since the launch of Safaricom M-PESA in 2007, countless players have entered the market to extend efficient payment services throughout the country. The list of companies that either provide services to mobile money systems in Kenya, or build on the existing services, is long, diverse, and continuously evolving (box III.2.1).

Source: UNCTAD, based on World Bank (2010b) and interviews.

Box table III.2.1. The mobile money ecosystem in Kenya

Type of activity	Enterprises
Mobile money platform	Airtel (formerly Zain), Essar Telecom (Yu Cash), MobiKash, MobiPay, Safaricom (M-PESA) Tangaza Limited, Orange Telecom (Orange Money)
M-money integration platform	Cellulant, CoreTEC, Craft Silicon, Intrepid Data Systems, Kopo Kopo, Tangazoetu Limited The Software Group, Zege Technologies, Web Tribe Limited
M-money e-commerce processing	ePay Kenya, PesaPal, Symbiotic Media Consortium, Tristar
Management Information System integrated with mobile money	Flexus Technologies
International remittances via local mobile money channel	Beyonic, Western Union/Safaricom
ATM infrastructure integrated with mobile money	Paynet Group, KCB Kenya, Equity Bank

Source: UNCTAD. Based on information provided by Kopo Kopo, March 2011.

Table III.4. Exports of computer and communications services, 2000 and 2009 ($ million, %)

	2000	2009	CAGR 2000–2009
Communication services (millions of dollars)	32 965	85 518	11%
Share of communication in total services (%)	*2.1*	*2.5*	
Computer and information services (millions of dollars)	45 790	195 515	18%
Share of computer and information in total services (%)	*3*	*5.6*	
Total services exports (millions of dollars)	1 544 364	3 467 633	9%

Source: UNCTAD. Based on IMF BoP data as available on 27 June 2011.

Note Computer and information services include news agency services. Communication services include postal and courier, as well as telecommunication services.

Table III.5. Top 10 exporters of computer and information services, 2009 ($ million, %)

Economy	Exports	Share of world total (%)	CAGR 2000–2009 (%)
India	46 687	23.9	29
Ireland	33 803	17.3	18.2
Germany	14 822	7.6	16.3
United States	13 378	6.8	10.1
United Kingdom	11 577	5.9	11.6
Israel	7 671	3.9	6.8
Sweden	6 858	3.5	21.5
Finland	6 701	3.4	47.5
China	6 512	3.3	38.1
Netherlands	6 118	3.1	20.2

Source: UNCTAD. Based on IMF BoP data.

they often survive by providing some type of innovative niche for locals – for example, by breaking down mobile top-up products to fit with small incomes, or with shared or mediated phone use (Burrell, 2010; Chipchase and Tulusan, 2007; Goodman and Walia, 2006; Rangaswamy, 2009b). Such niches are achieved through socio-technical appropriations. These can be technology changes (Barendregt, 2008; Galperin and Bar, 2006), but in many more cases they relate to very small adaptations of technology in commercial practices and connected arrangements where mobile products are used "outside the instruction manual" in order to better serve the bottom of the pyramid (Chipchase, 2009; Rangaswamy, 2009a). Thus, these micro-enterprises are crucial actors in the provision of mobile service to the poor (Anderson et al., 2010; Anderson and Kupp, 2008). Innovations in the telecommunications sector also support the development of business activities of the poor. Probably the best illustration is mobile money (chapters II and IV), with schemes such as M-PESA offering banking services to categories of the population and categories of enterprises that were previously unbanked (box III.2).

The margins for mobile-sector micro-enterprises are dependent on others in the value chain, which may impose limits on the potential for upgrading of products and processes. For example, mobile airtime vending is becoming a less viable product for micro-enterprises, due to the increasing price competition in

the industry. In Kenya, operators have looked to reduce commission levels in the value chain in order to reduce costs, with interviewees suggesting that this means that margins have dropped from 10 per cent to 4–6 per cent over the previous year, as competition between operators has increased (Foster and Heeks, 2011). There is an untapped potential for mobile-sector micro-enterprises to take advantage of the range of new products emerging in areas such as entertainment (e.g. downloading of ringtones), mobile money services (e.g. being an agent for services built on existing mobile money systems) and data (e.g. configuring, and advising on data use).

2. Other ICT services and ICT-enabled services

Improved ICT connectivity has reduced barriers to global services trade, creating new opportunities for firms to buy and sell services delivered electronically. Between 2000 and 2009, international trade in communication services almost tripled, and trade in computer and information services more than quadrupled (table III.4). Communication services in 2009 accounted for 2.5 per cent of total services trade, while the share of computer and information services was about 5.6 per cent. The potential value of ICT-enabled services has been estimated at around $475 billion (WTO, 2010). Less than 15 per cent of this was

Box III.3. Bringing micro-work to poor but talented workers in the South

Samasource was founded in 2008 as a non-profit social enterprise to tackle global poverty with micro-work. Its vision is to provide a bridge between poor but talented people on the one hand, and businesses that seek a competitively priced, qualified workforce and also care about ethical aspects, on the other.

After receiving projects from clients in the United States, most of which are big technology companies in Silicon Valley, Samasource breaks them down into very small and simple tasks. These are then distributed to 16 centres worldwide via an online work-distribution tool called SamaHub. After workers have completed the tasks online, the work is returned for quality control at head office before being delivered to the client. Tasks range from content generation and optical character recognition clean-up, to business listings verification and image-tagging. For example, Samasource workers may research and gather information on businesses or universities by aggregating content from the Web. Clients to date include Intuit, LinkedIn and Google.

Samasource focuses on providing employment especially to people who are socially disadvantaged, such as women, rural workers and youth. So far, some 1,200 jobs have been created in Haiti, India, Kenya, Pakistan, South Africa and Uganda. Over 1 million dollars in worker payments have been distributed to the field, and Samasource is committed to further increasing sales, international operations, and worker development. By 2012, it intends to reach 10,000 staff.

Source: UNCTAD, based on Samasource (http://www.samasource.org) and on a BBC News Africa article from 18 June 2011 entitled "How Silicon Valley outsources work to African refugees".

captured in 2007, indicating huge potential. According to WTO, computer and information services exports amounted to $185 billion in 2009 (WTO, 2010).

At the world level, India in 2009 led exports of computer and information services, with almost a quarter of the world total (table III.5). China was the ninth-largest exporter, with over $6.5 billion in that year. The other major exporters of computer services have mainly been developed countries. Developing and transition economies with significant exports include Malaysia ($1.4 billion), Singapore ($1.3 billion), the Russian Federation ($1.3 billion), the Philippines ($1.3 billion) and Argentina ($1 billion). In terms of growth between 2000 and 2009, exports of such services were particularly dynamic in some transition economies. For example, especially high annual growth rates were noted for Ukraine (57 per cent), the Republic of Moldova (55 per cent), Belarus (49 per cent) and the Russian Federation (41 per cent). Among LDCs, Uganda significantly increased its exports of computer and information services, albeit from a low level (reaching $36 million in 2009). Other developing countries that achieved significant forays into the computer and information services export markets between 2000 and 2009 include Costa Rica ($771 million), Morocco ($248 million), South Africa ($245 million), Sri Lanka ($245 million), Pakistan ($182 million), Uruguay ($180 million) and Egypt ($171 million).

New business models for international outsourcing are emerging on the back of better broadband connectivity, creating new opportunities for PSD linked to international trade in services. The outsourcing of "micro-work", including through "crowd-sourcing", is of particular interest in this context.[10] While still at an early stage, such outsourcing offers interesting prospects of PSD in low-income countries endowed with spare capacity among literate labour.

The outsourcing of "micro-work" essentially requires that a company breaks down activities into many very small tasks that can be performed outside by individuals and delivered through the Internet, or other media, against payment (World Bank, 2011). Tasks that can potentially be sourced in this way include elaborate professional services (such as computer programming), as well as simple tasks that require only basic skills and can often be performed very quickly against small payments. Micro-work is often sought and delivered by workers via specialized websites which serve as platforms, and which can either be commercially oriented, or have a charitable or development objective as in the case of Samasource (box III.3).

While micro-work is still at an embryonic stage of development, its growth potential is sizable, possibly reaching several billion dollars within the next five years (World Bank, 2011). Its inroads into developing countries have been quite spectacular in recent years. For example, in 2008, 76 per cent of the micro-workers of a leading platform (Amazon Mechanical Turk) were based in the United States and only 8 per cent in India. Two years later, the United States accounted for less than half (47

Box III.4. The role of freelancers in the Bangladeshi IT- and ICT-enabled services industry

According to the Bangladeshi Software and Information Services Association (BASIS), around 10,000 Bangladeshi free-lancers are active online. The vast majority of them work for clients in the United States and Europe – usually SMEs – but they also work for local-government institutions, non-governmental organizations (NGOs), and even individuals. They provide a range of ICT-related services, such as software development, graphic design, search engine optimization, social-media marketing, blogging, and data entry. Projects vary from building large e-commerce websites to doing product entry on eBay or posting positive feedback for companies on review websites.

Online portals such as www.freelancer.com, www.odesk.com and www.bworker.com, where freelancers can be hired on an assignment basis, are popular among "micro-workers" in Bangladesh, who export services over the web in an informal manner. Many of the freelancers have a day-time job or are students at IT faculties. The revenues generated by the most successful individuals can be in the tens of thousands of dollars, while the average is around a few hundred to a few thousand dollars. Although some freelancers work on high-value projects, which take months to complete, the most common situation is to be involved in small projects with multiple clients on a day-to-day basis.

Despite freelancers' low visibility in the country, BASIS reckons that they have now overtaken the formal IT- and ICT-enabled services industry in sales volume, although there are no official statistics to verify this. Indeed, until recently, the Central Bank of Bangladesh would consider payments related to these assignments and channelled through Western Union and the like as "remittances" and tax them accordingly.

However, a directive issued in May 2011 by the Central Bank of Bangladesh recognizes that these funds should be treated as export-related commercial income, which is tax-exempt. This is significant for the freelancers, who are now asking that PayPal be formally allowed as a means of electronic payment. A project funded by the Centre for Promotion of Imports from Developing Countries (a Dutch development agency) and being implemented by the International Trade Centre UNCTAD/WTO (ITC) is supporting this initiative by advocating with the Government of Bangladesh for a more business-friendly e-commerce environment.

Source: Information provided by BASIS and ITC.

---

per cent), while the share of Indian workers had surged to 34 per cent. Interestingly, the remaining 19 per cent of the work was carried out by workers in as many as 66 other countries (World Bank, 2011). Micro-workers are often freelancers looking for complementary income, as in the case of Bangladesh (box III.4). In order for micro-work to take off, mechanisms are needed to ensure that micro-workers are paid rapidly and accurately.

Up to now, the main vehicle to deliver micro-work has been computers connected to the Internet. However, with more widespread use of mobile broadband, the mobile phone may emerge as an attractive tool for certain activities. One firm, TxtEagle, is already outsourcing micro-work services through mobile phones in over 80 countries. The company provides marketing and consumer information services about emerging markets' consumers, and its employees are paid with airtime. It has been suggested that the target population could potentially exceed 2 billion people in developing countries (see box III.5).

If adequate ICT infrastructure is in place, micro-work can offer employment opportunities to people with basic levels of skills (such as literacy and familiarity with ICTs), and can be an avenue for the development of profitable market opportunities for businesses in both developed and developing countries. Its growth may well turn out to be exponential once the opportunities it offers become better known among both buyers and suppliers. The availability of micro-work services could trigger demand from business sectors that previously have not used them – in a similar way to the development of "traditional" BPO.

Micro-work is exposing young workers to entrepreneurship, and encourages them to further familiarize themselves with technologies; this can strengthen their skills and employability in other areas. Moreover, some workers may gradually upgrade their skills, and become able to tackle more complicated and better remunerated tasks. It should be noted that micro-work is often vulnerable to technological improvements or changes in the business model. For example, in the third-party gaming industry, new software has been developed to replace human labour on game sites. In the medium term, it is likely that human labour will be difficult to replace for some types of activities. Moreover, with the expanded use of smartphones, the role of micro-work may grow further.

> ### Box III.5. Crowd-sourcing via mobile phones: the case of TxtEagle
>
> TxtEagle, a United States-based company, offers crowd-sourcing and market research services in developing markets. Its platform enables businesses to collect information, data on the ground, and opinions, via mobile phones. TxtEagle uses the USSD protocol, which has the advantage of allowing for communication that is free of charge.
>
> Survey questions are sent to registered users, who receive free airtime in exchange for their answers. For example, one enterprise used the platform to collect information on road signs in the mobile users' local area, and put together a satellite navigation system. Another company used the TxtEagle platform to monitor television advertisements and check that local stations were broadcasting them correctly. The platform has also been applied to the translation of marketing materials into local dialects. Marketing activities to increase customer engagement – such as opt-in customer campaigns or the provision of incentives – are offered too.
>
> The company has reportedly partnered with over 200 mobile network operators, and has a presence in more than 80 countries. Recently, it raised $8.5 million of private funds to expand its operations. Mobile operators are compensated by the airtime purchases made by TxtEagle to pay its customers.
>
> *Source:* UNCTAD, based on information from TxtEagle.com, Evans (2011) and Bain (2011).

As is always the case with the introduction of new technologies and business models, micro-work also raises issues concerning possible negative effects, for example with regard to low levels of pay, work ethics, and working conditions. Cases have been noted where prison detainees have been forced to work until exhaustion to perform micro-work tasks such as "gold farming" on online video games for the profit of their guards.[11] There are also reports that micro-work is extensively used by spammers, who sometimes do not pay for the work conducted.[12] Further research is needed to better understand the full implications of this new phenomenon.

C. PSD OPPORTUNITIES IN ICT MANUFACTURING

Global manufacturing of ICT goods is highly concentrated, with a number of economies in East Asia accounting for an increasing share.[13] In 2009, seven of the world's top 10 exporters of ICT goods were in Asia, with China – by far the leading exporter – accounting for $356 billion worth of such exports. Asian economies are responsible for about two thirds of the global export market; China alone accounts for 25 per cent of the total (WTO, 2010). The recent adoption of a new definition of ICT goods has resulted in an even higher share for Asia of global ICT goods exports (box III.6).

Malaysia is among the few developing economies in which manufacturing accounts for the majority of the ICT-sector value added (fig. III.1). It is also one of the world's top 10 exporters of ICT goods. In 2009, more than one third of its merchandise exports consisted of ICT goods. In terms of employment, ICT manufacturing accounted for over 387,000 jobs in 2007 – approximately 80 per cent of the total ICT sector. Between 2000 and 2007, approximately 70,000 jobs in the production of television, radio and communication equipment were lost in Malaysia, while more than 30,000 new jobs were added in computer production. Global competition is fierce in this industry, from both existing and emerging players. For example, India has experienced one of the sharpest increases in ICT goods exports, which surged by 244 per cent from 2008 to 2009.

ICT manufacturing in other parts of the developing world is very limited; non-Asian developing economies accounted for less than 5 per cent of world exports in 2009.[14] Nonetheless, there are examples of ICT goods manufacturing in low-income countries. For example, Nigeria is home to a computer and component assembly company, Omatek, which is growing both in the local and the regional market.[15] In various other developing countries, assembling computers, laptops and other IT equipment is providing employment and economic opportunities. Local assembly can provide benefits in terms of reduced costs and tailoring of products to local or individual needs. In Peru, for example, informal assemblers accounted for 43.5 per cent of the sales of laptops and desktops in 2008 (UNCTAD, 2011b). Some ICT manufacturing activities are reported in the informal ICT sector, too. For example, the production of antennas for television reception (including satellite television) is frequently observed in Africa.[16] However, such production is constrained by technology evolution, which may make such products obsolete. Although there may be an opportunity

---

Box III.6. New ICT goods definition boosts Asia's share in ICT export statistics

The definition of what constitutes ICT goods was updated in 2009 and released by OECD in 2010. The change in definition entailed the removal of 79 product items, and the addition of 7. This resulted in a total number of 95 ICT goods items. For the world as a whole, the value of ICT goods exports in 2009 was about $173 billion,[a] 11 per cent less than would have been the case under the old definition.

Although for most exporters, the net impact of the change in definition implies a reduction in the total value of ICT exports, the magnitude of this reduction varies widely by country. In China, the top exporter of ICT goods, the new definition entailed only a small reduction in ICT goods exports, as the value of the goods added was worth 99 per cent of the value of the goods removed. By contrast, major ICT goods exporters in developed countries have been affected more. The United States, Germany, Japan and France saw some of the largest net declines in the value of their ICT goods exports. The change in definition will accelerate the trend of ICT goods exports shifting towards developing Asia (UNCTAD, 2009a and 2010).

Source: UNCTAD.

[a]   See UNCTAD (2011). Implications of applying the new definition of "ICT goods". Technical note no. 1. http://new.unctad.org/Documents/ICT%20sector/ICTA_TN_1_unedited.PDF.

---

to modify ICT components instead of importing them (given the modern modularization of devices), due to economies of scale and high costs of entry, it is unlikely that the trend towards the geographical concentration of ICT manufacturing in Asia will reverse any time soon.

D. POLICY IMPLICATIONS

As was noted in chapter I, several developing countries recognize the importance of including promotion of the ICT sector in their PSD strategies. Many see this sector as strategically important for the development of a competitive economy. Governments can facilitate expansion of the ICT sector by creating an enabling framework to address bottlenecks to its development. This involves a wide range of interventions in various policy domains, including liberalization and effective regulation of the ICT sector, enhancing trust in the use of ICT services (chapter II), providing training in ICT skills, nurturing ICT enterprises via incubation and by establishing technology parks, and using public procurement to create demand.

Priority-setting needs to reflect the kinds of activity that the Government wants to develop. For example, the nature of infrastructure and skills requirements varies considerably between activities aimed at servicing the local market and those aimed at servicing the international market. In order for policies aimed at promoting the ICT sector to be efficient, they should be well integrated in the overall PSD strategy.

1. ICT-sector liberalization and regulation

A key element in creating an investment climate that enables the use of ICTs is the liberalization and effective regulation of the ICT sector. As noted in chapter II, in countries with limitations on market entry, the roll-out of infrastructure and the uptake of ICT use among enterprises have typically been more limited than elsewhere. A more open market for ICT services allows private enterprises to enter, stimulates growth and investment, increases the availability of infrastructure and affordable services, and fosters innovation. At the same time, adequate regulation is required in order to reap full benefits from opening up.

Despite the rapid growth of the ICT sector in the past few decades, various constraints to its expansion remain. A number of countries have not liberalized the ICT sector fully, and even in those that have, barriers to entry may remain, in terms of high licensing costs or significant market power over key facilities that are hard to replicate. The role of Governments includes minimizing direct and indirect barriers to market entry, as well as providing adequate regulation of existing players. Limits on market entry through de facto or de jure monopolization of specific market segments, high administrative prices for licences or spectrum, complex and cumbersome licensing processes, and a lack of effective regulation for dealing with companies that have significant market power, constrain the effectiveness of the market.

Table III.6. Status of competition in telecommunications services, countries allowing competition in each market segment, 2010 (%)

	Competition	Partial/duopoly	Monopoly
Local services	56	14	30
International long distance	53	15	31
Leased lines	58	17	24
Mobile	62	28	10
Internet services	78	15	7
International gateways	58	24	18

Source: ITU.

According to ITU, most countries now allow competition in key ICT network services (table III.6). The most open market segments are mobile and Internet services, which have also been the two exhibiting the strongest growth over the last 10 years. By contrast, a number of countries have not moved to fully competitive markets, or still allow monopoly control over other segments. These restrictions limit market entry, and tend to hamper the ability of the economy to benefit from the reduced prices, innovation and market growth made possible by the combination of private-sector involvement and competition.

Access to different ICT services at affordable rates is essential to the development of various ICT producing activities. As the examples of such countries as India or the Philippines demonstrate, cheap and reliable broadband connectivity is essential for the development of an outsourcing industry. Likewise, increased availability and affordability of mobile services should lead to more jobs and business opportunities in the mobile sector, including the development of mobile applications, the provision of mobile money services, and the repair and sale of mobile phones and related accessories.

A survey of 17 African countries carried out by Research ICT Africa (RIA) (2010) identified seven aspects of ICT policy to promote affordable and quality ICT infrastructures: (a) market entry and open access (which should be technology-neutral); (b) allocation of scarce resources (such as spectrum); (c) interconnectivity; (d) regulation of anticompetitive practices; (e) universal service; (f) tariff regulation; and (g) quality of service. Only two of the countries (Botswana and the United

Republic of Tanzania) provided an ICT policy environment that was viewed positively by local actors, while in other countries it was, at best, viewed neutrally (Ghana, Tunisia and Uganda).

Improving the ICT policy environment is key to attracting local and foreign investment in ICTs, and to ensuring that the potential benefits materialize. One of the general policy recommendations is to ensure the effective autonomy of the regulator. Too often, especially in LDCs, regulators do not have enough political autonomy or the effective means to carry out their duties fully. Moreover, regulators and other authorities involved often lack the necessary capacity to implement appropriate measures in these areas. Building the capacities of ICT policymakers is thus important and requires international support.

2. Developing human resources

Developing a thriving ICT sector depends crucially on the availability of adequately trained human resources. Lack of the necessary skills is often cited as a barrier to the development of a local ICT industry, and serves as an effective barrier to attracting foreign investment. At the same time, in order for government or private-sector initiatives that aim at developing human resources to achieve their goals, it is essential to have a clear understanding of the precise needs of the enterprises in question. Matching supply and demand is necessary in order to ensure that skills developed through education and training are those that are sought by ICT enterprises. A poor match increases the likelihood of educated people having to look elsewhere for work, possibly contributing to brain drain.

In general, people who are ICT-literate have a higher chance of finding employment, as both companies and Governments need their skills in order to better participate in the knowledge-based economy. Governments should therefore seek to enhance digital literacy, by using the basic education system, beginning at primary school level, and by emphasizing lifelong learning through adult training programmes. Ideally, the public and private sectors, and academia and training institutions, should work together to develop national policies that focus on imparting appropriate skills that reflect the requirements of the ICT industry. The provision of free Internet access in public schools, universities and libraries can serve to broaden the use of technology and the Internet for entrepreneurs. At the same time, care should be

Box III.7. Promoting globally competitive infocomm manpower in Singapore

To support its fast-growing infocomm industry, the Government of Singapore has stressed the importance of developing a rich pool of globally competitive ICT human resources. To this end, the manpower development programmes under the national development strategy (iN2015) are focused on developing competencies in key sectors, developing globally competitive ICT professionals, and attracting, developing and retaining ICT talent. The Government is aiming for 80,000 new jobs by 2015, comprising 55,000 ICT and 25,000 non-infocomm jobs in the industry. By 2009, Singapore had reached the halfway mark, with more than 41,000 additional jobs created. A few of the related initiatives are presented below.

The *Critical Infocomm Technology Resource Programme* is a training incentive programme designed to equip infocomm professionals with critical and emerging skills. In April 2009 it was enhanced, to provide more funding for course and examination fees. Training courses are aligned with the National Infocomm Competency Framework, and more than 27,800 professionals have benefited from it since 2006. Some of the critical skills targeted for development by the programme include data integration and information management, infrastructure and network management, ICT in media and entertainment, IT services, business management and software development.

The *National Infocomm Competency Framework* articulates the competency requirements of key professionals. It seeks to widen and deepen the capabilities of Singapore's ICT professionals and to guide their career development and progression. Training courses are delivered through Continuing Education Training centres, which are expected to train up to 10,000 professionals over five years. The framework now offers about 250 job roles in areas such as infocomm security, data centre management, channels management, quality assurance, and portfolio management. The framework will be continually updated to cover new and emerging areas such as cloud computing, business analytics, green computing, next generation networking, and service science engineering.

The *Infocomm Leadership and Development* (iLEAD) programme aims to build a pipeline of experts in high-end, strategic growth areas such as business analytics, cloud computing, and green ICT. This is to ensure that Singapore's infocomm manpower capabilities keep pace with technological change. Organizations can use iLEAD to boost the capabilities of their existing employees and to take in new trainees.

The *Techno-Strategists Programme* aims to develop professionals with both technical and business knowledge of sectors such as financial services, healthcare, hospitality, retail, and interactive digital media. Training courses, workshops and certification examinations exist in five industry domains, and more than 1,000 professionals have acquired hybrid skills since April 2008.

As part of the effort to attract some of the best students to pursue a career in the ICT sector, two scholarship programmes have been launched. The National Infocomm Scholarship (NIS) provides "A" level students and polytechnic graduates with a government scholarship and valuable private-sector work exposure in top infocomm and end-user companies. About 180 students have so far been awarded the NIS. For outstanding "O" level students, the Integrated Infocomm Scholarship (IIS) was launched in 2009. This includes the opportunity for talented students to gain experience in major infocomm corporations locally and overseas. To date, 52 students have been awarded the IIS.

Source: Infocomm Development Authority (2010).

taken when seeking to leverage ICTs for educational purposes, as many initiatives in this area have failed to generate the results hoped for (see, for example, IADB, 2011a).[17]

The development of ICT professionals is a priority in many countries, including Singapore (box III.7) and Egypt (box III.8). In Cambodia, more than 3,000 software developers graduate every year, and the cost of hiring them is generally much lower than for software developers from China or India. Nevertheless, due to their skill levels being below international standards, they are still not competitive.[18] Here, as in many other developing countries, one of the challenges is to adapt the ICT curriculums taught in universities to reflect new

developments in the area of software. The Meltwater Foundation offers a three-phase entrepreneurial programme designed to foster software companies in Africa. It begins at the Meltwater Entrepreneurial School of Technology (MEST) campus in Accra, Ghana, with a two-year training programme. IT entrepreneurs with business ideas that are deemed to be viable then move to the MEST Incubator for assistance in getting their businesses off the ground.[19]

In UNECLAC's review of national ICT strategies in Latin America and the Caribbean, the software, applications and content industries were given special attention. UNECLAC underlined that new products depended increasingly on greater integration of hardware and

---

Box III.8. Boosting the number of ICT graduates in Egypt

Thanks to various initiatives, often in partnership with the private sector, the Government of Egypt has managed to increase the number of graduates with relevant skills for the ICT sector. The number of graduates that have received formal ICT training has increased significantly since 2006, when about 27,000 were trained. By May of 2011, there were already 40,000 graduates enrolled for formal ICT training.[a] The availability of trained technical staff graduating from Egyptian universities is expected to meet the demand of the market for several years to come. In the area of software development, the Software Engineering Competence Centre (SECC) has, since 2003, been delivering courses and offering advisory services to Egyptian companies to assess their maturity level. Over thirty companies have attended these courses and have achieved certification for Capability Maturity Model Integration (CMMI) maturity levels 2–5. By meeting the requirements of the SECC, Egyptian ICT companies can claim that they meet internationally acceptable criteria for software development, which helps them compete internationally. To date, SECC has focused particularly on lower-level certifications. Only a handful of Egyptian companies have so far achieved CMMI certification levels 4 or 5. SECC expects that it will take about another year for it to be able to provide level 4 and 5 certifications.

Source: UNCTAD (2011c).

[a] MCIT (2010). Egyptian ICT Indicators Portal. http://www.mcit.gov.eg/Indicators.aspx.

---

software components, and that the development of ICTs in the coming decade would be shaped by technology convergence. With a view to strengthening the software industry, the review made the following observation (UNECLAC, 2010: 28).

"From a national and regional public policy viewpoint, the short- and medium-term goal should be to resolve the main competitiveness gaps associated with the ICT industry, especially in the areas of human resource capacity, enterprise operational excellence, technology transfer, and the promotion of cluster initiatives."

Mexico has a comprehensive programme called PROSOFT to addresses specific challenges related to the human, regulatory, business, market and investment aspects of developing a domestic ICT industry. The programme contains a wide number of instruments, including some that deal with the promotion of human talent in software development and IT services. To improve the availability of trained/certified IT professionals, several concrete actions have been taken. *Mexico First*[20] is an initiative that financially supports (by up to 70 per cent) the certification of IT specialists and other skilled labour needed in IT- and ICT-enabled services. The programme aims to support the certification of 12,000 professionals annually. Applications can be made for a wide range of certifications, in the areas of multimedia, IT and BPO, as well as in English and project management. IT Talent is another programme, which supports the certification of graduates in competencies specifically required by industry. Five different profiles have been identified, and 48 people had been certified as software architects by April 2011.[21]

India's success in IT- and ICT-enabled services exports is partly explained by the local availability of a qualified workforce which is the result of a long-planned education strategy. In India, several companies are engaged in training and capacity-building activities, helping to support skills development for the IT/BPO market. Indian companies are also piloting BPO training activities and projects in rural areas, to assess the potential that this market represents for meeting the demand for outsourcing by hiring employees in rural areas directly while at the same time encouraging employment at the local and community level. Other Indian companies are also providing BPO certification directly.[22]

Development partners can make important contributions to the development of relevant ICT skills. For example, the German organization InWEnt has launched an initiative to support the capacity-building programme run by the Free Software and Open Source Foundation for Africa (FOSSFA) and by GIZ, which supports ICT SMEs and aims to encourage the growth of African ICT sectors. The programme specifically promotes free and open source business models, Linux administration certification, and innovative African free and open source software (FOSS) applications.[23]

In addition, a range of private-sector initiatives have been launched to speed up the development of ICT skills. For example, the Cisco Networking Academy programme delivers a learning experience to more than 900,000 students each year. Since 1997, over 3 million students from more than 165 countries have gained ICT skills through the programme.[24] Microsoft works with partners to create relevant training opportunities and innovative tools for people who are underserved by technology. As part of the "Microsoft Unlimited Potential" commitment, employability and workforce development programmes support organizations that work to ensure that individuals have the required IT skills.[25]

Beyond the ICT-specific training needs, the development of general entrepreneurship and management skills is also of the essence. This is one of the recognized challenges for ICT SMEs in Africa (Excelsior, 2011). Across the region, there are few skills development training programmes to help young entrepreneurs develop the necessary marketing, finance and operational tools needed to launch successful ICT enterprises. This also applies to basic activities that foster local adoption of ICTs, such as mobile and computer repairs and maintenance, running cybercafes etc. A few examples in this respect can be highlighted. The Success in Information Business programme, implemented by Jidaw Systems Limited, is dedicated to building human capacities for ICT entrepreneurship in Nigeria. It provides short courses on management that are specific to the ICT industry, for would-be business starters in the ICT sector.[26] In Zambia, Youth Resource Centres supported by IICD are deploying ICT in training curriculums. This includes promoting the operation of Internet connectivity as a potential area for entrepreneurship development. These schemes may contribute to helping Nigeria and Zambia benefit from a larger pool of workers with relevant skills who can then support ICT roll-out in the local private sector and create new ICT-related businesses. In Kenya, such basic skill-building partly comes through informal apprenticeships. There are, for example, successful ICT learning spaces in slum areas, such as the Digital Design School, NairoBits in Kibera, and the Mathari Resource Centre – which could be better supported or scaled up with appropriate support.[27]

3. Incubation and technology parks

To boost specific ICT enterprises, many countries have established various kinds of business incubators. Such initiatives may seek to overcome difficulties in raising local public- and private-sector awareness of the importance of supporting entrepreneurship and SME development in the ICT sector. They also aim at boosting the survival rate of start-ups by providing key services at their most vulnerable stage of development, and by fostering cooperation and emulation through geographical proximity benefits. They are typically geared towards supporting relatively sophisticated activities. Experience from developed countries show that enterprises that have benefited from business incubation have a higher rate of survival; the

same observation has been made for Brazil and China (United Nations Millennium Project, 2005). At the same time, some concerns have been raised about incubation, for instance regarding the extent to which benefits are sustainable, the potential for outreach, and the risks in "picking winners" (ibid.).

*Info*Dev, a donor-funded research, capacity-building and advisory programme, helps developing countries and their international partners use innovation and ICTs as tools for sustainable social and economic development.[28] One of its programmes is the Global Business Incubator Initiative, which aims to build capacity and to undertake research. The initiative was launched in 2002, with support from the Government of Japan. By April 2011, the network had 337 incubators in 93 countries. Most of the incubators target the ICT sector specifically, whereas others have a focus on agriculture, manufacturing, or other areas. InfoDev estimates that almost 17,000 SMEs have been incubated, that over 4,000 enterprises have graduated, and that more than 230,000 jobs have been created. An online incubator support centre (http://www.idisc. net) has been set up to give incubators the opportunity to network and to learn using knowledge tools designed for business incubators.

Recently, the Government of Finland, Nokia and infoDev jointly launched a new network of regional mobile applications laboratories (mLabs). Locations for the first five mLabs have been identified: Armenia, Kenya, Pakistan, South Africa and Viet Nam. For example, in the case of Kenya, the mLab for East Africa will be established by the *iHub Consortium, which includes the World Wide Web Foundation and the Nairobi School of Computing and Informatics. *iHub – Nairobi's Innovation Hub for the technology community – is an open space for technologists, investors, technology companies and computer specialists in the area. It focuses on young entrepreneurs, web and mobile phone programmers, designers and researchers. It is partly an open community workspace (co-working), partly a vector for investors and venture capitalists, and partly an incubator.[29]

There is a need for more systematic assessments of the extent to which incubators generate the results anticipated. For example, a more comprehensive assessment of the impact of individual incubators within the infoDev network could generate valuable insights into how and when incubators work the best. In Peru, incubators have had limited success in the establishment of technology-based enterprises (UNCTAD,

---

Box III.9. ICT park in Rwanda

Rwanda established an ICT park and incubation facility in Kigali in 2006. Kigali ICT Park is managed by the Rwanda Development Board, and promotes innovation, private sector development, capacity-building and sustainability. The Park offers a service package including subsidized office space, Internet connections, power, and other facilities. There are three main objectives: (a) incubation (for ICT start-ups); (b) technology production and exhibition (by ICT companies); and (c) the Multi-Disciplinary Centre of Excellence in ICT. At least six ICT companies have graduated from the Park, and another 12 are being incubated. There are plans to expand the scope and function of the Park in the coming years.

Source: UNCTAD, based on information provided by UNECA.

2011b). They have faced demand constraints in the form of a lack of participants, as well as limited opportunities to link with crucial institutions such as research institutions, or to access financial resources.

Many developing countries have established dedicated technology parks to provide internationally competitive ICT infrastructure and other facilities to foreign and domestic investors in technology-intensive industries. Among developing regions, Asia has been particularly active in using such policy instruments (Andersson et al., 2004). Well-known examples in Asia include Hsinchu Science Park (Taiwan Province of China), Zhongguancun Science Park in Beijing (China), the many technology parks dedicated to IT services in India, and the Multimedia Super Corridor (Malaysia). In recent years, the number of parks has also increased in Africa – examples being SMART Village in Egypt and the ICT park in Rwanda (box III.9).

Some initiatives seek to support ICT micro-enterprises engaged in less advanced activities. For example, the mobile operator Uninor's Hand in Hand Citizen Centres are a set of over 500 facilities across the State of Tamil Nadu, India, which are designed to allow female entrepreneurs to generate income and to deliver ICT training and support to other women in their communities.[30] Entrepreneurs are selected from self-help groups set up by the NGO Hand in Hand for women at the bottom of the pyramid. The women are given technical and business training, and loans for equipment which they repay monthly. The programme aims to empower local women with skills that will improve their income-generation and decision-making processes. At the same time, Uninor gains access to the rural market, and a point of contact with underserved customers. Mohanapriya is a 22-year-old entrepreneur working with a Centre in a rural village outside of Chennai. She and her mother sell mobile products and provide local women with ICT training, business training, and education on how to assert civil rights using ICT tools. The business allows them to make regular loan repayments and to generate a monthly income of 4000 INR ($88), a quadrupling of the income they had before joining the programme.

An important avenue to strengthen the competitiveness of small ICT enterprises is to promote improvements in quality. Where micro-enterprises are more clustered, such as in the case of urban handset vendors and repairers, local associations may be able to provide some controlling of quality and behaviours. In a Nigerian computer reseller cluster, such an association was able to improve and standardize quality somewhat among its members (Oyelaran-Oyeyinka, 2007). There is also room for policy to ensure behavioural standards. In the mobile money in Kenya, for instance, a policy to outline the roles and responsibilities of m-banking agents (signage, rates and qualifications) is pushing the value chain to enforce standards in order to preserve the reputation of the entire value chain (Dias and McKee, 2010). Moreover, the Digital Village scheme launched by the ICT Board of Kenya, which is still in its early stages, is seeking to work with existing ICT micro-enterprises and support them through loans and training to build digital centres in rural areas (Foster and Heeks, 2011). Another approach that has been taken by the United States-based social enterprise Inveneo aims to develop a network of certified local ICT enterprises that can deliver IT solutions to rural and remote regions of low-income countries (box III.10).

4. Using government procurement to create demand

States can play an active role in promoting a national ICT industry by expanding the demand for ICT services. In developing countries, the Government is often the largest ICT user. Consequently, the way in which it buys ICT goods and services influences overall demand for the local ICT sector. For example, UNECLAC recommends that Governments in Latin America and the Caribbean should encourage nationwide ICT-intensive modernization processes – for example via the automation of customs services, the digitization of transactions, public procurement, and traceability systems, and the use of mobile payments and services based on open data. Such reforms would open the way for domestic ICT enterprises to take better advantage of their innovation potential (UNECLAC, 2010).

The role of public procurement as a catalyst for local ICT industry development deserves more attention. As emphasized by Porter (1985), domestic demand is a strong stimulus to the competitiveness of local industry. Government ICT procurement represents an important part of domestic demand in low-income countries. At the same time, it is the nature of that demand (i.e. whether it is for cutting-edge, innovative ICT applications) as much as the size of the demand that matters. However, procurement rules relating to ICT goods and services should be designed in such a way that local ICT enterprises are given a real opportunity to qualify for the tender process. For example, Nigerian PC firms such as Zinok and Omatek were able to grow thanks to local procurement from the Government of Nigeria (Excelsior, 2011). It is important that government procurement is not seen as purely a question of financial investment, but also as a tool that can spur development of the local economy. Moreover, it is important to ensure that SMEs that are able to provide goods and services for government procurement are paid promptly, as they typically do not have the liquidity to extend credit over time.

Social outsourcing, as described in UNCTAD (2010), is a case in point. In India, several state Governments have made a deliberate decision not to route outsourced IT services work to large private-sector firms (sometimes subsidiaries of TNCs) but instead to channel it to social enterprises in poor communities. This deliberate procurement strategy aims at developing emerging ICT micro-enterprises, sometimes in rural areas (Heeks and Arun, 2010). A key problem facing small and new outsourcing firms – especially if they are located in rural areas – is to find enough clients to make the venture sustainable.[31] In such a situation, government procurement can act as a catalyst and help new market entrants to build sufficient scale and a track record that can subsequently be used in reaching out to new clients.

The introduction of e-procurement systems can act as an incentive for more SMEs to increase their use of the Internet as a business tool, and can thereby also create more local private demand for ICT consultancy services. The experience of Chile demonstrates that an e-procurement system backed up by strong policies on procurement can save government money and increase the quality of the goods and services procured, and at the same time can promote ICT uptake among SMEs and help to level the playing field in public procurement, so that more companies and not just large firms benefit (Chile Compra, 2008).

Box III.10. Building a network of certified small and local ICT enterprises

Inveneo is a non-profit social enterprise which aims to make ICT tools such as computers, telephony and Internet access available to people and organizations in rural and highly underserved communities of the developing world. In order to deliver the most sustainable ICT solutions for relevant organizations, Inveneo is building a network of in-country IT entrepreneurs who are recruited, trained and certified to provide local IT services to schools, hospitals, enterprises and Governments.

The Inveneo Certified ICT Partner (ICIP) programme is seeking to develop certified local technology companies that will have the necessary skills to deliver cost-effective installation and IT support services. By means of the programme, Inveneo has developed a network of over 76 partners in 24 developing countries – 18 of which are LDCs.

Inveneo continues to expand its network of partner companies. The preferred potential ICIPs are small ICT businesses with 3 to 20 full-time local employees and which have a track record in serving enterprise, government and/or school system clients over the last two or more years. They should also possess strong experience in at least three of the following technical areas: enterprise/school networking; basic Linux and open-source knowledge; Microsoft-certified; long-distance wireless networking; VoIP or rural power systems (battery and solar). In addition, they must be willing to commit two staff and the associated travel costs for two weeks of training, which is held on site in a rural location.

Applicants who wish to become ICIPs go through a rigorous recruitment and selection process. If they pass the screening, they benefit from intense training on rural ICT solutions, which consists of both classroom and hands-on field instruction, robust certification processes, and ongoing partner-support and management systems. ICIP partners have seen up to $2,000 a month in increased revenue through new clients acquired by virtue of being an ICIP.

Source: Inveneo (http://www.inveneo.org).

NOTES

[1] The information is available online at http://unctadstat.unctad.org/TableViewer/tableView.aspx?ReportId=1634.

[2] OECD data presented by Pierre Montagnier, OECD, at WSIS Forum 2011. 17 May 2011.

[3] See the summary of the discussion held at the Partnership session held during WSIS Forum 2011, available at http://new.unctad.org/upload/WSIS%20Forum%202011/WSIS_Session_summary_17052011.PDF.

[4] See IDATE (2010). World Telecom Services Market 2010: Global market worth 1,348.9 billion USD in 2009. 25 August. http://blog.idate.fr/?p=133.

[5] Source: World Bank and Public–Private Infrastructure Advisory Facility (2011). Private Participation in Infrastructure Projects database. 4 March. http://ppi.worldbank.org.

[6] See, for example, Business Wire (2011). Yankee group forecast shows global telecom spending rising for first time since financial crash. 25 May. http://www.businesswire.com/news/home/20110525005249/en/CORRECTING-REPLACING-Yankee-Group-Forecast-Shows-Global.

[7] All direct activity in the mobile supply chain is seen as being part of the supply side of the mobile sector. This approach diverges from the agreed definition of the ICT sector (OECD, 2009), which excludes vending and retailing. However, in developing countries, the actions and behaviours of such vendors very much reposition them as an active part of the sphere of production.

[8] See examples for Bangladesh, Kenya and Uganda in Deloitte (2008), GSMA (2009b), Ovum (2006) and UCC (2007).

[9] Bayala S, Kabore M and Traoré I (2009). Le sous-secteur informel des TIC au Burkina Faso: rapport de recherche. Research paper funded by International Development Research Centre (Canada). Also: Ndiaye SM, Niang A and Diongue K (2010). Le sous-secteur des TIC au Sénégal. Research paper funded by International Development Research Centre (Canada).

[10] Crowd-sourcing is the act of outsourcing tasks traditionally performed by an employee or contractor to an undefined, large group of people or community (a "crowd") through an open call.

[11] The Guardian (2011). China used prisoners in lucrative Internet gaming work. 25 May. http://www.guardian.co.uk/world/2011/may/25/china-prisoners-internet-gaming-scam.

[12] The Economist (2011). Turks of the world, unite! 24 May. http://www.economist.com/blogs/babbage/2011/05/repetitive_tasks.

[13] UNCTAD (2011). In wake of financial crisis, Asia's share of global ICT exports surges to record high. Press release. http://www.unctad.org/Templates/webflyer.asp?docid=14417&intItemID=1528&lang=1.

[14] Mexico is the main non-Asian developing-country exporter, accounting for 3.5 per cent of world exports of ICT goods. The remainder of the non-Asian developing countries account for less than 1.5 per cent of the total.

[15] See http://www.omatekcomputers.com/company_profile.html (accessed on 10 August 2011).

[16] Ouédraogo S, Bayala S, Niang A and Tankeu R (2010). Dynamiques et rôle économique et social du secteur informel des TIC en Afrique de l'Ouest et du Centre: cas du Burkina Faso, du Cameroun et du Sénégal. Research paper funded by International Development Research Centre (Canada). September.

[17] IADB (2011a) found that increased access to computers in schools by itself had had low returns in the Latin American and Caribbean region. In order for ICTs to have a positive impact, complementary inputs were critical – including hardware, software, electricity, teacher training, and technical and pedagogical support.

[18] Economics Today (2011). Using ICT to help rural areas. 16–30.

[19] See http://www.meltwater.org/about/.

[20] See: www.mexico-first.org/

[21] As reported at http://www.canieti.org/noticias/vista/11-04-04/Estrena_M%C3%A9xico_sus_primeros_Arquitectos_de_Software.aspx

[22] Hero Mindmine (2008). Global BPO certification. See http://www.heromindmine.com/index.html.

[23] See http://www.ict-innovation.org/.

[24] See http://www.cisco.com/web/about/citizenship/socialinvestments/docs/NetAcadBrief.pdf.

[25] See http://www.microsoft.com/about/corporatecitizenship/en-us/our-actions/in-the-community/workforce-development.aspx.

[26] See http://www.jidaw.com.

[27] See, for example, http://www.nairobits.com/.

[28] See http://www.infodev.org.

[29] See http://www.ihub.co.ke/pages/about.php.

[30] Information provided by the GSMA mWomen programme. See http://www.mwomen.org.

[31] Seehttp://ict4dblog.wordpress.com/2011/05/31/development-2-0-case-study-socially-responsible-outsourcing-to-rural-indian-telecentres/.

MAKING PSD INTERVENTIONS MORE EFFECTIVE
WITH ICTs

4

Governments and other organizations are engaged in many activities aimed at supporting the creation and growth of enterprises. However, the expanded scope for leveraging ICTs in this context has so far not been fully reflected in the strategies and policies of national Governments and their development partners. This chapter explores selected areas in which ICT use has the potential to contribute to making the business environment more enabling and PSD interventions more effective.

This chapter concentrates on three areas that are of high priority in the context of PSD interventions. Section A is concerned with the use of ICTs to make business environments more enabling. Section B focuses on ICT use in the delivery of business development and agricultural extension services, with special emphasis on training and advisory services and on making the relevant information more accessible. Section C examines how ICTs can be leveraged to improve access to finance – the biggest barrier to growth and development in micro- and small enterprises (MSEs).

A. HOW CAN ICTs HELP TO MAKE BUSINESS ENVIRONMENTS MORE ENABLING?

As noted in chapter I, in order to facilitate growth and development of the private sector, an important task for Governments is to make the investment climate and business environment as enabling as possible. The business environment can be seen as a subset of the investment climate – consisting of a complex set of policy, legal, institutional and regulatory conditions that govern business activities (box IV.1). While the investment climate has an overall effect on private-sector activities, the business environment is directly affected by government decisions at national, provincial and local levels. This section illustrates how ICTs can contribute in this context, with examples covering three areas, namely (a) facilitating business registration and licensing; (b) improving tax policies and administration; and (c) facilitating trade.

Governments and their partners, including bilateral donor and multilateral development agencies, are seeking to reform the business environment so that private enterprises are able to change their behaviour in ways that lead to enhanced economic growth through increased levels of investment and innovation, and to more and better jobs. This is done by reducing business costs (in order to increase profits or market share); reducing the risks associated with poor or frequently changing government policies, laws and regulations; and increasing competitive pressure through having new enterprises enter the market to stimulate market efficiency and incentives for innovation (DCED, 2008).

The relationship that is formed between government and business is a key aspect of the business envi-ronment. It can be improved through processes that make it more transparent, rules-based and efficient, thereby bringing down the costs of complying with regulations. The private sector devotes considerable time and effort to following administrative procedures and filling out forms. Therefore, the effective use of ICTs (e.g. using various e-government and auto-mated solutions) plays a role in improving this relationship. E-government applications can streamline processes and make them more efficient. If well implemented, e-government also enhances transparency, by systemizing and publicizing the procedures for government interactions, and reduces the scope for corruption. The likelihood of positive gains from the introduction of ICT-based solutions increases if they are implemented as part of broader initiatives to simplify regulation.

There are many "functional areas" of business environment reform (DCED, 2008: 14–15), such as (a) simplifying business registration and licensing procedures; (b) improving tax policies and administration; (c) improving labour laws and administration; (d) improving the overall quality of regulatory governance; (e) improving land titles, registers and administration; (f) simplifying and speeding up access to commercial courts and to alternative dispute resolution mechanisms; (g) broadening public–private dialogue; (h) improving access to market information; and (i) enabling better access to finance. There are also possibilities for ICTs to make a difference in areas not explicitly covered in this chapter, although the scope for beneficial effects is likely to vary considerably from area to area. Rather than covering all the areas, the remainder of this section gives special attention to the following three: (a) business registration and licensing; (b) tax administration; and (c) trade facilitation. Rather than claiming to be comprehensive, the analysis uses selected examples to illustrate how ICTs have contributed – or could

---

Box IV.1. Elements of the business environment

From a policy perspective, three broad subcomponents of the business environment can be identified:

(a) The *policy, legal and regulatory framework* refers to the range of policies, laws and regulations that affect business owners – men and women.

(b) *Administrative systems* refers to the ways in which policies, laws and regulations are enforced, and includes issues such as governance (public and private, corruption etc.).

(c) *National organizational arrangements* refers to the ways in which government and business represent themselves and communicate with each other, and includes the issues of social dialogue and public–private dialogue.

Source: DCED (2008).

contribute – to making business environments more enabling. Using ICTs to improve access to information is addressed in section IV.B, and access to finance is covered in section IV.C.

1. Improving business registration and licensing procedures

The process of registering an enterprise or obtaining a business licence can be improved by ICT use, by enhancing access to the procedures, automating them, and reducing the scope for corruption at both national and subnational levels.

ICT-supported reforms have contributed to important outcomes for private enterprises, particularly by speeding up the process of obtaining business licences and permits when these are made available online. Some 105 economies use ICTs for business registration services ranging from name search to entirely online registration. This includes New Zealand, which was the first country to introduce online business registrations in 1996 (World Bank, 2010a: 22). More recent examples are Colombia, where the introduction of an online company registration facility in 2008 has led to a 20 per cent annual increase in the number of registered companies, and Singapore, in which an online registration system has helped to save businesses an estimated $42 million annually (World Bank, 2010a: 22–23). The impact of such registration systems is more profound if they are introduced as part of broader reforms aimed at simplifying procedures. In Peru, for example, an integrated online system has been introduced, providing businesses with information such as registration status and a tax number. This

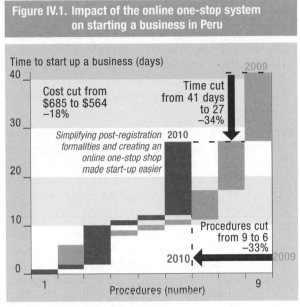

Figure IV.1. Impact of the online one-stop system on starting a business in Peru

Time to start up a business (days)

Cost cut from $685 to $564 −18%

Time cut from 41 days to 27 −34%

Simplifying post-registration formalities and creating an online one-stop shop made start-up easier

2010

Procedures cut from 9 to 6 −33%

Procedures (number)

Source: World Bank (2010a: 18).

has cut the number of procedures required to start a business, and has shortened the process by two weeks (fig. IV.1).

Automated registration procedures have been found to increase the number of new firms in an economy. A study of business registrations in 112 countries has shown that modernization creates a positive environment for starting new enterprises (Klapper and Love, 2011). The number of new businesses relative to the population ("entry density") was higher in countries where business registration could be carried out online. In addition, the average number of days and the costs to start a new business were much lower in locations with online registration (fig. IV.2).

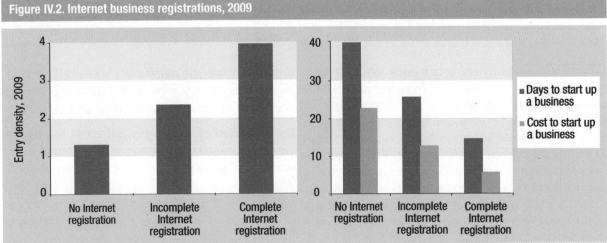

Figure IV.2. Internet business registrations, 2009

- Days to start up a business
- Cost to start up a business

Source: World Bank.

Box IV.2. Speeding up business registration at the local level in the Philippines

In many municipalities in the Philippines, it takes 3–5 days or more for a business to secure a permit to operate. The underlying reasons include excessive red tape and inefficiencies in the manual processing of applications. The situation is often aggravated by the rent-seeking practices of public officials. All of the above has meant lower government revenues and higher costs of doing business. Although investing in system informatization can help municipalities to improve the situation, many local government units lack the know-how and resources to implement such solutions.

The e-Governance for Municipal Development (eGov4MD) project, which is funded by the Canadian International Development Agency, is a collaborative initiative between the League of Municipalities of the Philippines, the Mayors Development Centre, the Canadian Executive Service Organization (CESO), and the Commission on Information and Communication Technology of the National Computer Centre (CICT-NCC). The project, which started in 2007, is also supported by the Department of the Interior and Local Government, and by the Department of Trade and Industry through its regional and provincial offices.

The project aims to improve local governance, increase the efficiency of public service delivery, and raise government revenues. This is to be achieved by building the capacity of selected e-ready municipalities nationwide, and implementing an open source-based software package consisting of a Real Property Tax System (RPTS), a Business Permit and Licence System (BPLS) and a Treasury Operations Management System (TOMS). The initiative also provides training for municipal personnel. Advisory services are delivered by CESO's volunteer advisers.

By early 2011, an enhanced eBPLS had been set up in 75 municipalities. Many of these reported 15 to 150 per cent increases in business permit revenues, large reductions in application processing times (from 2–3 days down to 1 hour), and increased user satisfaction. A number of the selected local government units had also updated or revised their revenue codes and streamlined the application process.

From April 2007 to October 2010, participating municipalities invested about PhP 28 million (approx. $636,000) in ICT hardware, excluding costs for capacity-building. About 40 CESO volunteer advisers were deployed, and 26 municipalities received training on eRPTS. More than 400 municipal department heads and staff were trained in open source technologies, the use of eBPLS, basic software programming, IT planning, and ICT project management. An NGO was established, comprising all municipal staff trained under the eGov4MD Project, to ensure sustainability and replication beyond the CESO partnership.

Venturing into e-governance requires long-term political support, institutional maturity, capital investment both in hardware and human resources, and a well-designed, visionary roadmap. Experience to date has shown the importance of political leadership in championing the process, from adopting municipal resolutions, sending staff to trainings, and allocating resources to procure the IT equipment needed, to having a project management plan.

The vision is that more municipalities will venture into e-governance, which will make them more competitive and business-friendly. The multi-stakeholder eGov4MD project is founded on a commitment to change. It is an initiative to break away from the status quo, to reform and to innovate. The League of Municipalities of the Philippines and its partners are searching for more local government units to join the initiative.

Source: Sagun (2011).

ICTs are also useful in helping to reduce corruption by making administrative processes more transparent, at both national and subnational levels. Automating interactions between businesses and the government limits the scope for human intervention and bribery, which results in lower business costs. For example, the introduction of automated processes for several e-government projects in India was linked directly to a decline in the incidence of corruption (fig. IV.3). It is worth highlighting that after the e-government projects were deployed, bribery reoccurred whenever the system was down. In the Philippines, the introduction of

e-governance at the municipality level significantly increased government revenue and shortened the time needed for obtaining a business licence (box IV.2).

Better regulations, and better access to regulations, can be an effective way to empower informal-sector enterprises. While in some cases informality is a conscious choice – a decision to avoid taxes and other obligations – it very often reflects a lack of awareness of the law or of the ways to comply with the law, or a lack of capacity to undertake the necessary procedures. Indeed, burdensome and poorly conceived

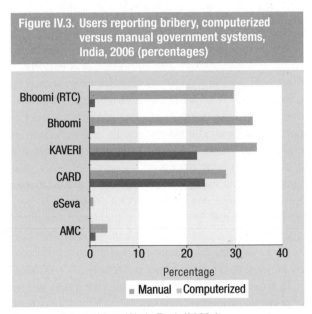

Figure IV.3. Users reporting bribery, computerized versus manual government systems, India, 2006 (percentages)

Source: Adapted from World Bank (2009a).

regulations have been found to be a major barrier to entry into the formal economy.[1] Legal empowerment measures – such as strengthening effective economic governance to make it easy and affordable to set up and operate a business, access markets, and exit if necessary – are indispensable for potential and emerging entrepreneurs. Informality narrows the fiscal space, and represents considerable revenue shortfalls for State budgets in developing countries. Informal

businesses make little contribution to the government budget. They pay no registration fees, no licence fees, no VAT on their sales, no corporate income tax, and no social contribution for their employees. Unregistered land and dwellings generate no registry or transfer fees, or local taxes. And yet, informal businesses often have to pay bribes, easily falling victim to officials who take advantage of informal operators' status and lack of awareness. Various e-government solutions and the effective use of ICTs in communicating with informal-sector enterprises can make an important contribution, as was found in an UNCTAD-led initiative (box IV.3).

2. Improving tax policies and administration

Reforms of the tax administration system in developing countries typically aim to improve compliance among MSEs, including in the informal sector. ICTs have proved to contribute to reforms of tax policies and procedures through the introduction of electronic filing of returns, electronic payment of taxes, and the provision of taxpayer services via the Internet.

In many developing countries, large businesses have been able to rely on online, IT-based systems for filing tax returns and making payments. In countries with widespread access to the Internet and mobile phones, the expansion of IT-based filing and payment opportu-

---

Box IV.3. UNCTAD's easy business formalization (micro-legalization) programme

UNCTAD has designed a programme to help Governments implement regulations suited to the needs of MSEs and to facilitate the formalization of informal businesses, based on international best practice. Advisory and capacity-building services are offered for:

(a)   Inventory and diagnosis of existing regulations applicable to the creation and operation of micro-enterprises (filling in tax declarations and paying taxes). This may be carried out via online applications such as the eRegulations system;

(b)   Simplification of existing schemes and/or the proposal of new, tailor-made regulations to minimize the number of steps and requirements for users and to maximize the legal and social benefits;

(c)   Organization of internal processing – within and among the administrations involved – with an emphasis on the use of eGovernment tools. For example, "iCREATOR" is an application that allows entrepreneurs to register their business online and helps Governments to monitor the flows of documents among the administrations involved. Smartcards are also used as a way to integrate government services;

(d)   Negotiation of partnerships for combined delivery of services with microfinance institutions and other providers of basic services to the poor;

(e)   Drawing up and execution of external communications to raise awareness among micro-enterprises;

(f)   Measuring results.

Source: UNCTAD (http://www.eregulations.org).

nities for the small business community is being considered. In Latvia, for example, around 20,000 taxpayers (80 per cent of which are SMEs) use a paperless, web-based secure e-tax declaration system (IFC, 2007a). In 1995, the Bureau of Internal Revenue in the Philippines introduced payment by mobile phone for small tax debts. Initially, the project was used for the payment of business registration fees, and it was subsequently extended to payments of income taxes and stamp duty (ibid.).

The Rwanda Revenue Authority has embarked on an initiative to enable businesses, in the future, to submit tax returns online. To cater for businesses without online facilities, the Authority plans to introduce Internet kiosks around the country that can be easily accessed and used by businesses, for a fee. The Authority also intends to introduce a facility for the online validation of tax clearance certificates to remove the need for companies to copy and notarize such certificates when they submit multiple tenders (World Bank, 2010a: 23).

Online filing of taxes saves time for enterprises, and when the tax process is properly redesigned for automation, it often results in a reduction of forms and procedures. Azerbaijan has reformed its tax system and introduced an online payment system. By September 2008, about 85,000 out of 200,000 active VAT payers (43 per cent) had switched to the Automated Taxation Information Service to file and pay their taxes. This system resulted in the removal of 15 payment procedures, and time savings equivalent to 576 hours per year (Hacibeyoglu, 2009).

3. Trade facilitation measures

In a globalizing world economy, a facilitative trade regime is vital for private investment and the development of the private sector. In this context, ICT-enabled solutions can serve an important role.

Development support in this field has typically shifted from trade-related technical assistance (e.g. export promotion and trade liberalization) to trade facilitation (to reduce transaction costs) and promoting awareness and knowledge among national institutions of the rules, procedures and institutions of the international trading system. This is especially important for growth-oriented firms that seek to expand into broader markets, both regionally and internationally.

Customs administrations play a central role in facilitating the smooth handling of exports and imports. The implementation of modern ICT solutions has significantly improved the efficiency of many customs administrations. Such solutions facilitate the completion and processing of customs declarations and other paperwork associated with importing and exporting. Electronic customs declarations have been shown to bring clearance times down and to reduce the time that goods have to stay at border crossings and in ports. Most importantly, this leads to a reduction in costs to business. In addition, government revenue is boosted through improved collection of taxes. Automated customs systems, such as the Automated System for Customs Data (ASYCUDA) (box IV.4), play an important role in this regard. Moreover, the introduction of ICT-based solutions has helped to remove opportunities for corruption among customs officials, by increasing the level of accountability (IFC, 2007c). ICTs provide audit trails for the monitoring and review of administrative decisions, and minimize face-to-face contact between customs personnel and clients.[2]

Despite the documented success of ASYCUDA and other automated customs systems, developing countries (particularly LDCs) continue to face multiple challenges related to customs automation. Key concerns include the lack of financial resources for infrastructure and equipment, insufficient awareness and training, compliance risks, and resistance to change. In this respect, securing continued support from international donors is vital in order to ensure further improvements to trade facilitation efforts in this area.

B. HOW CAN ICTs BE USED TO SUPPORT BUSINESS DEVELOPMENT SERVICES?

The provision of business development services (BDS) and extension services to rural enterprises can be made more effective by applying ICTs.[3] In the context of services delivery, ICTs play two important and related roles: they can be used to extend the reach of the services offered, and they can reduce the transaction costs associated with the delivery of the services.

BDS and extension services are typically provided to nascent enterprises to improve their survival rates and to foster expansion that leads to job creation and economic growth. As noted in chapter I, many MSEs in developing economies are confronted with internal barriers to their operations and growth prospects,

---

Box IV.4. Automated customs to support PSD: the case of ASYCUDA

ASYCUDA is a computerized customs management system that covers most foreign trade procedures. The system handles customs declarations, accounting procedures, and transit and suspense procedures, thereby generating valuable trade data that can be used for statistical economic analysis. The ASYCUDA software, which has been developed by UNCTAD, takes into account the international codes and standards developed by international bodies, and can be configured to suit the national characteristics of individual customs regimes. It provides for electronic data interchange (EDI) between traders and customs in accordance with EDIFACT (EDI for Administration, Commerce and Transport) rules and in compliance with the World Customs Organization (WCO) Data Model.

ASYCUDA was first developed for West Africa, in response to a request from the secretariat of the Economic Community of West African States (ECOWAS) to assist in the compilation of foreign trade statistics in their member States. The development of this management system has aided the reform of customs clearance processes in many developing economies and has encouraged the integration of regional economic communities. By the end of 2010, there were some 67 operational ASYCUDA technical assistance projects, and the programme was present in 90 countries, 41 of which were in Africa.

In Madagascar, the new TradeNet system connects trade organizations, using the ASYCUDA platform to share information and transmit documents electronically (Fjeldsted, 2009). The results included a reduction of three weeks for importing a container and 72 hours in customs clearance time. Customs receipts doubled, and corruption was reduced. Similarly, in Liberia, ASYCUDA first came into use at the end of 2009. Between December of that year and October 2010, port transit time fell from 49.7 days on average to only 3.8 days. Moreover, one year after the introduction of the automated system, the monthly revenue collected had increased by more than 50 per cent.[a]

Source: UNCTAD.
[a]   Comparisons between December 2009–February 2010 and December 2010–February 2011.

---

including limited organizational and financial management skills, and limited business experience and technical or production skills. In response, a range of services is offered by various development agencies to overcome these obstacles.

In the late 1980s and early 1990s, a conceptual distinction was made between financial and non-financial services provided to enterprises, in an effort to achieve greater sustainability through specialization.[4] Financial services referred to the range of financial mechanisms that are used to help enterprises start up and expand (e.g. loans, banking services, revolving funds and microfinance), while non-financial services referred to virtually everything else. Thus, BDS has come to embrace the following micro-level development instruments: training, counselling and advice, developing commercial entities, technology development and transfer, information, and business linkages. Within each of these, various ICTs have been used to enhance outreach and efficiency (Anderson, 2008). Services in the BDS field serve small enterprises in much the same way as agricultural extension workers serve farmers (Gibson, 1997).

The remainder of this section focuses on the BDS areas of training, advisory services and market information provision – domains in which effective use of ICTs

can make a difference. As shown below, this potential has most often been realized in the agricultural domain.

1. ICT use in training and advisory services

There are several ways in which ICTs can be used to enhance the delivery of training and advisory services: (a) making business development toolkits available online; (b) leveraging the Internet to make agricultural extension services more interactive and participatory; (c) helping small-scale producers meet certifications and other requirements, via information systems, in order to boost exports; and (d) providing mobile-based business support services. Regrettably, there is little systematic evaluation of the effectiveness of ICT use in these areas. However, reflecting the varying needs and capabilities of the different beneficiaries of such support services, it is advisable to explore a range of ICT tools – including radio, Internet, and mobile telephony.

One way of leveraging ICTs is by making various kinds of business development toolkits (containing generic advice, business planning guidance and templates), as well as self-assessment and business diagnostic tools, available online. While such standardized tools can serve a useful role in informing the user about relevant areas of business development, PSD practitioners need to be wary of the risks of supply-oriented services and the delivery of programmes that do not respond to a clearly defined demand.[5] A study of Internet-based business support services for small businesses in Cape Town, South Africa, found a discrepancy between the views of the agencies involved in providing the services and those of the beneficiaries (Mitrovic and Bytheway, 2011). Although the providers were able to point to a number of outputs (such as numbers of visitors to websites, attendees at workshops), they lacked awareness of the actual impact on business performance that had come about as a result of the services extended. Many enterprises interviewed were also unaware of the services that were available, and those that were aware of the services found them to be ineffective in delivering benefits.

Many agricultural extension services have leveraged the Internet as a way to increase interactivity and participation (Richardson, 2003). Internet-based services might be more successful at making support services available via local sector-specific intermediaries, rather than directly. Indeed, there have been many failed attempts at reaching the poor through web-based solutions, especially in countries with limited Internet penetration and low levels of literacy (De Silva and Ratnadiwakara, 2009).

Some extension services draw on a combination of ICT tools. The Collecting and Exchange of Local Agricultural Content (CELAC) project, for example, seeks to share good practice in the areas of crop and animal farming to farmers in seven districts of Uganda.[6] It uses SMS (text messages), as well as other multimedia communications including online and hard-copy newsletters. The use of community radio call-in programmes is integrated into the service, as is the use of drama on videocassette and DVD to portray farming practices and challenges encountered in farming (UNCTAD, 2010). In the Plurinational State of Bolivia, a daily radio programme gives information about production technologies and the treatment of diseases, on the basis of listener requests sent via telephone and chat. Selected information is also available on request via an SMS service which is currently being used by a pilot group of 1,000 persons, including, in particular, SMEs and traders.[7]

ICTs can also be used to help small-scale producers meet certification and other requirements in order to boost exports. ICTs are helping the Organic Produc-

ers and Processors Association of Zambia (OPPAZ) to enhance its ability to respond to increasing demand for high-priced ecological products. With support from the International Institute for Communication and Development (IICD), OPPAZ implemented a database in 2009 containing information required for organic certification (e.g. volumes, quality, inputs, and production methods). Farm inspectors now use hand-held mobile devices with GPS to collect data and produce accurate maps of the plots monitored. The organic producers' association in the Plurinational State of Bolivia (Asociación de Organizaciones de Productores Ecológicos de Bolivia (AOPEB)), in the same year, introduced an ICT-enabled solution to support its internal certification system for 35,000 organic producers. In this case, trained producers collect field data using a laptop that has mobile Internet and connects to a central database at headquarters. While the complexity and high costs of collecting data often impede the participation of smaller-scale producers, the use of ICTs has made the certification more effective and efficient. Some 75 per cent of the participants found that both certification costs and the time needed in order to comply with the certification requirements had fallen considerably. About 70 per cent of the participants found that prices and incomes had increased as a direct result of ICT use, and OPPAZ and AOPEB both experienced a 20 per cent increase in their membership.[8]

The rapid growth of mobile access suggests significant potential for mobile-based business support services. In the *Information Economy Report 2010*, the Jigyasha 7676 helpline was highlighted as a successful, demand-driven approach to providing advisory services to small-scale famers in Bangladesh. This initiative was developed jointly by Banglalink – the second-largest mobile operator in Bangladesh – and Katalyst (UNCTAD, 2010: 103). A review of African countries found a range of related initiatives delivering various forms of support services to small enterprises, small farms and the self-employed via mobile telephones (Donner, 2009). The study concluded that there were more services targeting agriculture than small enterprises; in fact, it found no instances of mobile-based BDS to non-agricultural enterprises. The same study mentioned Kenya's National Farmers Information Service, which invites farmers to call in on their mobile phones to interact via voice menus with a database with answers frequently asked questions. As in the case of Jigyasha 7676, the content is tailored to the specific needs of the users, and the communication costs are borne by the farmer.[9]

Box IV.5. Fighting pests and diseases: the case of the Digital Early Warning Network

The eradication of pests requires large-scale, collective efforts, which can be facilitated by ICTs. In the Lake Zone of the United Republic of Tanzania, farmers from ten districts have been participating in the Digital Early Warning Network, which has trained them to recognize the symptoms of cassava mosaic disease and cassava brown streak disease. The network is part of the Great Lakes Cassava Initiative, which aims to improve the livelihoods of more than a million farmers in six countries of the Great Lakes region. Armed with mobile phones, these farmers now "crowd source", or send out monthly text messages to researchers, about disease incidence. In return, they receive advice on how to cope with the disease. When more than 10 per cent of the members of a group spot a disease that was not present previously (or that has become more prevalent), a project team visits the area to verify the information and advise farmers on what steps to take. Each group of farmers is given a topped-up phone card that is used to send the text messages. The groups meet monthly to discuss observations and share experiences.

Source: Information provided by FAO and IFAD.

In Uganda, the Community Knowledge Worker initiative, supported by the Grameen Foundation, provides advice to farmers via the Internet and mobile phones. Farmers can visit the community knowledge worker closest to them to access crucial information about best practices in farming (as well as information about market prices and the weather). The community knowledge worker sends an SMS-based query or uses a custom-built application to query a database directly from a mobile phone. The content is provided by agriculture research organizations and is reviewed by a panel of experts. There are currently 98 community knowledge workers, each of whom reaches between 500 and 1,000 farmer households.[10]

One critical area in which small-scale farmers look for advice is plant protection, to save crops from diseases and pests. Smallholder farmers are often unaware of plant diseases or are unable to accurately assess them. Among other things, plant diseases reduce agricultural productivity and raise costs. By using mobile phones and radio frequency identification technology (RFID), it is now possible to provide farmers with better knowledge regarding what diseases or pests to monitor, and how to respond if these are found. New technological solutions can help small-scale producers to identify, track and protect their crops, animals and livelihoods. To give some examples, ICTs are being used for locust surveillance from Mauritania to India, for cassava disease management in central Africa, and for large-scale pest reporting in Uganda and the United Republic of Tanzania – with positive results (box IV.5).

In order for projects that aim at providing advisory services for rural enterprise development to be effective, and to ensure that relevant knowledge and expertise is represented, working in some form of partnership is often recommendable. Large and small agricultural firms alike have an interest in controlling water, diseases and pests, and therefore often also have an interest in partnering with government agencies. Meanwhile, rural communities themselves already have considerable complementary knowledge. Vast differences in ecological and agronomic conditions make farmers' knowledge indispensable for projects to improve smallholders' productivity. As in the case of the Digital Early Warning Network (box IV.5), ICTs enable two-way communication, ensuring that local knowledge is acquired and utilized appropriately. In addition to creating opportunities for information and knowledge dissemination, they offer ways of capturing local expertise.

Rigorous impact evaluations of the effectiveness of ICT-enabled agricultural extension work are rare and much needed (Aker, 2010). However, a recent study has looked specifically at the effects of ICT use on such services to marginalized farmers in rural India (Fu and Aktar, 2011). In this case, the delivery of agricultural extension services involved using GPRS-compatible phones and employing village workers (local youths known as "munnas") to speedily communicate Short Dialogue Strips (audiovisual dialogues between agricultural experts and farmers on local agricultural problems, issues and knowledge). Detailed analysis has shown that, as a result of this approach, farmers have gained in awareness and agricultural knowledge. Over 75 per cent of farmers said that mobile phone-assisted services were useful, over 86 per cent viewed these services as faster than the agricultural services that were previously available, and over 96 per cent were using more agricultural advice since they had been exposed to the new mobile-based services.

There is a lack of systematic evidence on the incidence of ICT-based training, advisory and extension services to urban and rural enterprises, and even less information on the impact of such initiatives. Nevertheless, based on anecdotal evidence and the few impact assessments that have been carried out, some preliminary observations can be made. Firstly, there is scope for many more training and advisory projects to make use of ICT-based solutions. Secondly, such projects are likely to be more effective if the intended users are consulted during the design and implementation phases. In general, the more that services are tailored to the precise needs of their beneficiaries, the more valuable they are. Thirdly, there is an advantage in forming partnerships between relevant stakeholders. Involvement by the private sector in the provision of training and advisory services can help ensure that the services offered are demand-driven (Committee of Donor Agencies for Small Enterprise Development, 2001).

2. Enhancing access to relevant information

The area of business development services where ICT applications have been used the most is in the provision of information about the market. In this area too, most of the focus has been placed on information related to agricultural enterprise, typically with the goal of helping farmers to transition from subsistence to commercial agriculture (Okello, forthcoming). Given the prevalence of poor people in the rural areas of low-income countries, such services may be of particular relevance from a poverty reduction perspective (UNCTAD, 2010).

Better access to market information has been found to help small-scale farmers improve their productivity and to support other rural entrepreneurs along the agricultural value chain (UNCTAD, 2010). ICT use in-

creases the chances of essential information reaching farmers when they need it, which enables them to make better-informed decisions, and to adjust their practices and optimize their use of scarce resources (see, for example, box IV.6). In addition, ICT solutions are allowing Governments and development partners to monitor agricultural productivity and rural enterprise development, make more accurate projections, and improve planning. Some of the more innovative developments are found in Africa. The potential of ICTs for enhancing access to information is illustrated here by looking at some examples from Africa, namely ZNFU4455 in Zambia, the Ethiopia Commodity Exchange and the Kenya Agricultural Commodity Exchange, and Kenya's DrumNet projects.

a. Making markets work better: the case of rural enterprises in Zambia[11]

ZNFU4455 is a market information service in Zambia that is open to all smallholder producers and traders. Launched in 2006 by the Government of Zambia, with assistance from the International Fund for Agricultural Development (IFAD) and in cooperation with the Zambia National Farmers' Union (ZNFU), the service provides accurate and up-to-date agricultural and market information reported by the buyers and covering the entire value chain. This allows smallholder producers to make better-informed decisions about what to grow, the volumes required, storage, processing, marketing, and investment opportunities.

Its main objective is to make markets work better for smallholder producers and traders. The service covers 180 traders and their offers for 15 commodities. To find the best available price, producers and traders send an SMS to 4455 containing the first four letters of the commodity and the relevant district or province. They immediately receive a text message with the best prices and with codes designating the po-

---

Box IV.6. Using multiple ICTs to provide market information to 300,000 producers and entrepreneurs in the Plurinational State of Bolivia

In the Plurinational State of Bolivia, an ICT programme run by the Government of the Department of Santa Cruz reaches out to producers, traders and companies using a combination of Internet, radio and mobile services. Thanks to this integrated approach and the widespread dissemination, the ICT programme has become a reference point for all actors along the value chain – i.e. small-scale producers, SMEs, and large-scale traders and supermarkets – enabling them to make better-informed business decisions. Around 60 per cent of the beneficiaries have indicated that they now know better where to sell, and 45 per cent feel that they are able to negotiate better prices and improve their income. Households also use the information to choose the lowest-priced products on the market.

Source: IICD.

tential buyers. After selecting a bid, the farmer sends a second SMS with the buyer's code. The farmer then receives a text message containing the buyer's name and phone number. Finally, the farmer phones the buyer directly and starts trading. Each message costs about $0.15. The service is easy to understand and use, and it provides information upon request rather than pushing content onto farmers.

This demand-driven service has improved market efficiency. Its business model rests on revenues generated from advertisements and sponsorships, and it leverages several different ICTs including SMS, Internet and radio. The radio programme is broadcast in English as well as seven local languages. Importantly, ZNFU4455 enjoys full government support, and is now an integral part of the national agricultural policy. Zambia's good mobile phone coverage in rural areas, and the fact that the service is hosted in a credible institution such as ZNFU, have contributed to its success. Since its launch in August 2006, ZNFU4455 appears to have strengthened the bargaining power of smallholder producers, by providing them with better access to markets and allowing them to deal with traders on a more equal footing. Farmers also benefit from lower transaction costs, and by producing higher-value outputs, reaching wider markets, and avoiding overproduction. Meanwhile, policymakers in Zambia have benefited from more up-to-date information, which is used to identify trends in the price fluctuations and to flag food-security challenges.

b. Ethiopia Commodity Exchange: revolutionizing Ethiopian farming[12]

The Ethiopia Commodity Exchange (ECX) was launched in 2008. Through the use of ICTs, it is contributing to making agricultural practices in the country more productive. The ECX is seeking to create an integrated agricultural information system, using ICTs to disseminate data and information to farmers across the country and to establish a database with up-to-date world market prices on commodities. This ICT-based marketplace serves the entire value chain: farmers, traders, processors, exporters and consumers.

Agricultural markets in Ethiopia have been characterized by high transaction costs and risks. With only a third of output reaching the market, commodity buyers and sellers have traditionally only traded with people they know. Trade took place on the basis of visual

inspection, as there was no way of assuring product quality or quantity. This drove up market costs as well as consumer prices. Small-scale farmers, who account for 95 per cent of Ethiopia's agricultural output, came to the market with little information, and were at the mercy of merchants in the markets they knew, poorly equipped to negotiate prices or reduce their risk.

The new exchange, which is a partnership of market actors, the Members of the Exchange and the Government of Ethiopia, automated the system from beginning to end, from warehousing to clearing and settlement of payments to the delivery of commodities. By bringing integrity, security and efficiency to the market, the exchange has become visible throughout the supply chain, resulting in real-time price transmission, improvements in the quality of exports, and better returns for farmers. During its first 1,000 days, ECX traded over a billion dollars worth of commodities, including four million bags of goods handled and delivered. It processed 69,000 transactions involving 450 ECX members.[13]

ECX traders now have an incentive to win local producers as clients and to provide information to them about how to benefit from the market. Whereas producers previously had an incentive to degrade the quality of their produce by adding water or even dirt to increase its weight, the dissemination of information about the new quality system and the possibilities of getting higher prices for better quality have led to a significant increase in the supply of high-quality coffee, and also sesame.

Price information from the exchange is transmitted to local farmers through several ICT channels. ECX uses SMS, Interactive Voice Receiver (IVR) services, community information centres, electronic display boards, and its own website, as well as traditional media such as radio, television and the print media. Although knowing about prices does not automatically give small-scale farmers a competitive advantage, better access to information implies a reduced disadvantage vis-à-vis more informed market players. Enhanced market transparency has made small-scale farmers better able to negotiate prices. They can now also get a market premium for adding value to their products, and are no longer restricted or captive to local markets. Farmers are now also able to use future prices for planting decisions and for collateral.

c. DrumNet and KACE: two Kenyan market information services[14]

The DrumNet and Kenya Agricultural Commodity Exchange (KACE) projects are two market information services in Kenya that operate in overlapping areas but differ in terms of geographic coverage. DrumNet consists of projects implemented in two Kenyan provinces and focuses on sunflowers and French beans. KACE has nationwide coverage. The impact of both services was recently assessed in an independent study.

The DrumNet project was launched in 2003, with the primary objective of shortening the value chain of targeted commodities and improving farmers' revenues. It aimed to replace numerous intermediaries by using a mobile phone-based platform to provide market information to the project's partners. The partners include farmers organized into smallholder farmer groups averaging 30 members per group, a financial organization (Equity Bank), a buyer, and an agro-input dealer. The farmers in western Kenya grow sunflowers for sale to Bidco Oil Ltd., while the farmers in central Kenya grow French beans for sale to Kenya Horticultural Exporters, a leading exporter of fresh produce.

In both the central and western regions, production and market information is sent via an SMS from DrumNet's central computer-based platform in Nairobi (Okello et al., 2010). Smallholder farmers participating in the project pay a commission to DrumNet in return for agricultural information and other services. The fees are recovered upon sale of the beans or sunflowers. The link between farmers and DrumNet goes through a member selected by the group to act as "transaction agent". Information from DrumNet is then sent via SMS to the agent, who is expected to relay it to the members. The agent also confirms by SMS to DrumNet that the information has actually reached the group.

The KACE project was first launched in 1996 as a commodity exchange with an auction floor located in Nairobi. Its goal was to provide a forum to bring sellers (farmers) and buyers together, and thereby to eliminate the many intermediaries and reduce the transaction costs. The commodities traded included staple and non-staple food crops, livestock, livestock products and cash crops. In 1998, KACE launched a website through which subscribing buyers and sellers could place bids for commodities. The company also initiated a mobile phone-based information-provision programme with nationwide coverage. By means of this service, sellers (farmers) and buyers have been able to obtain commodity prices in different markets by sending an SMS to KACE at a cost of K Sh 5 (about $0.05). Furthermore, KACE runs a nationwide radio programme which allows buyers and sellers to offer bids for commodities during the broadcast.

KACE has a team of people who collect prices from wholesalers at different times in the morning. The data collected are sent (usually by e-mail) to KACE's head office in Nairobi, which processes the information and publishes average prices for major markets on its website and computer-based platform. The prices for each day become available for download from the website or via SMS at about noon each day. KACE also runs market information points under franchise in some major towns in western Kenya. Each market information point has a computer with an Internet connection, and hence can be used by farmers (sellers) and buyers to download information.

An assessment of these two projects found that both had generated a number of benefits for the farmers involved:

(a) DrumNet members had achieved significantly higher sales volumes and agricultural income than their counterparts.

(b) Farmers using the KACE services were spending significantly less on travel and search costs than those who had not used these services.

(c) Participation in ICT-based projects had improved market access/commercialization and had led to more efficient use of agricultural inputs.

(d) Furthermore, the use of ICT tools had led to an overall improvement in market efficiency, as indicated by lower margins being paid to intermediate traders in areas where ICT tools were being used.

Both projects faced challenges in terms of financial sustainability. The poor economic status of farmers sometimes encouraged them to engage in opportunistic behaviour that undermined project sustainability. Moreover, certain factors related to the physical environment reinforced this tendency, further affecting the project's ability to recover its loans and performance. In addition, inflexible business regulations and the lack of an enforceable legal framework also worked against the projects. The study suggested that in order to ensure long-term sustainability, an enabling socio-economic environment, a supporting legal framework, and flexible strategies were needed.

3. Concluding observations

In summary, the use of ICTs to extend the reach of BDS to nascent and growing enterprises appears to be expanding, but from a low level. This practice is more developed in agriculture than in other sectors, but even in agriculture there is room for greater use of ICT-based solutions.

In the case of ICT use to make training and advisory services more effective, the results from the studies available underline the importance of tailoring the services to the precise needs of the beneficiaries. This makes it essential to develop a good understanding of the situation of the enterprises concerned and to involve them in project design and implementation. The various examples cited above also show the power of using a combination of different ICT tools rather than opting for any single technical solution. This is particularly important in low-income countries characterized by varying levels of connectivity and by dissimilar capabilities and needs among enterprises. Projects that make use of broadcast media, such as radio, are particularly appreciated by people who have less capacity to read. More educated users indicate greater satisfaction with projects that utilize computers and the Internet. Broadcast media and mobile phones remain vital for reaching out to less privileged members of society.

The expanding use of mobile phones among MSEs offers considerable scope for the delivery of BDS, including to rural enterprises, and for the use of mobile phones in combination with other ICT tools. There are good reasons for BDS providers to explore this field further to expand their client base and to reduce the costs of delivering relevant services. More services could be built around text messaging, such as allowing entrepreneurs to (a) ask for information about public services and to comment on them; (b) make payments of fees and taxes; and (c) receive alerts about weather forecasts and market prices. This approach is conducive to making services more demand-driven and tailored to specific needs of users. At the same time, more research and rigorous impact assessments are needed, in order to identify best practices in terms of ICT use geared towards enhancing the effectiveness of BDS.

C. HOW CAN ICTs BE USED TO ENHANCE ACCESS TO FINANCE?

Limited access to finance is one of the most frequently mentioned barriers to the growth and competitiveness of MSEs (e.g. Schiffer and Weder, 2001; CGAP, 2010; IADB, 2011b: chapter I). There are many reasons for this situation, including policy distortions in the financial sector, lack of know-how in banks, information asymmetries, and the relatively high risk associated with MSE operations (Mohini et al., 2006). MSEs generally face greater difficulties in obtaining credit than larger enterprises (Beck, Demirgüç-Kunt and Maksimovic, 2002), and the problem is most accentuated in economies with poorly developed capital and financial markets and with a large proportion of unbanked, or underbanked, people and entrepreneurs. An improvement to the financial system that would help to relax some of the limitations on accessing finance would therefore be particularly beneficial for MSEs.

ICTs may play a role in this context. The emergence of mobile money systems is creating new possibilities for MSEs to access financial resources at reduced cost.[15] Firstly, the introduction of mobile money systems makes it possible for MSEs to receive and transfer – in real time – very small amounts of funds at low cost across long distances (even internationally). In this way, mobile money can act as a lubricant in the economy and can contribute to a more efficient allocation of available capital by enabling funds to flow wherever they are most needed. Secondly, mobile financial services can offer a way to bring down the otherwise high transactions costs related to the processing and administration of small loans, and thereby alleviate a significant disincentive for banks and other lenders to extend credit to MSEs. The introduction of various kinds of mobile money systems has potential implications for banks and microfinance institutions (MFIs), and also for other lending sources. It also raises several policy issues. The following sections examine these possibilities in further detail.

1. Mobile money services

As noted in chapter II, mobile money deployments in developing countries are spreading rapidly. These are still early days for mobile money services, which makes it difficult to assess the potential of this phenomenon. In fact, out of the known deployments, more than half have been launched either in 2010 or in 2011, and many more are expected to be introduced in the near future. Most deployments were introduced with the primary goal of offering person-to-person transfers, rather than targeting businesses. Moreover, as most MSEs in low-income countries remain excluded from the formal financial sector, retail banks and mobile operators have little knowledge of their financial needs (Bångens and Söderberg, 2011). Thus, there is still limited information with regard to the impact of such schemes on the performance of MSEs.

The nature of the services offered by the various existing and planned schemes differs considerably. Three broad categories of services can be distinguished, from basic to more sophisticated ones: (a) money transfer services (domestic and/or international); (b) payment services (for airtime top-ups, bills, salaries, and other goods and services); and (c) financial services (savings, credit, insurance). Domestic money transfers, airtime and bill payments are the three most common services currently offered. Relatively few deployments cater for transactions such as repayments of loans from MFIs (section IV.C.2) or international money transfers (section IV.C.3). However, much innovation is under way, and many new types of services are emerging.

Even basic money transfer or payment functions can have a major impact on the way in which MSEs operate. The value chain for MSEs often involves providers across a dispersed geographic area, making the ability to transfer money efficiently of critical importance in order for an enterprise to be able to manage its cash flow and expedite the fulfilment of supplies and goods. In the absence of mobile money transfers, an entrepreneur in a low-income economy may have to choose from a number of less competitive options, such as the following (Bångens and Söderberg, 2011: chapter II):

(a) Traditional money transfers via Western Union, MoneyGram, banks, and post operators, which are often considered expensive and/or inconvenient;

(b) Informal or local solutions, such as sending funds by bus, which can be costly, and unsafe due to the risk of theft; or

(c) Delivering the money in person.

In addition, the mobile money system approach makes it possible to move funds in real time, when the need arises, rather than in the form of lump sums of cash that have to be amassed before a planned transfer can take place. This feature is significant for

entrepreneurs who make business transactions with buyers or suppliers in distant regions.

Several business models are used to supply mobile money services. Firstly, the mobile phone may be used as an additional channel (in the same way that users can access their accounts via the Internet), as in Mexico (box IV.7). This approach tends to face lower regulatory barriers, but may be less successful in reaching the unbanked. Secondly, some services allow users to load money into an electronic account operated through a mobile phone that can store, transfer or redeem value, with limited involvement by banks (the electronic money account is operated by the mobile network operator). The M-PESA system in Kenya is an example of such a scheme. Thirdly, there may be combinations of the first two options, as in the case of SMART, in the Philippines. Fourthly, a third party may provide an electronic account that can be operated via a mobile phone or by using a prepaid card. While this approach has so far had little traction (Germany, BMZ and GIZ, 2011), some examples are emerging. Yo! Payments is a mobile payments aggregation service in Uganda which enables businesses to receive payments from their customers via mobile money, and to make mobile money payments to any mobile money account holder. It aims to interconnect all mobile money providers and financial institutions worldwide and to provide Yo! Payments account holders with a unified method of receiving payments from any customer who has a subscription to any mobile money service provider or has a bank account.[16]

What model is implemented depends – among other things – on the relative market power of the different telecom and financial players, the nature of the services to be provided, and the regulatory environment. In Africa, MNO-led initiatives predominate, due to low levels of banking penetration and high levels of mobile penetration. In Latin America, card and point of sale (POS)-based approaches (banking agents equipped with POS terminals where customers can use their bank cards, generally prepaid) are more common. In Asia, third party-led models (either card- or phone-based) often operate under the licence of a partner bank (Germany, BMZ and GIZ, 2011).

As the network of people and enterprises using mobile phones to make financial transactions expands, and the platform becomes pervasive, the demand for services to extend beyond transfers grows too. From the perspective of MSEs, mobile solutions may be of interest, for example to handle merchant, bill and sal-

---

Box IV.7. Mobile financial services in Mexico: opportunities and challenges

Mobile financial services are still at a nascent stage in Mexico, but the market holds significant potential for their application. In contrast to the case of Kenya, mobile financial services in Mexico are being introduced by the banks rather than by the mobile network operators (MNOs). The Government has made significant reforms that seek to leverage mobile phones and third-party agents (banking agents or "corresponsales") for enhanced financial inclusion. To this end, the new regulatory framework enables financial institutions to develop transactional accounts targeting low-income customers and to use third-party agents to serve those segments. These accounts could be linked to a mobile phone in order to use it as a transactional channel. The use of mobile phones for money transactions is still limited, though this may change as mobile financial services develop.

In 2010, Mexico had a mobile penetration of 81 subscriptions per 100 inhabitants (annex table II.1). Less than 60 per cent of the population have a bank account (Mexico, Ministry of Finance, 2011), and 57 per cent of municipalities lack a presence of any kind by a formal financial services provider (either commercial, development, microcredit, or cooperative banks) (CNBV, 2010). In addition, many households (particularly those with low incomes) receive remittances but have limited access to financial services. Internet banking has yet to become widely adopted; only 12 per cent of Internet users with a bank account currently use Internet banking (CNBV, 2010). Thus, there should be opportunities for mobile applications to help expand the geographical and functional coverage of financial services and to reduce operational costs associated with financial transactions.

The new regulatory framework developed in 2009–2010 establishes improved conditions for financial inclusion. Firstly, it enables the use of third-party "banking agents", and secondly, it enables "niche" banks to emerge, which can take deposits leveraging the development of e-payments. The new framework opens the possibility for conducting small financial transactions through accounts linked to a mobile phone number. Additionally, this new regulation also enables four different types of accounts with proportional know-your-customer requirements for account opening commensurate with the level of risk. Specific information on these new account types (based on transactional level and requirements for identification) are expected to be released during 2011.

The current regulatory framework allows for shared business models where MNOs provide the operative platform. However, it does not permit MNOs to offer financial services. Deposit-taking (be it redeemable or for the purposes of payments) remains a banking activity. Some new business models are emerging to leverage mobile networks:

(a) Government welfare transfers through point of sales terminals located in hundreds of community shops (affiliated to Diconsa, a government agency that supports the distribution of basic goods). Bansefi, a national development bank focusing on low income customers, distributes government aid through these shops, using a card storing digital fingerprints together with wireless point of sales terminals.

(b) A banking institution and the national energy company are partnering in order to provide customers with electronic accounts that can be operated via a smart card (for point of sale payments and automatic teller machines) or via mobile phones to make low-value transaction payments.

(c) As at April 2011, four banks were providing mobile services (as an added service feature) to their existing clients, who in most cases already have Internet banking services. Mobile transactions are managed using a traditional electronic funds transfer linked to a debit account number rather than to the mobile phone number.

In order for the development of mobile payments and Internet banking to play a bigger role for small-scale businesses and entrepreneurs, the design of future mobile money services will need to take advantage of the new regulatory framework. It will also require detailed information on their actual access, their use, and their needs.

Source: UNCTAD, based on Chatain et al. (2011), CGAP and Dalberg Global Development Advisers (2010), CGAP (2009a), and interviews in Mexico with CNBV and experts from the private sector and civil society.

a   SOFIPOS is short for Sociedades Financieras Populares (popular financing companies).

---

ary payments (box IV.8). In terms of rolling out more sophisticated financial services – especially credit, savings and insurance – MNOs will need to partner with banks, MFIs, insurance companies, or other institutions that have the expertise and a licence to deliver such products. For banks, the main driver for offering mobile money services may be to expand outreach, acquire customers and reduce costs, while mobile operators see it as a way of strengthening customer loyalty, and, to a lesser extent, increasing ARPU and acquiring new customers (Germany, BMZ and GIZ 2011).

Box IV.8. Mobile money services for MSEs in Africa: the case of Orange Money

Orange Money is one of the providers of mobile money in Africa, and has been launched in six countries, namely Côte d'Ivoire, Kenya, Madagascar, Mali, Niger and Senegal. There are plans to extend such services to all countries where Orange has obtained a licence to provide mobile telephony.

The nature of the services offered by Orange Money varies by country, reflecting the local market situation and the bank–Orange partnership. According to the company, Orange Money is the market leader in four of the six countries, and is in second position in Niger and fourth position in Kenya. In the latter market, where Safaricom (M-PESA) has a dominant position, Orange has decided to offer an out-of-the-ordinary service and has therefore partnered with Equity Bank to develop an Orange Money account, called Iko-Pesa, that is linked directly to a bank account. This account allows consumers to load and send money, and to deposit it and withdraw it into/out of their Equity bank account, and also to apply for, process and receive loans, via their mobile phones. Subscribers can also use this system to pay utility bills and to buy consumer goods from certain retail stores.

For the mobile operator, revenue is generated directly from the use of the mobile money services offered. There can also be indirect revenues, as a result of greater customer loyalty or by attracting new clients. Various service applications are of potential interest to MSEs:

(a) *Money transfers from buyers to suppliers* can save travel time, reduce transaction costs, and reduce the need to move around with cash.

(b) *Differentiated accounts* can allow companies to accommodate B2B use, by allowing larger amounts to be stored or transferred with the Orange Money Account. This solution requires agreement from the central bank.

(c) *Merchant payments,* for which there is always a cost involved. Some merchants have to pay to obtain cash. If they can use electronic payments, costs can be reduced and they can avoid moving cash around. Merchant payments may be relevant for very small restaurants, as well as for large enterprises. Hundreds of shops already accept payments via Orange Money in the six countries where the service has been launched.

(d) *Bill payments,* e.g. for electricity, water, and pay TV (large enterprises).

(e) *Salary payments,* e.g. for staff working for Orange.

Some banks regard these new services as new competition, and are lobbying regulators to limit the ability of MNOs to provide services that have traditionally been the realm of banks. So far, central banks in Africa have generally shown openness to the entry of MNOs in this area. However, in developing new money services in a country, it is important for central banks to have a good understanding of the risks involved with different kinds of services.

Source: UNCTAD, based on an interview with Orange.

2. Mobile solutions to international remittances

International remittances represent a potentially important source of finance for MSEs that are inadequately serviced by the formal capital markets. In 2009, officially recorded flows totalled over $414 billion worldwide, of which more than three quarters ($316 billion) went to developing countries. In more than 20 countries, remittances accounted for over 10 per cent of GDP; and in 10 of these countries they accounted for over 20 per cent of GDP.[17] Recent research has found that the high costs associated with international remittances, especially those that are sent to sub-Saharan Africa, are likely to be reducing the amounts transmitted as well as their development impact (AfDB and World Bank, 2011). High costs are often the result of exclusivity agreements between banks or post offices and international money transfer companies, low levels of financial market development, and the small number of companies that are engaged in remittance transfers.

Some evidence suggests that remittance flows can have a positive effect on business investment and entrepreneurial activities (AfDB and World Bank, 2011: 63):

(a) In urban Mexico, about one fifth of the capital invested by 6,000 microenterprises was financed by remittances (Woodruff and Zenteno, 2001);

(b) In rural Pakistan, the propensity to invest in agricultural land has increased with international remittances (Adams, 1998);

(c) In the Philippines, households that received remittances were more likely to start relatively capital-intensive entrepreneurial activities (Yang, 2008);

(d) In Egypt, overseas savings were associated with more entrepreneurship and investment (McCormick and Wahba, 2001 and 2003); and

(e) The growth impact of remittances has tended to be stronger when the level of financial development is weaker (Giuliano and Ruiz-Arranz, 2009).

Innovative, mobile-based solutions represent an attractive option to facilitate more remittances and greater development gains in Africa. As noted recently (AfDB and World Bank, 2011: 73):

"The technologies have the potential to vastly improve access to both remittances and broader financial services, including low-cost savings and credit products, for African migrants and remittance recipients."

Many countries in which the highest proportion of GDP is accounted for by international remittances also enjoy high rates of mobile phone penetration (table IV.1). Nevertheless, out of the 109 known mobile money deployments, only eight allow cash out via a customer or agent mobile account; another 15 are preparing for such services (CGAP and Dalberg Global Development Advisers, 2010).[18] Only two of the existing systems have been in operation for over a year, namely G-Cash and Smart, both in the Philippines (ibid.). Among the 15 countries included in table IV.1, only Jamaica was able to accommodate international remittances to mobile phones. This suggests clear potential to leverage mobile solutions for international remittances.

In the latter half of 2010, Vodafone and Telenor both announced plans to introduce new services into their mobile money systems, including international remittances (Menon, 2011). Vodafone Qatar and Philippines-based Globe Telecom announced that they would jointly enable a money transfer service between their two networks. Vodafone Money Transfer account holders in Qatar will be able to send funds directly from their mobile phones to Globe subscribers in the Philippines.[19] Over 200,000 Filipinos now live and work in Qatar. Their remittances sent back home during the year 2009 amounted to more than $185 million. Telenor Pakistan expanded its "easypaisa" mobile money service, with an international transfer service offered

Table IV.1. International remittances as a share of GDP in 2008, and mobile cellular subscriptions per 100 inhabitants in 2010, economies with a high reliance on remittances		
Country	Remittances as a share of GDP, 2008 (%)	Mobile cellular subscriptions per 100 inhabitants, 2010 (%)
Tajikistan	49.6	86.4
Tonga	37.7	52.2
Republic of Moldova	31.4	88.6
Kyrgyzstan	27.9	91.9
Lesotho	27.0	32.2
Samoa	25.8	91.4
Lebanon	25.1	68.0
Guyana	24.0	73.6
Nepal	21.6	30.7
Honduras	20.4	125.1
Haiti	20.3	40.0
Jordan	19.0	107.0
El Salvador	17.2	124.3
Bosnia and Herzegovina	14.8	80.1
Jamaica	14.5	113.2

Source: Remittances data, Development Prospects Group, World Bank and ITU World Telecommunication/ICT Indicators database.

in collaboration with Xpress Money (United Kingdom). Senders of funds from abroad can transfer their money through the wide network of Xpress agents present in more than 80 countries.[20]

One of the first challenges is to facilitate a more rapid roll-out of mobile money systems that can handle international remittances; current deployments affect only a fraction of total remittance flows. Another challenge is to reduce the costs associated with using the services. At least for certain remittance streams, the price of sending money via mobile schemes appears to be similar to that of using cash remittances, despite the fact that reliance on mobile phone transfers gets around the need to develop distribution networks (AfDB and World Bank, 2011). This may partly reflect a lack of competition in the paying network. The following regulatory challenges have been identified as potentially restricting the launch and growth of relevant solutions (CGAP and Dalberg Global Development Advisers, 2010: 14):

(a) Regulations that dictate the type of organizations permitted to send international money transfers and how they are allowed to operate;

(b) Compliance with know-your-customer/anti-money laundering requirements, which affect the type of agent and customer acquisition;

(c) Regulations that restrict the involvement of non-banks in financial transactions and affect the types of activities that non-banks can engage in, or how money is held.

3. Microfinance and ICTs

Microfinance plays an important role in providing financial services to unbanked or underbanked entrepreneurs in low-income countries. The idea behind microfinance and microinsurance is to adapt services to populations that have been excluded from the formal financial system and the risk-management schemes of mainstream banking. Subsistence farmers and small-scale entrepreneurs in the informal sector are often viewed by traditional banks and insurance companies as low-profit and high-risk clients. This is an important constraint for MSE development in many low-income economies, and makes it pertinent to consider the scope for ICT solutions to make microfinance and microinsurance more inclusive and effective.

Relatively few mobile money services have so far been used to facilitate MFI loan disbursements and repayments, partly due to the diverging priorties of MFIs and MNOs (Germany, BMZ and GIZ, 2011). As one study notes (Kumar et al., 2010: 1):

> "...MFIs and successful m-banking businesses occupy different worlds today...The MFI world focuses on creating low-cost, human-driven infrastructure, while the m-banking world is tied into and uses payment systems infrastructure. It is not surprising then that these two worlds have not yet aligned."

Services offered by MFIs are based on frequent contacts with their clients. Face-to-face meetings are considered important to building and nurturing the social capital that is the basis for creating trust and assessing credit risk. By using appropriate technology, MFIs might be able to reduce somewhat the need for physical meetings, enable the processing of a higher number of transactions at lower cost and risk, and extend the reach of their services.[21] Many MFIs conduct numerous transactions daily, and frequently have daily collections of cash. Their members include owners of small businesses, vendors and farmers, whose working days are long and for whom daily trips to a bank mean lost time and higher costs.

The efficient collection of savings and of credit instalments is crucial to the financial sustainability of MFIs. In this context, they often rely on commercial agents to find new clients and to service existing ones. One of the challenges faced by MFIs that rely on paper-based collection and tracking systems is to mitigate money leakage and fraud. When a client pays the commercial agent in cash, the transaction is typically noted in the client's savings or credit notebook as well as in that of the commercial agent.[22] Occasionally, the amount declared to the MFI falls short of the total sum of cash collected. If a significant discrepancy is noted between the MFI's accounting and the client's expectation, it may be the result of fraud or embezzlement on the part of the agent. Such situations create collateral damage and can be hard to remedy. Indeed, a substandard system for tracking payments can in itself encourage fraudulent behaviour – ultimately with serious consequences for an MFI. A substandard system makes published financial results less reliable, lowers the willingness of lenders to fund MFI activities, and may possibly result in higher interest rates being charged. Finally, it undermines trust in the MFI–client relationship.

Technology can help to improve the tracking of payments. Ideally, MFIs should be able to handle the flow of data between members, service suppliers, microcredit (or microinsurance) units and investors in an integrated manner. This can be done by streamlining routine business processes such as customer registration, loan or claims management, and implementing systems.[23] Technological solutions may include the use of smart cards (box IV.9) and/or mobile devices.

The success of M-PESA has led some MFIs in Kenya and the United Republic of Tanzania to adopt mobile solutions for loan repayments and sometimes for savings. Examples include Tujijenge Tanzania, which makes it mandatory for all repayments on individual loans of less than $1,800 to be made via M-PESA, and the Small and Micro Enterprise Programme (SMEP) in Kenya, which in 2009 allowed its 51,000 customers to make mobile loan repayments and savings contributions (Kumar et al., 2010). These systems have made it possible for MFIs and savings and cooperative credit organizations (SACCOs) to offer their customers more

Box IV.9. Using smart cards to improve the efficiency of MFIs

When exploring technological solutions to some of the challenges facing MFIs, smart cards are often the first option to be considered as a partial replacement for paper-based systems (Gerelle and Berende, 2008).[a] For example, Tegona, a Swiss company, has developed a smart card solution consisting of two parts: the front office and the back office. The *front office* is responsible for the tracking of credit and debit operations. Each agent is equipped with a point of sale terminal, which transmits all transactions to the back office, using general packet radio service (GPRS) (via GSM operators).[b] To make transactions more secure, every client receives a chip card when opening his/her account or when subscribing to an insurance product. The *back office* involves the monitoring of the transactions, and the management of the client portfolio, particularly with regard to savings, credit or insurance, and connects the information to the MFI's Management Information System. The back office solution is offered as Software as a Service (SaaS), which means that the MFI does not need to make large investments in equipment or software, or to enter system maintenance costs into its bookkeeping.

The front office terminals allow the MFI to reinforce agents' presence among clients. Apart from the collection of savings and credits, they make it possible to answer locally clients' concerns and needs, giving them immediate access to account statements, credit instalment details, provisioning and withdrawing.

Pilot studies of the system undertaken in Côte d'Ivoire in 2010 have revealed a number of positive effects. Firstly, better and more secure cash management has made agents more efficient by allowing them to concentrate on the commercial representation and on the growth of the portfolio. It has also reduced the time to market during the creation of a new partnership. The amount of fraud has also dropped significantly, which has expanded the space for new products and reduced the level of risk. Secondly, a more proactive local attitude has helped some MFIs to generate a more dynamic and stable cashflow while at the same time reducing outstanding debts. Thirdly, computerization and automation of the tracking of operations has significantly improved customer relationship management, by way of better business intelligence related to asset and risk management. Finally, further growth in the portfolio of customers and in the payments that they generate, as well as enhanced customer loyalty, have helped to lower the portfolio management costs. Lower costs should eventually allow the whole sector to expand.

But the implementation of such a system is not without costs and challenges. First, smart cards need to be issued, which introduces an additional step when an account for a new client is being opened. Various improvements are currently being explored in this context, with the aim of simplifying and shortening the process, by replacing the memory card form factor by a smart sticker (using RFID), for example on the back of a mobile phone. The recent introduction of mobile phones embedded with NFC technology could further simplify the process. However, the deployment of that technology will take time. Smart card or RFID technology can be alternatives to today's standard mobile phone payment schemes in countries that lack reliable ID cards. The introduction of new technology and habits to clients is another challenge. People need to be trained how to use the system in order to trust it.

Source: UNCTAD, based on information provided by Tegona.

[a]   A smart card (or chip card) can be defined as any pocket-sized card with embedded integrated circuits that can process information.

[b]   Several MFIs have piloted the use of point of sale terminals to distribute loans and accept borrowers' repayments (Gerelle and Berende, 2008).

convenient, affordable products, while simultaneously increasing efficiency, security and transparency in the back office. Another example is the Kenya Agency for the Development of Enterprise and Technology (KADET), which has also linked up with the M-PESA platform. At the end of 2010, nearly half of KADET's clients were making loan repayments and savings deposits using mobile phones. Previously, they made their payments at a bank branch where KADET held an account, entailing up to one day of travel for those located in remote areas. KADET plans to expand its range of services to include loan approvals via SMS,

offering loan disbursements via mobile money, and sending repayment reminders by SMS (Capsuto, 2011).

In order to seize opportunities from mobile money systems in microfinance, the institutions involved need to integrate one (or multiple) mobile money systems with their management system, so that transactions made are automatically assigned to the corresponding customer account and posted to a back-office database. MFIs with a large customer base in countries with a high penetration of mobile money users are the best

Box IV.10. Bringing smaller MFIs into mobile microfinance: the Kopo Kopo case

The dynamism of mobile money services in Africa is attracting entrepreneurs in developed countries to innovate locally and develop new business solutions. Kopo Kopo, an enterprise that was incorporated in the United States in August 2010, chose to place its headquarters in Nairobi, Kenya, to serve the sub-Saharan market. By offering a Software-as-a-Service platform for integrating mobile money systems with banking and enterprise resource planning software, the company seeks to enable small MFIs and SACCOs to leverage mobile money systems.

To test its new software application, Kopo Kopo decided to run a pilot project in Sierra Leone. As in many other low-income countries, banks are few and far between in Sierra Leone. For example, there are only 2.3 bank branches per 100,000 adults (ibid.). While other companies (e.g. Web Tribe, The Software Group and Zege Technologies) had already offered mobile money integration services in East Africa, Kopo Kopo was the first to do so in Sierra Leone. The pilot project, which involved Hope Micro, an MFI, and Splash Mobile Money, commenced in January 2011 in the Greater Freetown area. The goal was to enable Hope Micro borrowers to repay their loans via Splash instead of making cash repayments at the Hope Micro Central Office, thereby benefiting borrowers in terms of less time spent away from their businesses and less money spent on taxi fares.

At the outset, a business process analysis was undertaken, with the aim of understanding how incorporating Splash might change employee roles and responsibilities in Hope Micro. Of the various employees involved, the cashiers, data entry personnel and loan officers required the most retraining. The cashiers were trained to recruit borrowers into the pilot when they arrived to pick up their loan disbursement cheques. The data entry personnel were trained in how to use the service to download mapped transactions and import them to Hope Micro's management information system. Finally, the loan officers were trained to escort borrowers through all the processes necessary to make a loan repayment via Splash.

Once everyone understood their new roles and responsibilities, Hope Micro started to process loan repayments via Splash. The first round of repayments required a loan officer to call each participating borrower one day before a repayment was due, to set a time to meet the next day, and then to accompany the borrower to the nearest Splash agent to assist with the cash-in, send the loan repayment, and log the transaction ID in the loan repayment booklet.

Borrowers immediately saw the advantages of using the mobile service over repaying in cash. For example, one borrower found that she could save Le96,000 (about $24) over the life cycle of her loan by avoiding taxi fares. With most borrowers spending hours in traffic each week to make loan repayments, the mobile solution also freed up time to keep businesses open longer. One client estimated that she would save a full working week over the life cycle of her loan.

There were also challenges. The Splash agent network, for instance, struggled to serve Hope Micro customers. On several occasions, Splash agents turned borrowers away because they either lacked the electronic float necessary to perform a cash-in (the process where a borrower converts cash to electronic currency) or because there were too few Splash customers to make it profitable. Getting Hope Micro staff to champion and take ownership of the pilot was another challenge. Although cashiers and data entry personnel were enthusiastic, only a few loan officers actively encouraged their borrowers to use Splash. As a result, many borrowers were not well enough informed to understand the purpose and possible benefits of the pilot. Other challenges included finding borrowers for the pilot, teaching borrowers to protect their Splash PIN numbers, and dealing with faulty SIM cards.

Despite such hurdles, the system is being managed and scaled by Hope Micro. It remains to be seen if Splash will be of sufficient benefit to the institution. In order for other MFIs in Sierra Leone to integrate with Splash and extend mobile financial services throughout the country, a clear business case has to be proved. Hope Micro needs enough borrowers in order for the cost savings from increased efficiency (e.g. lower cash management costs and fewer full-time data entry personnel) to outweigh the expenses involved with changing business processes and buying the new technology.

Source: UNCTAD, based on information from Kopo Kopo.

positioned to reap cost savings from leveraging such systems. MFIs that operate in markets where there is already an established market solution are likely to reap the benefits (e.g. SMEP in Kenya). By contrast, for the many MFIs that have a small customer base and low transaction volumes, the initial costs may make mobile solutions a less attractive option. One way for even small MFIs and SACCOs to overcome some of these set-up costs may be to apply a Software-as-a-Service platform for integrating existing mobile money services with their enterprise resource planning software. Such systems are currently being developed and piloted in Africa (box IV.10).

While relatively few MFIs have so far integrated mobile money systems into their operations (Kumar et al., 2010), this situation should change in the next few years as more evidence emerges from those systems that have been implemented. There is scope for improving the outreach to remote areas, reducing transaction costs, improving customer service, and reducing fraud, with the help of mobile technology. Adequate attention should be given to learning from early adopters, in order to identify best practices for additional MFIs to effectively exploit ICT solutions in their operations.

4. Policy challenges and opportunities with mobile money

It is still too soon to assess the impact of mobile money solutions on access by MSEs to financial services. On the one hand, MSE owners and managers have seen advantages from using these new technologies and approaches, as a more secure and affordable means for making financial transactions. Uptake is likely to accelerate as the network of business users expands and when services are adapted to the needs of relevant enterprises. On the other hand, even if transaction costs are reduced, other issues affecting the decisions of financial service providers remain. Demands for collateral, business experience, and a lending history will continue to influence the decisions of financial service providers. Moreover, to date, most mobile money systems have mainly focused on basic money transfers rather than on credit services or international remittances. Thus, there appears to be scope for expansion. This makes it important to consider what policy challenges and issues Governments should address in order to ensure positive outcomes from the introduction of mobile money services.

Most mobile money deployments are in developing countries. Thus, Governments in those countries (including several LDCs) face the challenge of pioneering new legislation and regulation related to the use of mobile money. This situation contrasts with most other policy domains, where developed countries are ahead in terms of policy design and implementation. Against this background, it is essential that policymakers and regulators understand the potential benefits and risks. Challenges include the creation of enabling environments that facilitate the roll-out of services that are in demand, but that also help avoid possible negative effects. The international community can play a role in supporting the development of sound regulatory frameworks and relevant institutions, as illustrated in a recent report for the German Development Cooperation (box IV.11).

The introduction of mobile money services into an economy that lacks a strong financial sector and is characterized by many unbanked people can produce both good and bad effects. While various benefits already have been discussed, consideration must also be given to the risks. At the same time, it may not be desirable to aim for fully developed regulations prior to permitting the launch of mobile money operations. Instead, many developing countries have opted for a "test and learn" approach, by which conditional approvals are granted which allow the regulators to observe market developments before issuing regulations that are based on actual identified risks and not on conjecture. This concept is also reflected in the G20 Principles on Financial Inclusion.[24]

As regulations evolve, there may be reason to examine the effect on bank accounts and deposit bases, which may serve as consumer and commercial lending resources. There should be an understanding of the use of reserves, both in the promotion of safety and soundness and in monetary policy. Strengths of traditional and well-developed bank-based payment systems may need to be reproduced or adapted for a non-bank mobile money environment, including know-your-customer and anti-money laundering requirements, traceability, a restitution structure that is consistent and understandable, ensuring the continued solvency of a system, the availability of a government "backstop" for emergencies, establishment of trust in the system through vetting and oversight as well as during times of adversity. This will become increasingly pertinent as the use of mobile money systems scales up.

Box IV.11. How German Development Cooperation can support the successful roll-out of branchless banking services

In a 2011 study, German Development Cooperation assessed the potential role for development partners to assist developing countries in the area of mobile money and other branchless banking services. In view of the experience to date, it has identified several ways in which its active involvement could make a difference:

(a) Provision of advice to market players and regulators, related to realizing an overall conducive framework addressing all core aspects of branchless banking

(b) Resource centre: Bridging existing knowledge gaps in order to avoid future failures in new projects. This would involve the development of practical tools to support market assessments, agent network sizing, segmentation etc.

(c) Supporting Governments in leveraging branchless banking. Enabling Governments to reap the fruits of these initiatives (e.g. through government-to-person payments) should result in increased global interest in branchless banking.

(d) Being a partner for private initiatives. German Development Cooperation could act as a catalyst between MFIs, banks, MNOs and technology vendors. The support could include product design support for specific segments, ICT enhancements for MFIs, funding pilot projects, technical support to third-party providers, and support in setting up viable agent networks.

(e) Linking branchless banking to other development objectives in order to enhance its impact.

Source: Germany, BMZ and GIZ (2011).

The use of mobile money services entails both legal and policy considerations, which may have domestic as well as cross-border implications. In addition to the issues already addressed, a preliminary checklist of selected policy and legal issues in mobile money services can be identified. For the sake of convenience, this is separated below into broad categories related to systems oversight, user-related concerns, crime and security considerations, and infrastructure issues (Field, forthcoming). The discussion that follows is not intended to be comprehensive or applicable to every situation, but rather to serve as a starting point in considering policy areas in need of attention to ensure the successful introduction of mobile money services.[25]

a. System oversight

Regulation of mobile money is a challenge for developing countries, not least because it traverses two previously distinct and independent sectors – communications and finance. When MNOs approach their conventional communications regulator with mobile money ideas, they are typically referred to the financial regulator for approval. In most cases, a start-off requirement is that the MNO must partner with a financial institution whose activities are already regulated by the central bank using existing legislation. In all cases, the financial institution holds the actual cash deposits, against which "e-value" is issued, and therefore, by proxy, the same system of regulation is extended to mobile money.

Differing national views of the nature of electronic money, and what it means to issue electronic money, have produced several different approaches to regulation. For some States, electronic money is the electronic equivalent of a national currency and therefore should be issued only by the State. For others, electronic "money" represents only one part of the service of moving value from one owner to another. That service may be composed of a number of steps – some of which could be carried out by banks or non-banks – which bring efficiencies to the process. Under this view, the goals of regulation would be to ensure the safety and soundness of the entire payment system, consumer protection, and other social objectives.

Under either view, the nature and the extent of regulation and supervision of mobile money services need to be considered. Non-bank mobile money providers (such as MNOs) are normally not regulated comprehensively in their payment services, though some Governments have utilized existing "money transmitter" or similar laws to regulate non-bank providers. Key issues include the need to determine the *location* of the virtual services and the appropriate *jurisdiction* – among government agencies (e.g. banking vs. telecom) and with respect to courts. Transparency is paramount. For services with a cross-border aspect, international harmonization, such as adoption of treaties or conventions, may come into play. In designing regulations, a balance must be sought between encouraging experimentation that can lead to new approaches, and maintaining economic stability.

Risk allocation can be addressed through proactive regulation, or can be left to private agreement between the parties, or can be addressed via a combination of the two. It is appropriate to allow risk allocation to vary by kind of service, usage, parties, and possibly even system architecture, since each variation may change the relative power of the parties and their ability to detect and prevent loss. Generally, there should be incentives for the party with the ability to improve the system over time to act. It is important not to overregulate, as this may hamper the establishment of new services. Regulation should be calibrated in light of the nature of the financial services (e.g. transfers, payments or savings), and the risks associated with each of these (Dittus and Klein, 2011).

The goal of promoting commerce and the need for liquidity in a payment system are significant. Moreover, mobile money services may be useful in advancing related e-government goals, such as the collection of taxes, duties and fees (including taxation of e-transactions), procurement, and payment obligations by Governments (benefits, salaries, grants/loans, subsidies).

Identity management must be addressed too – either on a case-by-case basis by the service provider, or more comprehensively. This may include recognition of electronic signatures, as well as other aspects such as website authentication and account authorization services. Regulatory consideration must be given to system security and resilience, including the identification and banning of bad payers, the evaluation and supervision of systems, mitigation of the risk of system collapses (which may include public safety nets), and contingency planning.

Addressing these and other concerns will increasingly require effective collaboration between communications and telecommunications regulators; while one is an expert in the financial aspects of mobile money, the other better understands the facilitating technology. Currently, in many countries, contacts do exist between individuals working at the two regulators, but there is often no formal institutional link between the two types of regulators. In the United Republic of Tanzania, the Bank of Tanzania and the Tanzania Communications Regulatory Authority have signed a formal Memorandum of Understanding to collaborate on the regulation of mobile money.

b. User issues

There is a spectrum of consumer protection concerns, which may vary based on social expectations. The most important is how to protect customer funds in cases where a non-bank is the e-money issuer. Non-banks are rarely subject to the kind of prudential regulation that applies to banks, so when non-banks issue e-money, regulators are likely to be concerned about ensuring adequate protection for customer funds (Tarazi and Breloff, 2010). General concerns include the relative obligations of the counterparties, banks, and MNOs and their agents, including loss allocation as well as protection against fraud, user error, and system error or loss.

Particular attention is being given to regulating MNO agents, since effective mobile money models require cash in/cash out points located near the customer (Tarazi and Breloff, 2011). Key issues include who can be an agent, what kind of services agents should be allowed to provide and on what terms, and the extent of bank liability for agents. There is no one-size-fits-all regulatory solution for the provision of mobile money services via agents, and markets are experimenting with various approaches to find out what works. Although this process may produce results consistent with customer interests, regulators should view this as an argument supporting a light-touch regulatory approach, not a presumption that regulation is unnecessary (ibid.).

Effective dispute resolution is an integral part of any successful payment system (at least, if alternatives are available). Countries vary with regard to whether there should be negligence or strict liability standards for losses due to the unauthorized use of devices or access codes. An independent and trusted judiciary and/or arbitration-type process may be called for, especially when considering integration into global markets. Issues of payment raise issues of insolvency and related risks. It may be necessary to characterize prepaid "money" and to recognize the special risk for prepay customers who may be financially unable to afford other payment plans.

A variety of issues relating to personal privacy are also of significant concern in most consumer payment systems. Matters of data mining, and of carrying a transaction history and other information with an electronic payment, may be problematic. Related issues include confidentiality and data protection, as well as anonymity. There may, however, be valid reasons for using mobile payment data for economic, social or even health research. Since money transfers often involve buying and selling, there are also concerns related to e-contract enforceability, distance selling (language, disclosures), and applicable law and jurisdiction.

c. Crime and national security considerations

Money laundering presents a critical set of issues in any payment system. Systems must be built in a way that discourages such practices and allows for some form of monitoring or review. The Financial Action Task Force (FATF), an independent, intergovernmental body, has issued guidance in this area,[26] dividing mobile services into four categories:

(a) Mobile financial information services for viewing accounts only, without the ability to conduct transactions. These are considered low-risk.

(b) Mobile banking and securities account services tied to existing accounts. These are likely to be regulated and supervised.

(c) Mobile payment services allowing payments to be made by non-account holders. These come under the widely varying controls and supervision of non-traditional financial institution payment service providers.

(d) Mobile money services which offer the ability to store value on mobile phones in the form of phone credits or airtime, or by other means, are still unregulated and unsupervised in many countries.

Terrorist financing presents similar issues, including issues of anonymity, traceability, and supervision. Risks may be mitigated through the technical establishment of value limits, as well as through appropriate monitoring. Customer due diligence and the adoption of know-your-customer principles also play a significant role. Currently, there are no uniform international standards for low-risk e-payment products, but the FATF has issued a Guidance Paper on Financial Inclusion, outlining how several countries around the world apply a risk-based approach to branchless banking (FATF, 2011).

Ways to discourage other uses of electronic money for criminal purposes – such as tax evasion, fraud (by issuers or others), theft and hold-ups, blackmail, kidnapping and piracy, bribery and gambling – should be built into any system, and should be addressed in law.[27] Similarly, corruption at all levels, as well as the

requirement for government and financial transparency, must be addressed. Depending on the technical architecture of a mobile money system (e.g. the value that is resident on the mobile device, as opposed to "in the cloud"), the seizure of phones and devices at borders by customs, or other seizures by police, may have financial implications.

d. Infrastructure policies

Various other related public policies will greatly affect the success of mobile money services. Some of these are best addressed within the private sector, while others may require government intervention.

In the area of standards and technical coordination, policies may need to be negotiated between and among device manufacturers, issuers, merchants and banks. Increased bandwidth requirements also need to be addressed. In certain situations, there may be benefits from considering offline approaches to payment or even dedicated networks.

A State may wish to promote competition in mobile money services. Issues of cooperation, barriers to entry, and intellectual property sharing then come into play. For consumer protection, monetary policy or other reasons, security and system resilience may need to be encouraged or required.

The development and operation of a successful mobile payment system requires the use of "cutting edge" technologies. It will be necessary to identify appropriate technologies and to address their use locally. There may be conflicts involving export restrictions, and patent and other intellectual property policies; there may also be restrictions on the use of certain encryption techniques. Furthermore, there may be reasons to promote or allow partnerships with foreign experts or investors.

New technological systems do not function in a vacuum. If mobile money systems are to be fully beneficial, additional infrastructure may be needed in order to support hem. This may include transport infrastructure and delivery systems, customs processing, financial settlement and netting systems, judiciary and regulatory efficiency and independence, and legal regulation of payment systems (particularly where mobile systems have "leapfrogged" prior technologies and no appropriate laws covering payment systems exist). There might also be a call for public education and awareness-raising, including technical and legal instruction. Additionally, some societies may be faced with an underdeveloped corporate culture, undeveloped debt, credit and equity markets, or underdeveloped legal frameworks.

* * * * *

Mobile money services promise widespread benefits for private sector development, and particularly for MSEs that are currently poorly catered for by existing financial services. If well managed, these services have the potential to contribute to much-improved financial inclusion (G20 Financial Inclusion Experts Group, 2010). Governments and their central banks should take the opportunity to explore ways to absorb these enterprises into the mainstream via mobile-based commercial and financial transactions. If well managed, mobile money systems have great potential to improve and expand markets, create jobs, and build a middle class.

In order to capture the full potential in this area, dedicated research is needed in order to extract lessons from the early adopters. Donor support is important, to help countries that are eager to implement appropriate frameworks capable of addressing the issues outlined in this section. As summarized by the German development agency (Germany, BMZ and GIZ, 2011: 8):

"Success will require building partnerships between mobile operators, financial institutions, retail organizations and other ecosystem members, and establishing new delivery models. It will require building a corpus of knowledge, sharing lessons, and leveraging all resources that are available. Most importantly, it will require organizational commitment and sharp execution by service providers. Only then will branchless banking be truly transformational."

NOTES

[1]   See, for example, UNDP's work on legal empowerment of the poor, at http://www.undp.org/legalempowerment/.

[2]   Automated customs systems can be programmed to select randomly from a roster of available customs officers in order to check customs declarations, thereby minimizing opportunities for collusion (IFC, 2007c: 53)

[3]   The term "business development service" was first coined in 1997 by the international Committee of Donors for Small Enterprise Development, which defined it as "services that improve the performance of the enterprise, its access to markets, and its ability to compete. [This includes] a wide array of business services, both strategic and operational. BDS are designed to serve individual businesses, as opposed to the larger business community" (Committee of Donor Agencies for Small Enterprise Development, 2001: 11).

[4]   This long-time separation between BDS and financial services is not uncontested. There is growing evidence of improvements gained through a more integrated approach (Sievers and Vandenburg, 2004).

[5]   The importance of tailoring activities to the demand of users has been highlighted many times. See, for example, Miehlbradt (1999) and UNCTAD (2010).

[6]   See http://www.celac.or.ug/.

[7]   Information provided by IICD.

[8]   Information provided by IICD.

[9]   See also Hellström (2010), which mentions the following examples from East Africa: MPAIS in Rwanda and Uganda, Farmer's Friend in Uganda, and Question Box in Uganda.

[10]   See http://www.grameenfoundation.applab.org/ckw/section/data-collection-info-services-technology.

[11]   This section is based on information provided by FAO and IFAD.

[12]   This section is based on information provided by UNECA.

[13]   See ECX:1000 perfect days. Available at http://capitalethiopia.com/index.php?option=com_content&view=article&id=14135:ecx1000-perfect-days&catid=12:local-news&Itemid=4.f

[14]   This section is based on Okello (forthcoming).

[15]   In this section, the term "mobile money systems" refers to all kinds of mobile platforms that can facilitate services such as money transfers (domestic and/or international), payments, and financial services (e.g. savings, credit, insurance).

[16]   See https://payments.yo.co.ug/index.php/component/content/article/44-about-yopayments/60-what-is-yo-payments.

[17]   See http://www.migrationinformation.org/datahub/remittances.cfm.

[18]   The eight deployments are M-Via (Mexico), Paymaster (Jamaica), Maroc Telecom (Morocco), M-PESA (Kenya), Zap (East Africa), Banglalink (Bangladesh), G-Cash (Philippines) and Smart (Philippines).

[19]   See http://www.cellular-news.com/story/46363.php.

[20]   See http://www.cellular-news.com/story/45114.php.

[21]   For example, ICT solutions can be used for remote updates, sending reminders, providing training, and collecting payments.

[22]   An agent may collect money from 50 to 100 clients per day, each of them entrusting the agent with, say, up to 20 per cent of his/her daily gross revenue.

[23]   See, for example, http://www.microinsurancefacility.org/en/thematic-pages/technology.

[24]   Knowledge: Utilize improved data to make evidence-based policy, measure progress, and consider an incremental "test and learn" approach acceptable to both regulator and service provider. Principle 7 of the G20 Principles on Financial Inclusion (http://www.g20.utoronto.ca/2010/to-principles.html).

[25]   This section draws significantly on the forthcoming publication by Field.

[26]   Financial Action Task Force (2010). Money laundering using new payment methods. October. Available at http://www.FATF-GAFI.org. See also: FATF 40 Recommendations. Standards for money laundering. Available at the same website.

[27]   For certain systems, a need may arise for government-to-government sharing of information. This commonly arises in tax evasion and money laundering investigations, but also may arise in other situations.

LEVERAGING ICTs TO SUPPORT WOMEN'S ENTREPRENEURSHIP

5

Exploring how ICTs can be used to support women entrepreneurs is important for several reasons. Firstly, women's entrepreneurship represents untapped potential for PSD. While women-owned MSEs have been found to be less profitable than MSEs owned by men (Alturki and Braswell, 2010; GTZ, 2010; IFC, 2007b; IFC, 2010; Ilavarasan and Levy, 2010; ILO, 2008b), this gender-based difference seems to disappear for larger ventures. In fact, some evidence suggests that among medium-sized and large enterprises, those owned by women are equally or more productive than those owned by men (GTZ, 2010). This makes it important to identify and address possible barriers constraining the growth and upgrading of women-owned MSEs. Secondly, a number of key barriers to growth are specific, or particularly constraining, to women entrepreneurs. As will be shown in this chapter, ICTs can be used to help overcome some of these. Thirdly, ICTs have, so far, seldom been used systematically to make initiatives aimed at supporting women's entrepreneurship more effective. Against this background, this chapter discusses how ICTs can be used to address the above-mentioned barriers. It provides recommendations to stakeholders interested in using ICTs to support women-owned MSEs more effectively, and explores relevant initiatives.[1]

A. BARRIERS FACING WOMEN ENTREPRENEURS IN DEVELOPING REGIONS

Women-owned MSEs in developing countries can largely be divided into subsistence-based enterprises and growth-oriented enterprises. The focus of the former tends to be on making a stable income, without necessarily seeking to expand the economic activity. The latter kind of enterprise is characterized by greater entrepreneurial drive and a stronger desire to grow (Levy et al., 2010). Currently, most women-owned MSEs in developing regions belong to the first category, operating informally in activities that require limited skills and training, such as smallholder farming, petty trading, street vending and beauty services (Naituli et al., 2008; World Bank, 2009b; Ilavarasan and Levy, 2010; IFC, 2010; Banerjee and Duflo, 2011).

Both groups are affected to different degrees by a number of barriers that are specific to women-owned MSEs and that ICTs can potentially help overcome:

  (a) Women-owned MSEs often face greater difficulty in accessing financing from formal sources, such as banks and traditional lending institutions;

  (b) Women entrepreneurs tend to have less time to spend on their business due to family responsibilities and the biased division of labour in the household;

  (c) Women often have less physical mobility, affecting their ability to access opportunities and markets, and to network and build their businesses; and

  (d) Women have less access to skills and training.

Additionally, in many countries, patriarchal social structures limit the freedom of women to engage successfully in business. In these instances, while innovative ICT-enabled initiatives could be used to reduce these effects to a certain degree (practical gender interests), more overarching initiatives are required to address broader societal issues.[2]

1. Access to finance

Accessing affordable, suitable finance is a key challenge for most MSEs, and even more so for women-owned MSEs. This problem is a function of many factors; three of the most pertinent are described here. Firstly, traditional collateral, such as proof of property ownership, is often required by banks. In many countries, however, customs, social practices or even laws do not allow women to own property. In 43 countries in Africa, 23 in Asia and Oceania, 5 in Latin America and the Caribbean, and 2 in Eastern Europe, women are reported not to have equal rights with men to acquiring and owning land (UNDESA, 2010). In most African and many Asian countries, although equal property-ownership rights are stipulated by law, the prevailing customary practices[3] (which in a number of cases take precedence over statutory law) prevent women from having control over the shared property of the married couple, or even over the property that they brought into the marriage (UNDESA, 2010; OECD, 2006b; EIU, 2010). There is little that ICTs can do to address such legal barriers.

Secondly, the majority of women entrepreneurs in developing countries have limited awareness of where and how to access financial services, and mostly lack a bank account (UNDP, 2008b; World Bank, 2010a). For example, in Viet Nam, the Government has launched a number of initiatives to assist women entrepreneurs, including opening special branches at Sacombank (the country's largest privately owned commercial bank), and starting a programme dedicated to women in rural areas at Agribank (the country's largest state-owned commercial bank). However, as only about 10 per cent of Vietnamese have a bank account, the effectiveness of these policies has been limited (EIU, 2010). Thirdly, many women entrepreneurs in developing regions are considered by banks to be high-risk, low-profit customers, as they operate informal businesses in low-growth sectors of the economy (ibid.).

Consequently, various studies have found borrowing from friends and family to be the primary source of loans for women entrepreneurs. For example, a study of women entrepreneurs in Nepal found that such loans made up 85 per cent of women's borrowing (UNESCAP, 2005). Microfinance is another viable option, as it does not require traditional collateral. However, it has been noted, for example in India and Kenya, that while microfinance loans may be suited to the needs of subsistence-based women-owned MSEs, they are often less well adapted to the needs of growth-oriented ones (ILO, 2008b; Banerjee and Duflo, 2011).[4]

2. Time constraints due to family responsibilities

Most women entrepreneurs in developing countries suffer from a biased division of household labour along gender lines, and bear the burden of running a business as well as taking care of domestic chores, children and the elderly.[5] Balancing these responsibilities with running a business is one of the most frequently cited challenges for women entrepreneurs.[6] Often the woman is the primary caregiver for the family, and has to dedicate time to help family members who fall ill. In effect, with less time to devote to the business, she is likely to lose out on income, especially if she is the primary or only worker in the business. Ironically, although most women entrepreneurs in developing countries end up working longer hours than men, they often have less time to dedicate to their business. This also means that they have less "discretionary time" for activities that are important to their business, such as learning new skills or technologies, networking, or searching for information about market opportunities (ILO, 2008a; Gill et al., 2010). Unsurprisingly, the extent to which they become members of business associations is far less than that of men (World Bank, n.d.).

3. Restricted physical mobility

Women-owned MSEs in developing countries are often disadvantaged by restrictions on women's physical mobility, which are rooted in social norms, customs, and family responsibilities. Restrictions due to social norms range from constraints on appropriate places for a woman to visit and the times at which she can be out of the house, to female seclusion in certain countries of South Asia and the Middle East, where women are required to avoid any interaction with males who are not their relatives (Esplen and Brody, 2007). For example, women in Saudi Arabia are prohibited from driving, have restricted access to public transportation, and require permission from a male family member to travel overseas (Alturki and Braswell, 2010). Additionally, a woman entrepreneur's mobility may also be constrained by family obligations.

The impacts of such restrictions on women-owned MSEs range from discouraging women from starting a business because of the association with dishonour and shame when a woman works outside of her home (Esplen and Brody, 2007) to putting constraints on participation by women in activities that are crucial for business operation and growth, such as accessing markets, creating networks or obtaining training (Bolton and Thompson, 2000). Finding and accessing markets is frequently cited as one of the main areas where women entrepreneurs have more difficulties than men (Alturki and Braswell, 2010; GTZ, 2010; IFC, 2007b). They may be restricted to accessing information and business opportunities from within their immediate physical surroundings (neighbourhood or city) (OECD, 2006b). A study of women micro-entrepreneurs in Mumbai, India, found them to be less likely than male entrepreneurs to have customers from outside that city: only 3 per cent of the women reported having customers "at a distance" (compared with 20 per cent of their male counterparts) and only 1.5 per cent of them ever contacted businesspeople who live in different areas of the same city by mobile telephone (Levy et al., 2010). Women entrepreneurs in Saudi Arabia have been found to be less likely than those in other countries in the region to be involved in international trade: only 21 per cent of the 264 women-owned businesses (202 registered and 62 unregistered) that participated in a study were importing, exporting, or both (Alturki and Braswell, 2010).

4. Limited skills and training

Most women-owned MSEs in developing countries have limited skills and training, which constrains their choice of business activities, as well as their ability to meet the needs of their business. For example, a survey of entrepreneurs in Kenya in 1999 showed that although the numbers of men and women owning micro-enterprises were almost equal (670,727 men compared to 612,848 women), most women (74.7 per cent) were in trade-related businesses that did not require formal skills (Munyua and Mureithi, 2008). It has also been documented that in developing countries, women are concentrated in low-profit, low-growth, informal businesses (IFC, 2010; Ilavarasan and Levy, 2010; Naituli et al., 2008; World Bank, 2009b). In addition to having limited time available for training, many of these women entrepreneurs are unlikely to have received basic education – further constraining their access to suitable skills and training. Although inequality has been reduced in terms of access to primary education, women still make up two thirds of the world's 774 million illiterate adults (UNDESA, 2010). It could be argued that their lack of basic education, coupled with time constraints, results in situations whereby even those who are motivated and entrepreneurial are trapped in informal economic activities, lacking the resources and training to grow.

B. ADDRESSING THE BARRIERS

There are multiple ways in which the use of different ICT tools can assist women-owned MSEs in overcoming some of the barriers highlighted above.

1. Choice of ICT tools

There is limited information on how ICT use among entrepreneurs varies by gender. Radios, mobile phones, PCs, the Internet, telecentres and Internet cafes (and sometimes a combination of these) appear to hold potential for reaching women entrepreneurs in developing regions and for meeting their needs. Women-owned MSEs' needs for and potential benefits from different ICTs vary greatly, as illustrated by a study of 77 urban women-owned MSEs in Kenya (box V.1). Furthermore, subsistence-based businesses have different needs compared to businesses that are growth-oriented. For example, business skills training related to marketing and business planning may meet the training needs of growth-oriented businesses, but may only rarely meet the training needs of subsistence-based enterprises (Banerjee and Duflo, 2011).

While *radio* is the most widely diffused ICT tool in many developing countries, including the poorest communities without electricity, radio use has certain limitations. It provides one-way communication, making it challenging to give feedback and to receive information tailored to the needs of the listener. Furthermore, it may be difficult for women entrepreneurs to reconcile radio schedules with their other business responsibilities, with domestic chores, and with caring for family members. However, the combined use of radio and mobile phones in a rural context has, in some cases, helped to improve access by rural women entrepreneurs to information or business skills training (Radloff et al., 2010; SEWA, 2011). For example, the Women of Uganda Network (WOUGNET) is a membership organization that uses ICTs to support women. In the northern province of Apac, it uses a combination of community radio and mobile phones to improve its access to rural women entrepreneurs. Special radio programmes are broadcast via a local community station called Radio Apac, and the content of the shows is designed to suit the needs and capacities of the listeners. The women gather in groups to listen to the radio, and each group has a mobile phone that is used to pose questions to the radio station. Women find the programme useful, as it is easy to participate in, and

does not require them to travel or acquire complex technical skills (Okello, 2010).

The widespread uptake of *mobile phones* means opportunities for reaching and supporting women entrepreneurs. A survey of 662 urban micro-enterprises, carried out in 2009 in Mumbai, found that nearly every woman who owned or managed a micro-enterprise had a mobile phone (Ilavarasan and Levy, 2010). Similarly, all urban, women-owned MSEs (including informal enterprises) in the Kenya study (box V.1) owned a mobile phone or a SIM card (Nguyen, 2011).

While the value of *computers* and the *Internet* is high, especially for growth-oriented enterprises, these are less in demand as business tools by women in subsistence-based businesses and by women operating in areas with an unreliable electricity supply (UNCTAD, 2010; Esselaar et al., 2007; Donner, 2006; Molony, 2007). The study of women entrepreneurs in Mumbai found that businesses with up to five hired workers saw no need for a computer (Ilavarasan and Levy, 2010). *Telecentres* and *Internet cafes* provide shared, cost-effective access to PCs and the Internet. However, there are limitations associated with using such centres to support women entrepreneurs. For example, in a survey of urban micro-enterprises in Mumbai, few business owners, and no women business owners, visited Internet cafes for business purposes (Ilavarasan and Levy, 2010). This may have been the result of various factors – including not needing PC access for the business, lacking time, or the Internet cafe environment being inappropriate for women. The latter point may apply especially where the premises are used primarily by young men practising online gaming or viewing adult content (Chawla and Behl, 2006; Rangaswamy, 2007; Ilavarasan and Levy, 2010; Kleine, 2010).

2. Overcoming barriers with ICT-based support

Few studies have looked specifically at the scope for ICT-based interventions to support women's entrepreneurship. Moreover, few current initiatives in this area appear to be taking full advantage of ICTs.[7] For example, a review of the projects listed in IFC's Women in Business programme found no reference to ICT usage (IFC, 2011). Similarly, out of the vast range of activities coordinated by ILO and aimed at supporting women's entrepreneurship, very few references are made to the potential of ICTs, and the number of

Box V.1. Understanding the diverse ICT and business needs of women-owned MSEs in Kenya

The findings from in-depth interviews with women in Kenya who own MSEs in Nairobi and Kisumu, and from practitioners who work for various business-support organizations, underline the importance of developing a clear understanding of the information needs of different categories of MSEs. The research was undertaken in 2010 and covered 77 women-owned MSEs. The respondents were primarily in the trade and services sectors, and were grouped into four categories: self-employed micro-enterprises (0 employees), micro-enterprises (1–5 employees), very small enterprises (6–15 employees) and small enterprises (16–50 employees). The study found that the nature of the respondents' information needs and communication needs, their ICT usage, and the resources they had available to meet their needs, varied considerably. As discussed below, the diversity of needs largely corresponded with the number of employees, the type of business, and the educational level of the owner.

Respondents with 0–5 employees (whose enterprises could largely be described as subsistence-based) indicated the need for information on basic business skills, such as how to identify products or services, how to carry out bookkeeping, or where to obtain capital. Capital constraints, lack of business skills, bad debts, fluctuations in pricing and revenue due to seasonality of products, and family burdens all contributed to their financial struggle. These respondents reported meeting their information needs through personal experience, watching other people around them, and word of mouth via face-to-face meetings. Most either owned or had access to a mobile phone. Access to radio was ubiquitous too, but few used it to obtain business information. These respondents' information searches were limited to the immediate physical environment, i.e. what they could observe or who they could talk with in their surroundings.

Entrepreneurs with 6–15 employees reported information needs that were primarily concerned with how to market products or services, and how to retain skilled employees. The need to obtain information about accessing affordable finance remained a priority for some respondents, however the majority of respondents at this level stated that their priority was to obtain information related to the marketing of their business. Several respondents had attended a number of business skill training courses, and indicated a demand for further training in specific areas of business management, for example sales and marketing, or strategy. Most also requested information on the success stories of other businesspeople, in order to draw inspiration from them and learn from their experiences. These respondents met their information needs through face-to-face conversations, phone calls, newspapers and television.

The information needs of entrepreneurs with 16–50 employees included those that have been mentioned above, but also how to access export markets, and how to increase the efficiency and effectiveness of operations. This could involve creating management information systems and obtaining detailed reporting and monitoring on the business operation. Respondents with this level of information needs mostly called for "just in time" information on how to deal with business problems at hand.

Source: Nguyen (2011).

Initiatives that currently seek to leverage ICTs for their delivery is small. An extensive search for ICT-enabled initiatives returned only a few relevant programmes. So, in general, very little information is available on the existing programmes, and very little evidence is available on their impacts, making a rigorous and systematic evaluation of initiatives highly desirable in future research. The following discussion should primarily be seen as a first endeavour to identify key areas in which the use of ICTs should be further explored, in order to make efforts at facilitating the creation and expansion of women-owned MSEs more effective.

a. Access to finance

There are a number of ways for ICTs to help lower the barrier to accessing financing for women entrepreneurs. Key factors constraining their access to finance are a lack of information about credit schemes, and a lack of financial literacy (ILO, 2008a). ICT tools including mobile phones, radio and the Internet can be used to address this situation, by delivering information and training on these topics. For example, mobile phones are being used in an initiative to provide 4,000 women entrepreneurs in Nyanza, Kenya with increased access to financial services, and to financial literacy and business management skills training. The initiative was developed to address the problem where, even when banks create special facilities to support SMEs as a result of government encouragement, women may not be able to take advantage of the schemes due to a number of factors, including insufficient information about the schemes, lack of collateral or even lack of a bank account, or not meeting the requirements set by the bank (Cherie Blair Foundation for Women, 2011).

As has already been discussed, family and friends are an important source of funding for women entrepreneurs. Mobile remittance services, such as those discussed in chapter IV, section C, can make the process of soliciting such funds faster and more cost-effective. For example, in Kenya, M-PESA has made it easier for rural women to receive funds from their husbands and other contacts in the city (CGAP, 2009b). Before the advent of mobile money, they had to travel from rural areas by bus to the city or to the post office in the local town in order to collect the money – a process that, due to poor transportation, could take up to a week, which is time that women entrepreneurs often do not have. With mobile money, they can request the funds via the telephone, and receive the money at a nearby mobile money agent.

Many women-owned MSEs in developing countries are vulnerable to personal risks – such as sickness of family members, divorce, separation, or accidents, which, if realized, could lead to women having to spend the capital that they intended to use for their business, limiting the growth of the business, or in extreme cases, even leading to the collapse of the business (ILO, 2008a). The design and implementation of innovative mobile micro-insurance schemes geared to the needs of women entrepreneurs could be devised to assist them in addressing these risks, thereby increasing their confidence in accessing finance. The case of Kilimo Salama (cited in chapter II) has demonstrated that it is possible to use mobile money systems innovatively to increase the reach and affordability of insurance programmes, although little is yet known about their effectiveness. An extensive search has failed to detect any case where mobile phones or other ICT tools have been used for women-focused micro-insurance initiatives, however. Perhaps similar products could be developed to meet the needs of women entrepreneurs. Such insurance could cover the costs associated with life's events where the burden falls heavily on women – for example childbirth, or lost income from caring for a sick child or relative (Iskenderian, 2011). One such example of a women-specific insurance product is Ri'aya (Caregiver) Micro-insurance, from the Microfund for Women, which was launched in Jordan in April 2010. One year later, it had a customer base of 13,000 women (Microfund for Women, 2011). ICTs are currently not used for Ri'aya. However, leveraging mobile phones for this and similar schemes could increase their reach to more women.

b. Limited time and physical mobility

Making information available via ICTs is one way to help women entrepreneurs avoid the need to travel, thereby helping to deal with their time poverty, and with constraints on their mobility. For example, community radio is used by the Toro Development Network in Uganda to broadcast selected commodity prices on a weekly basis, helping women smallholder farmers save time on lengthy trips into town to obtain such information. This project has been funded by Gender, Agriculture and Rural Development in the Information Society (GenARDIS) – a small grants fund that was started in 2002 to support initiatives that use ICTs to empower rural women (Radloff et al., 2010).

ICT tools are also used to reduce the need for travel related to business transactions such as purchasing. For example, in Kenya, women business owners increasingly use their mobile phones to make payments through M-PESA, which allows them to save considerable time and cut down on the need to travel to buy stock or other inputs. Instead of having to travel long distances, they can place orders via the telephone, pay with M-PESA, and get the goods delivered through the public transport service (Cherie Blair Foundation for Women, 2011). Although the benefits from ICT use in this case are similar to those that businesses owned by men would receive, the impact is potentially greater on women, as women may be affected more acutely by particular constraints (e.g. limited mobility or lack of time).

ICTs can also be effective in enhancing awareness of and providing access to existing business development services, which may otherwise be out of reach to woman entrepreneurs due to their time and physical mobility constraints. For example, SEBRAE – a business development organization in Brazil – works with a network of cybercafe owners who are trained to support clients in accessing SEBRAE's business support services which are available online. For women entrepreneurs, the online availability of SEBRAE's services, coupled with the assistance of a trained person to help them use the service, could be particularly helpful.[8]

Similarly, ICT tools can improve access by women entrepreneurs to markets and opportunities that were previously out of reach. For example, mobile phones have been used by the Mikocheni Agricultural Research Institute to enable women farmers in the village of Peko-Misegese, United Republic of Tanzania, to obtain higher prices for their crops by reaching a wider range of potential buyers in other towns that they previously did not have access to (Radloff et al., 2010). Similarly, business development organizations can assist members to create a Web presence that allows them to promote and sell their products and services to customers in markets that are currently out of reach to them due to their physical mobility constraints.[9]

The use of mobile phones, e-mail and Web-based video calls (such as Skype) may allow women-owned MSEs to substitute for face-to-face meetings (which may be unfeasible due to mobility constraints), enabling them to build business relationships. Mobile phones have been found to strengthen business and social relationships, allowing women entrepreneurs to expand the geographic area within which they can do business, and to access opportunities (Ilavarasan and Levy, 2010).

c. Limited skills and training

As has already been noted (chapter II), ICT tools can help entrepreneurs increase their productivity through improved access to skills and training needed for their businesses. For example, Huduma Kwa Wakulima (Kenya Farmers Helpline), from Kencall, allows farmers to call a phone number and get responses from experts to specific questions about farming and livestock. Approximately 43 per cent of the calls are from women farmers who, prior to the helpline, rarely received any assistance from agricultural professionals (Cherie Blair Foundation for Women, 2010).

A variety of ICT tools (most notably radio and telecentres) have been used by the Self-Employed Women's Association (SEWA) to reach its 1.3 million members. SEWA believes that the radio remains an important ICT tool for supporting and training its members, who listen during work. SEWA has found radio to be particularly effective in delivering training to women with no literacy or technical skills, or electricity for that matter, in the most remote villages in India. In addition, telecentres are used by SEWA as community learning centres (CLCs) to offer ICT training, childcare, disaster mitigation activities, and a village database containing information on the local economy and SEWA member profiles. Recently, these facilities have been extended to rural and remote areas, through the use of mobile CLC vans that contain a number of personal computers and have Internet connectivity and appropriate software (SEWA, 2011).

Furthermore, ICTs can be better exploited to deliver training in a way that is suitable for women entrepreneurs. In a study of growth-oriented women entrepreneurs in the United Republic of Tanzania (Stevenson and St-Onge, 2005), "just in time" training, where relevant topics are delivered on demand, was found to be the preferred method for obtaining skills and training for women entrepreneurs, as opposed to the traditional two-to-five-day courses held in classrooms, where participants need to take time away from their businesses. It was also recommended that follow-up sessions should be conducted after the training, in a one-on-one format. This supports the point that time constraints are one of the key barriers that limit women entrepreneurs' access to skills and training. ICTs are conducive to the delivery of such training programmes where the content is delivered on demand through mobile phones or PCs, allowing access whenever and wherever convenient. The Cherie Blair Foundation for Women has started using mobile phones to send follow-up messages to women entrepreneurs participating in its training programmes, and to connect women entrepreneurs. However, as the project only began in June 2010, little information is available so far on its impact (Cherie Blair Foundation for Women, 2011).

C. POLICY RECOMMENDATIONS

To date, insufficient programme or policy attention has been given to the application of ICT tools in existing or new initiatives supporting women entrepreneurs. This seems to be an untapped potential. ICTs should be used as an enabling tool that enhances the effectiveness of existing initiatives. For example, organizations supporting women entrepreneurs should explore ICT-based solutions as an additional strategy, to complement face-to-face meetings for trade-promotion activities. In addition to organizing trade missions to other countries or markets, or trade fairs that only a limited number of women entrepreneurs have the resources to participate in, online meetings could be arranged between women entrepreneurs on the one hand, and potential business partners or customers from foreign markets on the other. These meetings could aim at initiating new business relationships, and could subsequently support the women entrepreneurs with follow-up activities.

Any initiatives aimed at supporting women-based entrepreneurship using ICTs should be tailored to the specific needs of the intended beneficiaries – whether they are aimed at making incomes sustainable or at facilitating growth. In order for services to be accessible and relevant, they need to be based on an understanding of the specific information, knowledge, and support that are demanded. Support programmes addressing SMEs in general (such as the well-known SME Toolkit produced by IFC) run the risk of not being specific enough to be useful to some beneficiaries. Each subgroup of women-owned MSEs has different needs and capabilities, and it is important to adjust the support accordingly. For example, informal micro-enterprises with fewer than five employees are unlikely to have access to computers or to need Web-based services or information (Ilavarasan and Levy, 2010). Most likely, they are less interested in business skills training or marketing, but more interested in the basics of what to buy and sell and how to get finance. Meanwhile, enterprises of 10–15 employees with computers are more likely to have growth-related needs – such as learning how to expand their markets, learning new business skills, and upgrading their ICT skills (box V.1).

A needs assessment should therefore be the starting point for the development of new ICT-based initiatives, and an ongoing impact evaluation should be used to inform decisions. The high and rapidly increasing penetration rate of mobile phones amongst women entrepreneurs, including those in subsistence-based enterprises, presents an opportunity to obtain feedback and information that would allow policymakers

and agencies to develop a clear understanding of their situation. It is important that initiatives take into consideration the capabilities, circumstances, context of usage and preferences of the target group, in order for them to be effective (as highlighted in box V.1).

An illustration of the problem of insufficient assessment of needs is the case of the Cameroon Chamber of Commerce, Industry, Mines and Crafts, where a multimedia centre with Internet facilities that was created for its members who are women entrepreneurs in the textile sector went largely unused. A major reason for this was that the centre was designed without understanding the specific situation of its target users, resulting in the centre being located in an area that was difficult to get to by public transport and had opening hours (8 a.m.–4 p.m.) that were inconvenient for women entrepreneurs. Furthermore, although most of its target users were unfamiliar with the Internet, there was no training organized for them to learn how to use the centre. Finally, its existence was not well promoted (Busken and Webb, 2009).

It is worth noting that lessons from the field have highlighted the need for training programmes to be developed that take into account the limited skills and training, and even the basic level of education, of most women who own MSEs. Hence, lessons from programmes produced by IICD (box V.2) and GenARDIS (Radloff et al., 2010) underscore the need for skills development, and to involve women entrepreneurs in content development.

Box V.2. Supporting women entrepreneurs with ICT: lessons from the field

The International Institute for Communication and Development (IICD) and its partners have suggested a number of lessons learnt in using ICT to support women entrepreneurs based on the organization's experience with the implementation of 54 ICT programmes for producers and entrepreneurs in nine countries in Africa and Latin America. IICD found that female participants in its programmes were held back by a combination of low levels of literacy and technical skills, complex cultural barriers such as unequal access to information compared to men, and an overall lack of power and self-esteem. Furthermore, programmes supporting entrepreneurs often did not include relevant information for female producers and entrepreneurs, and overlooked their participation in content-generation, exacerbating the challenges for this group.

A number of approaches were reported to be helpful in addressing barriers constraining women entrepreneurs, including:

(a) Paying attention to the specific information needs of women entrepreneurs, and involving them in content-generation;

(b) Using audio and multimedia to overcome low levels of literacy;

(c) Tailoring training locations and timings to suit female beneficiaries; and

(d) Ensuring that trainers are gender-sensitive in terms of the training methodology – for example, giving participants group assignments rather than individually oriented training.

Source: UNCTAD, based on information provided by IICD.

Finally, the absence of systematic, evidence-based impact evaluation is observed in current initiatives using ICTs, including those focusing on women entrepreneurs. A search for evidence of impact, even among the above-mentioned programmes, returned mostly success stories and brief anecdotal reports. There is a need for more comprehensive evaluations that are based on empirical evidence, and that provide a realistic picture of the programme's impact for the majority of its recipients and not just isolated success stories.

NOTES

[1]   For a broader discussion on how to apply a gender lens to issues related to science, technology and innovation, see UNCTAD (forthcoming).

[2]   A distinction can be made between "practical gender interests" (responses to address women's immediate perceived needs without challenging women's subordination) versus "strategic gender interests" (efforts at creating more satisfactory, alternative arrangements to those which exist) (Molyneux, 1985). Under this categorization, the discussion in this section focuses mainly on ICTs' role in addressing practical gender interests.

[3]   Customary practices are unwritten rules and norms established by long usage (based on customs and cultures) (EIU, 2010).

[4]   Several factors make microfinance less attractive to growth-oriented businesses. Microfinance involves small loans that need to be repaid quickly. The interest rate is considerably lower than that charged by informal money lenders (which is the alternative for a women entrepreneur who does not have collateral or relatives and friends who can lend the money), but it is considerably higher than bank rates. MFIs typically require weekly meetings, which is time-consuming.

[5]   On average, women worldwide spend about two hours a day on domestic work — twice as much time as men. In less developed regions they can spend up to five times as many hours as men on unpaid domestic work (UNDESA, 2010). Additionally, caring for relatives alone takes up an average of 55 minutes of a woman's day in Asia (ibid.).

[6]   In-depth interviews with women-owned MSEs in Ghana, for example, found that "balancing work and family life" was considered the area in which the women faced the greatest barriers, compared with their male counterparts (IFC, 2007b).

[7]   For example, at a recent workshop on women's entrepreneurship organized by the World Bank, ICTs were not mentioned in the programme – despite the work carried out within the Bank on ICT4D (http://go.worldbank.org/XI1101SN20).

[8]   Information provided by SEBRAE.

[9]   There are numerous services available that enable a business to set up a website and promote and sell its products, including free and fee-paying, and not-for-profit and commercial services. Examples include Open Entry, Etsy, Shopify, and Amazon Marketplace.

6

POLICY
RECOMMENDATIONS

Developing a thriving private sector is a priority for Governments in most developing countries. The private sector is an indispensable source of job creation, government revenue and economic diversification, all of which are key factors in achieving sustainable economic growth and development. From the perspective of facilitating PSD, this report has underlined the potential contributions that effective use of ICTs — in the private and the public sector – can make. While ICT use is not a panacea, it represents an untapped potential to accelerate progress in regard to PSD. The scope for leveraging such technologies has been greatly enhanced by recent changes in the ICT landscape, with many more MSEs now being exposed to affordable interactive communication tools.

The previous chapters have provided illustrations of how PSD has been affected by ICTs in the framework of four interfaces: (a) the development of ICT infrastructure; (b) enhanced business use of ICTs; (c) the ICT sector; and (d) using ICTs to make PSD interventions more effective. In view of that analysis, ICTs have a clear role to play in government interventions at each level (table VI.1).

At the *macro level*, contributions from ICTs are related to reforms that make the investment climate more competitive and open. Promoting the development of a competitive ICT infrastructure generally requires the liberalization and appropriate regulation of the telecommunications sector, and the mobilization of private investment. The drive towards greater global economic integration, and the need for developing economies to compete within this framework, further underscore the importance of ICT use in this context, especially as part of efforts to reform the business environment. As noted in chapter III, there is still scope for regulatory improvements in this area in many developing countries.

Meso-level interventions aim to create a more enabling business environment. Future business environment reform processes should build on the substantial body of knowledge that has been developed with regard to using ICTs to connect citizens and enterprises with their Governments, in a number of fields. These include the improvement of specific regulatory functions – such as business registration, filing tax returns, and trade facilitation – and of the ways in which private enterprises and their representative organizations liaise with Governments. At this level, Governments should also consider how to create a regulatory environment that supports the roll-out of mobile money services and related applications, which can alleviate some of the financial barriers that are faced particularly by MSEs.

ICT-related *micro-level* interventions may improve the productivity and competitiveness of private firms in two principal ways. Firstly, Governments can create the conditions in which it makes sense for enterprises to invest in and use ICTs, and in which the ICT sector is able to respond to the demands of the business community. They can establish the relevant ICT infrastructure, and facilitate the opening and functioning of relevant ICT markets. Secondly, providers of business-development and financial services can improve the delivery of support to enterprises with ICTs. When applied effectively, ICTs reduce the costs of deliver-

ing the services, and extend their outreach to client groups that would otherwise be hard to service.

Against this background, Governments and their development partners that are involved in policy formulation should take a holistic and comprehensive approach to leveraging ICTs for PSD. On its own, new technology is likely to have a limited effect on private sector development. Broader reforms are necessary in developing countries to provide the appropriate physical and policy frameworks. The potential of ICTs cannot be fully realized without adequate infrastructure and skills and a commitment by government to free and open markets. Governments can work with the private sector to create an investment climate that encourages the use of ICTs within private firms and also across the government bureaucracy. When carefully integrated into reform processes and considered as part of a wider reengineering process, ICTs stand the best chance of contributing to cost reduction, to the promotion of transparent, rules-based systems, and to better communication between the public and private sectors.

When exploring the potential role of ICTs in supporting PSD, the diverse and multi-faceted needs of enterprise have to be placed at the centre of the analysis. All enterprises value access to relevant and timely information, as well as the possibility to communicate effectively with customers, suppliers and peers, and with government authorities. As firms grow and their capabilities are enhanced, their demand for effective storage and processing of information is accentuated, too. Nevertheless, the extent to which improved access to a certain technology will make a difference depends on the enterprise itself, and also on the context in which it operates. Are relevant ICT tools and services available and affordable? Does the enterprise have sufficient knowledge about how to use the technologies and applications? Can it find relevant content, services and support that match its precise requirements, and can it influence their supply? To what extent are its clients and suppliers ICT-proficient? Is the government – at national or subnational level – making effective use of ICT solutions in its dealings with the private sector?

In some areas of intervention, considerable experience has already been built up and there is ample evidence to guide the policy directions to follow. This applies, for example, to policies that are aimed at creating an open and competitive environment that is conducive to extending relevant ICT infrastructure at affordable prices. By contrast, some opportunities for ICT use

Table VI.1. Overview of levels of policy intervention and relevant technical areas

Level of policy intervention; technical areas	Potential ICT contribution
Macro level: Creating a competitive and open investment climate	
Investment climate reforms, including: – Macroeconomic stability – Budget and financial management – Guiding productive structural change (industrial policy) – Investing in human resource development – Infrastructure and utilities development and management – Open and competitive markets – Restructuring of state enterprises	– Liberalization and effective regulation of telecommunications and related markets – ICT skills development – Competition policies to ensure that ICT services are affordable
Meso level: Creating an enabling business environment for business growth	
Business environment reforms, including: – Policy, legal and regulatory framework – Administration – Business representation and dialogue – Access to finance – Public–private dialogue – Facilitating innovation and knowledge systems	– Using ICTs to improve the interactions between government and the private sector, e.g. in the form of e-government and public–private dialogue – Using ICTs to promote transparent, rule-based business regulations – Using ICTs to facilitate business registration, tax administration and trade – Improve legal and regulatory frameworks to facilitate e-commerce/m-commerce/mobile money and related applications
Micro level: Improving the productivity and competitiveness of private firms	
Address internal constraints of enterprises – Micro-enterprise development – SME development – Women's entrepreneurship – Formalization of informal enterprises – Attract foreign investment – Entrepreneurship promotion – Value chains and clustering	– Creating incentives for private enterprises to invest in ICTs to improve their competitiveness, e.g. by reducing business/transaction costs, accessing information, reducing risks, enhancing communication – Using ICTs to make business development and extension services more effective – Using ICTs to improve the access of enterprises to micro-finance and other financial services.

Source: UNCTAD.

to contribute to PSD have only emerged in the past few years, and in these cases there is still very little track record. Examples include the roll-out of new mobile money services with related applications, the introduction of m-government services, and the growing outsourcing of micro-work. In these cases, more analysis and testing of new approaches is needed, in order to adequately assess the potential and to identify best policy practices.

In light of these findings, the following policy recommendations are made with a view to seizing the untapped potential of ICT use to enable and accelerate PSD:

Strengthening the ICT infrastructure

Promote affordable access to relevant ICTs. When setting priorities for strengthening the investment climate, carefully consider what improvements in the ICT infrastructure are required in order to support various private-sector activities. Micro-enterprises in rural areas may, first and foremost, need to ensure basic connectivity, which now means access to mobile voice networks. Mobile penetration has greatly improved,

but large parts of the rural population in LDCs still lack access to a mobile signal. Meanwhile, enterprises seeking to engage in e-commerce or exports, or to become part of global value chains, increasingly require access to affordable and reliable broadband connectivity. In developing countries with limited fixed telecommunications infrastructure, mobile broadband is likely to offer the most cost-effective solution to bridging connectivity gaps. In order to speed up the roll-out of mobile broadband, countries need to allocate spectrum and to license operators to provide the service. Indeed, almost 50 developing and transition economies have yet to launch mobile broadband services.

Enhancing ICT use in enterprises

Enhance investment in and use of ICTs by private firms. Further efforts are needed to support the adoption of ICTs by private enterprises. There is growing evidence that firms (including MSEs) that invest in and apply ICTs are in a better position to become more productive, competitive and profitable. This is because ICTs can reduce the costs of business transactions, provide tools for better business management, and enhance the capacity to get goods and services to the market. However, the benefits from the different uses of ICTs are not distributed uniformly. The value to an enterprise of having access to a certain technology depends on its size, industry, and market orientation. Many MSEs, including in the informal sector, are hesitant about investing in some ICTs; this may reflect educational, literacy and cost barriers, or simply that they do not see the relevance of using such tools in their business. The major exception to this is mobile phones. Most MSE owners and managers in developing countries already own and frequently use a mobile phone – increasingly for business purposes. Obtaining market information and building customer relations appear to be the prime business needs that are catered for through mobile phone use.

While much benefit from enhanced affordable access to relevant ICTs will be the result of appropriation by the private sector itself, independent of any particular government or donor intervention, the chances for such gains increase when the regulatory environment is conducive to the use of ICTs by enterprises. Governments and development actors need to learn from private sector experience and intervene in ways that help enterprises and civil society to seize opportunities created by developments in technology. Moreover, care should be taken not to crowd out private-sector service providers when launching government initiatives, and rather work with the market.

Include ICT modules in business training programmes. Many entrepreneurs in developing countries, and especially in LDCs, lack the necessary capacity or awareness to take full advantage of ICTs. Thus, even if they have access to mobile phones or the Internet, they may not know how best to leverage them for their business operations. One way to address this issue is to integrate ICT skills development into general business-management training curriculums. Depending on the beneficiaries targeted, such training may range from providing advice on how to use mobile phones as a business tool to more advanced training in how to use various technologies and applications to improve operational management, customer relationship management, or resource planning.

Adopt regulatory frameworks that help to enhance confidence in the use of new technology or the new application of known technology. A prerequisite for more widespread uptake of ICTs for commercial purposes is that enterprises and consumers trust the

systems. In many countries, adequate legal frameworks still need to be adopted and enforced in order to unleash the full potential of electronic transactions. The need to act is accentuated by the increased use of mobile devices for commercial transactions, which raises new regulatory issues. As this is particularly relevant for low-income countries – where mobile platforms are the main enabler of electronic transactions for businesses, Governments and consumers – support from the international community is highly desirable.

Promoting the ICT producing sector

Facilitate the expansion of the ICT sector. A thriving ICT sector services local markets and is often a source of local innovation and dynamic entrepreneurship. Thanks to technological change and new business models, many more employment opportunities are emerging in the ICT sector of low-income countries. As part of their efforts to promote PSD, Governments should carefully consider how best to tap into the new opportunities presented, for example by social outsourcing, micro-work, and mobile-sector microenterprises. While the liberalization of ICT markets and increased competition have contributed to an expansion of this sector in most countries, faster ICT growth and employment creation can be facilitated through policy interventions aimed at:

(a) improving the availability of the skills needed in the ICT sector;

(b) stimulating ICT uptake among local firms, including MSEs;

(c) providing appropriate ICT infrastructure and regulatory frameworks that help create confidence among enterprises and consumers;

(d) promoting and clustering entrepreneurship and innovations through incubation and ICT parks; and

(e) using government procurement to create demand among local ICT enterprises.

Leveraging ICT use to make PSD interventions more effective

Make ICT use an integral part of business environment reforms. ICTs have been found to play a useful role in enhancing, extending, and contributing to the sustainability of business environment reforms. The core of this effort is around improving the governance of the economy, and the interactions between the Government and the private sector. Chapter IV showed how ICTs contribute to improving the legal and regulatory governance of the private sector, by simplifying and codifying rules and regulations, reducing compliance costs and promoting transparency. In order for the introduction of ICTs into business environment reforms to have the greatest impact, however, there is a need to shift from passive government information systems to more interactive ones. If ICTs are used simply to scan or digitize paper-based systems or to place basic information on the Internet, the beneficial effect may be minimal. Such approaches can be taken further by creating more interactive systems in which business owners and managers are enabled to use online facilities to register a business, file tax reports, and pay fees. When applied effectively, ICT-based solutions have led to major reductions in the time it takes to register a company or obtain a licence, and to increases in government revenue and greater transparency.

Examine the relationship between ICTs and enterprise formality. In many developing countries, informal-sector enterprises account for a very large part of the private-sector activity. Better regulations, and better access to regulations, can be effective ways of empowering informal-sector enterprises. Lowering the bar (making it easier, less costly and less time-consuming to register companies) may enhance the willingness of companies to formalize. However, there appears to be value in better understanding how informal enterprises can be made aware of the process and benefits of formalization – especially through ICTs that they are already using, such as mobile phones. Since ICTs have been able to connect formal and informal businesses to market opportunities, it should also be possible to use these technologies to connect them to government programmes and services.

Leverage ICTs in the delivery of business development services. Chapter IV showed how ICT use can extend the reach of business development services (BDS) to new and growing enterprises, partly by overcoming the "tyranny of distance", and by reducing the cost of service delivery. Some BDS providers have used the Internet to provide information and guidance to clients. However, few such initiatives have drawn on the potential of the Internet as a more dynamic and interactive mechanism for information, training and advisory services. Although innovative practices are more widespread in the agricultural sector, even in that sector there is still potential for further expansion in ICT use. Greater use of mobile phones by MSE owners

and smallholder farmers in developing economies offers scope for novel ways of providing BDS. While the use of mobile phones offers great scope for extending BDS to enterprises that are typically unaware of service providers, or are too far away from them, few conventional BDS providers have so far integrated the use of such technology into their programmes. At the same time, rather than opting for any single technical solution, BDS providers may leverage the power of using a combination of different ICT tools.

Leverage mobile money services to create more inclusive financial markets. Mobile money services hold great promise to enable cost reductions in the provision of financial services, especially to MSEs that are currently poorly catered for. In some developing countries, including LDCs, mobile money systems have quickly been embraced by small-scale business owners and managers as a more accessible, secure and affordable way of making financial transactions. However, there is a large untapped potential for mobile money services, and mobile provision of micro-finance and other financial services to be leveraged for PSD. The level of uptake and the impact on enterprises varies from country to country. In this context, attention should be paid to the extent to which various mobile money services – most of which were launched as person-to-person services – can be adapted to the situation and specific needs of MSEs. States and their central banks should take the opportunity to explore ways of absorbing these enterprises into the financial system through mobile transactions. Developing-country Governments (including in several LDCs) will be expected to pioneer new legislation and regulations to make sure that maximum gains for society are reaped from the use of mobile money. In order to capture the full potential in this area, dedicated research is needed to extract lessons from the early adopters. The international community should play an important role in supporting the development of sound regulatory frameworks and relevant institutions.

Recognize the gender dimension. To date, little programme or policy attention has been given in existing or new initiatives to the application of ICT tools to support women entrepreneurs. This is an untapped potential. While ICTs may do little to redress underlying societal structures that hamper opportunities for women entrepreneurs, they can contribute with regard to several practical gender-related issues. As stressed earlier, some barriers to enterprise growth and development are particularly pertinent to women entrepreneurs. Four specific challenges, which the use of ICTs can help to address to some extent, are (a) access to finance; (b) limited skills and training; (c) lack of time due to family commitments; and (d) limited physical mobility. ICTs should be used as an enabler to overcome these challenges and to enhance the effectiveness of existing initiatives. For example, organizations supporting women entrepreneurs should explore ICT-based solutions as an additional strategy, to complement face-to-face meetings for trade promotion. Moreover, lessons from the field highlight the need for training programmes to be developed that take into account the limited skills and training, and even the basic level of education, of most women who own MSEs. In addition, women entrepreneurs should be invited to participate at the content-development stage of relevant initiatives.

Overall recommendations

Reflect ICTs better in PSD strategies. To date, most national PSD strategies, as well as those developed by donor agencies, make relatively few references to the role of ICTs. While there is a general view that ICTs contribute to business productivity and competitiveness, the details on how this can be promoted are typically scant. PSD strategies should explicitly recognize that ICTs can contribute to the development of the private sector through interventions at micro, meso and macro levels. Interventions should also acknowledge the importance of a multi-level response to this topic and not treat ICTs in isolation, thus acknowledging the four ICT–PSD interfaces.

Develop guidelines for donors. In collaboration with UNCTAD and other relevant organizations, the Donor Committee for Enterprise Development could develop guidelines for donor and development agencies, and their programme partners (i.e. developing-country Governments and business membership organizations), on how to integrate the ICT dimension in future PSD strategies. Such guidelines would help to establish a bridge between the donor assistance which relates to PSD and that which relates to ICT for development.

Interventions need to be demand-driven. In order to enhance the likelihood that the spread of ICTs will contribute to the development of the private sector, the design and implementation of policies must be grounded in a solid understanding of the specific needs and situations of a range of different enterprises. In this context, attention should also be paid to MSEs, as these

face particular barriers and challenges. Moreover, as has been shown in earlier chapters, even within the group of MSEs, there are wide differences in needs and capabilities. Thus, the diversity of the private sector as well as that of ICTs must be carefully factored in when Governments, donors and other stakeholders develop policies, strategies and specific interventions aimed at leveraging ICTs for PSD. In this context, policymakers and practitioners should actively seek the input and engagement of enterprises in programme design and implementation. Their direct involvement brings relevant experience to the fore, and helps to focus interventions on outcomes that are of higher value to end-users.

Leverage partnerships. A more demand-driven approach to policy interventions adds importance to the development of effective partnerships between Governments, donors, the private sector and civil society. Lessons should be learned from the experience to date with regard to partnership implementation in the field of ICT for development. Five success factors have been identified for such partnerships (Geldof et al., 2011), namely (a) paying detailed attention to the local context and ensuring the involvement of the local community in the implementation; (b) setting clear and agreed development outcomes; (c) building sustainability and scalability into the design of the partnership; (d) creating a foundation of trust, honesty, openness, mutual understanding and respect; and (e) having a supportive wider ICT environment in place, both in terms of policy and infrastructure.

Devote adequate resources to measurement and impact assessment. An absence of systematic, evidence-based impact evaluation has been observed in current initiatives using ICTs to promote PSD. A lack of data and of resources to undertake rigorous assessments has led to excessive reliance on "success stories" and anecdotal evidence. There is a need to accelerate the production of reliable and internationally comparable statistics that examine ICT use by both enterprise and government. In this area, the international community can support the existing efforts being undertaken by the Partnership on Measuring ICT for Development. With a view to developing a richer base of knowledge, it can also finance more comprehensive project and policy evaluations based on empirical evidence conducted through independent research. Such initiatives are needed to provide a more realistic picture of possible impacts and to generate valuable knowledge for future policymaking and interventions.

REFERENCES

Adams RH (1998). Remittances, investment and rural asset accumulation in Pakistan. *Economic Development and Cultural Change*. 47:155–73.

ADB (2000). *Private Sector Development Strategy*. Manila.

ADB (2006). *Private Sector Development: A Revised Strategic Framework*. Manila.

AfDB (2008). Strategy update for the bank's private-sector operations. Prepared by the Infrastructure, Private Sector, Water and Regional Integration.

AfDB and World Bank (2011). *Leveraging Migration for Africa: Remittances, Skills, and Investments.* AfDB and the World Bank. Washington, D.C.

Aker J (2010). Dial "A" for agriculture: using information and communication technologies for agricultural extension in developing countries. Tufts University, Economics Department and the Fletcher School. Medford MA02155.

Alturki N and Braswell R (2010). Businesswomen in Saudi Arabia: Characteristics, challenges, and aspirations in a regional context. Available from www.monitor.com/Expertise/BusinessIssues/ EconomicDevelopmentandSecurity/tabid/69/ctl/ArticleDetail/mid/705/CID/20102207132025370/ CTID/1/L/en us/Default.aspx.

Analysys Mason (2010a). Assessment of economic impact of wireless broadband in India. Report for GSMA. November.

Analysys Mason (2010b). Assessment of economic impact of wireless broadband in South Africa. Report for GSMA. December.

Anderson G (2008). Integrating mass media in small enterprise development: Current knowledge and good practices. Employment Sector. Employment Working Paper No. 2. ILO. Geneva.

Anderson J and Kupp M (2008). Serving the poor: Drivers of business model innovation in mobile. *Info*. 10 (1):5–12.

Anderson J et al. (2010). The last frontier: market creation in conflict zones, deep rural areas and urban slums. *California Management Review*. 52(4):6–28.

Andersson T et al. (2004). *The Cluster Policies Whitebook*. Holmbergs i Malmö. Malmö, Sweden.

Bain R (2011). The power of text in the developing world. *Research*. Source: TxtEagle, 20 January 2011. Available from http://www.research-live.com/features/the-power-of-text-in-the-developing-world/4004395. article.

Banerjee A and Duflo E (2011). Poor economics: A radical rethinking of the way to fight global poverty. *Public Affairs*.

Bångens L and Söderberg B (2011). Mobile money transfers and usage among micro- and small businesses in Tanzania. Available from http://www.spidercenter.org/.

Barbarasa E (2010). *Catalyzing support for small and growing businesses in developing countries: Mapping the policies of international development donors & investors*. Aspen Network of Development Entrepreneurs. Washington, D.C.

Barendregt B (2008). Sex, cannibals, and the language of cool: Indonesian tales of the phone and modernity. *The Information Society*. 24(3):160–170.

Baumol WJ (2010). *The Micro Theory of Innovative Entrepreneurship*. Princeton University Press. Princeton.

Bayala S et al. (2010). Dynamiques et rôle économique et social du secteur informel des TIC au BF. Rapport de recherche RAP.R.TIC INFOR 3.1. Yam Pukri. Ouagadougou.

Beck T et al. (2002). Financing patterns around the world: The role of institutions. Policy Research Working Paper 2905. World Bank.Washington, D.C.

Bolton WK and Thompson JL (2000). *Entrepreneurs: Talent, Temperament, Technique.* Butterworth Heinemann. London.

Broadband Commission (2010). A 2010 leadership imperative: The future built on broadband. Available from http://www.broadbandcommission.org/outcomes.html.

Burrell J (2010). Evaluating shared access: Social equality and the circulation of mobile phones in rural Uganda. *Journal of Computer-Mediated Communication*. 15(2):230–250.

Busken I and Webb A (2009). *African Women & ICTs: Investigating Technology, Gender and Empowerment*. International Development Research Centre. Available from http://www.idrc.ca/openebooks/399-7/#page_133.

Bylund P (2005). International Desktop Study. SMEs and poverty reduction. An update for the Centre for Enterprise Development.

Calandro E et al. (2010). Comparative sector performance review 2009/2010: Towards evidence-based ICT policy and regulation. Volume two. Policy Paper 2. ResearchICTafrica.net.

Capsuto T (2011). Mobile payments: The devil is in the details. KIVA Blog. KIVA.

CGAP (2009a). Notes on branchless banking policy and regulation in Mexico. March.

CGAP (2009b). Poor people using mobile financial services: Observations on customer usage and impact from M-PESA. Available from http://www.cgap.org/gm/document-1.9.36723/BR_Poor_People_Using_Mobile_Financial_Services.pdf.

CGAP (2010). *Financial Access 2010: The State of Financial Inclusion Through the Crisis.* CGAP and the World Bank Group. Washington, D.C.

CGAP and Dalberg Global Development Advisers (2010). *Improving Access and Reducing Costs of International Remittances through Branchless Banking Solutions*. Available from http://www.cgap.org/gm/document-1.9.49049/Dalberg-CGAP_Intl_Remit_Branchless_Banking_Findings.pdf.

Chatain PL et al. (2011). *Protecting Mobile Money against Financial Crimes. Global Policy Challenges and Solutions.* World Bank. Washington, D.C.

Chawla D and Behl R (2006). Perception study of cybercafé users. *Global Business Review*. 7(1):17–41.

Chen M (2005). The business environment and the informal economy: Creating conditions for poverty reduction. International Conference on Reforming the Business Environment: From Assessing Problems to Measuring Results. Committee of Donor Agencies for Small Enterprise Development. Cairo.

Cherie Blair Foundation for Women (2011). Input to the Information Economy Report 2011. E-mail correspondence.

Chile Compra (2008). ChileCompra, the Public Procurement Bureau facilitates access to the public sector. Available from http://www.chilecompra.cl/english/whatischilecompra.html.

Chipchase J (2009). Mobile phone practices and the design of mobile money services for emerging markets. Available from http://www.janchipchase.com/publications.

Chipchase J and Tulusan I (2007). *Shared Phone Practices: Exploratory Field Research from Uganda and Beyond*. Available from http://janchipchase.com/content/presentations-and-downloads/shared-phone-practices/.

Committee of Donor Agencies for Small Enterprise Development (2001). *Business Development Services for Small Enterprises: Guiding Principles for Donor Intervention*. Washington, D.C.

Comisión Nacional Bancaria y de Valores (2010). Reporte de inclusión financiera. Junio 2010.

Commonwealth of Australia (2000). *Private Sector Development through Australia's Aid Programme*. Australian Agency for International Development. Canberra.

DCED (2008). *Supporting Business Environment Reforms: Practical Guidance for Development Agencies*. 2008 edition. DCED. Cambridge. Available from www.enterprise-development.org.

De Silva H and Ratnadiwakara D (2009). Using ICT to reduce transaction costs in agriculture through better communication: A case study from Sri Lanka. LIRNEasia. Colombo. Available from http://www.lirneasia.net.

Deloitte (2008). Economic impact of mobile communications in Serbia, Ukraine, Malaysia, Thailand, Bangladesh and Pakistan. Report for Telenor ASA. Available from www.telenor.rs/media/TelenorSrbija/fondacija/economic_impact_of _mobile_communications.pdf.

Deutsche Bank Research (2010). Enterprise 2.0: How companies are tapping the benefits of Web 2.0 – Digital economy and structural change. *Economics*. No. 78. 8 September. Available from www.dbresearch.com.

Devi P (2008). E-governance for small and medium enterprises in a developing country like Fiji: Potentials and problems. In: Bhattacharya J, ed. *Critical Thinking in e-Governance*. SIGeGOV. Available from http://www.csi-sigegov.org/critical.html.

Dias DB and D McKee (2010). Protecting branchless banking consumers: Policy objectives and regulatory options. Focus Note 64. CGAP. Washington, D.C.

Dittus P and Klein M (2011). On harnessing the potential of financial inclusion. BIS Working Paper No. 347. Bank for International Settlements, Monetary and Economic Department. Basel.

Donner J (2006). The use of mobile phones by microentrepreneurs in Kigali, Rwanda: Changes to social and business networks. *Information Technologies and International Development*. 3(2):3–19.

Donner J (2009). Mobile-based livelihood services in Africa: Pilots and early deployments. In: Fernández-Ardèvol M and Ros A, eds. *Communication Technologies in Latin America and Africa: A Multidisciplinary Perspective*. IN3:37–58. Barcelona.

Donner J and Escobari M (2009). A review of the research on mobile use by micro and small enterprises (MSEs). In: Heeks R and Tongia R, eds. *ICTD 2009 Proceedings*. Carnegie Mellon University:17–26. Doha.

DPI (2003). Report of the International Conference on Financing for Development. Monterrey.

Duncombe RA and Heeks RB (2002). Enterprise across the digital divide: information systems and rural micro-enterprise in Botswana. *Journal of International Development*. 14(1):61–74.

Duncombe RA and Molla A (2009). The formalisation of information systems in sub-Saharan African small and medium-sized enterprises. *African Journal of Information Systems*. 1(2):1–29.

Economist Intelligence Unit (2010). Women's economic opportunity: A new global index and ranking. Economist Intelligence Unit. Available from http://graphics.eiu.com/upload/WEO_report_June_2010.pdf.

El-Shenawy N (2011). *Statistical compilation of the ICT sector and policy analysis in Egypt*. Orbicom. Montreal.

Esim S (2001). *See how they grow: business development services for women's business growth*. International Center for Research on Women. Washington, D.C.

Esplen E and Brody A (2007). Putting gender back in the picture: rethinking women's economic empowerment. BRIDGE. Available from www.bridge.ids.ac.uk/reports/BB19_Economic_Empowerment.pdf.

Esselaar S et al. (2007). ICT usage and its impact on profitability of SMEs in 13 African countries. *Information Technologies and International Development*. 4(1):87–100.

Eurostat (2008). Final report – Information Society: ICT impact assessment by linking data from different sources. Eurostat. Luxembourg. Available from http://epp.eurostat.ec.europa.eu/portal/page/portal/information_society/documents/Tab/ICT_IMPACTS_FINAL_REPORT_V2.pdf.

Eurostat (2010). *Europe in Figures – Eurostat Yearbook 2010*. Available from http://epp.eurostat.ec.europa.eu/cache/ITY_OFFPUB/KS-CD-10-220/EN/KS-CD-10-220-EN.PDF.

Evans J (2011). TxtEagle raises $8.5 million to give 2.1 billion a voice. TechCrunch. 12 April.

Excelsior (2011). *Transforming the East African ICT Sector by Creating a Business Engine for SMEs*. InfoDev (World Bank), HIVOS, DFID. Washington, D.C.

Field RL (forthcoming). Development implications of mobile money. Forthcoming in: *The Lydian Journal*. Available from http://www.pymnts.com/Development-Implications-of-Mobile-Money/.

FATF (2011). *Anti-Money Laundering and Terrorist Financing Measures and Financial Inclusion*. FATF/OECD. Paris. Available from www.fatf-gafi.org/dataoecd/62/26/48300917.pdf.

FinScope (2006). *Pilot Study Survey Highlights Including BSM Model: FinScope Small Business™ Gauteng 2006*. FinMark Trust & Gauteng Enterprise Propeller. Johannesburg.

Fjeldsted K (2009). Trade reform gives Madagascar a competitive edge. In: *Celebrating Reform 2009*. World Bank. Washington, D.C. Available from www.doingbusiness.org/reforms/case-studies/2009/trade-reform-in-madagascar.

Foster C and Heeks R (2011). Employment and the mobile sector in developing countries. Paper prepared for UNCTAD (mimeo).

Fu X and Aktar S (2011). The impact of ICT on agricultural extension services delivery: evidence from the rural e-services project in India. QEH SLPTMD Working Paper. University of Oxford. Oxford.

G20 Financial Inclusion Experts Group (2010). *Innovative Financial Inclusion: Principles and Report on Innovative Financial Inclusion from the Access through Innovation Sub-Group of the G20 Financial Inclusion Experts Group*. 25 May. Available from www.ausaid.gov.au/publications/pdf/G20financialinclusion.pdf.

Galperin H and Bar F (2006). The Microtelco opportunity: Evidence from Latin America. *Information Technologies and International Development*. 3(2):73–86.

Gelb A et al. (2009). To formalize or not to formalize? Comparisons of micro-enterprise data from Southern and Eastern Africa. Working Paper No.175. Center for Global Development. Available from http://www.cgdev.org/content/publications/detail/1422458.

Geldof M et al. (2011). What are the key lessons of ICT4D partnerships for poverty reduction? Systematic Review Report for DFID.

Gereffi G (1999). International trade and industrial upgrading in the apparel commodity chain. *Journal of International Economics*. 48 (1):37–70.

Gerelle E and Berende M (2008). Technology for microinsurance: Scoping study. Microinsurance Paper No. 2. MicroInsurance Innovation Facility, ILO. Geneva.

Germany, BMZ and GIZ (2011). *The Transformative Role of Mobile Financial Services and the Role of the German Development Cooperation.* GIZ. Eschborn.

Gibson A (1997). Business development services core principles and future challenges. *Small Enterprise Development*. 8(3):4–14.

Gill K et al. (2010). *Bridging the Gender Divide: How Technology Can Advance Women Economically*. ICRW. Available from http://www.icrw.org/publications/bridging-gender-divide.

Giuliano P and Ruiz-Arranz M (2009). Remittances, financial development and growth. *Journal of Development Economics.* 90 (1):144–52.

Goodman J and Walia V (2006). *A Sense of Balance: A Socio-Economic Analysis of Airtime Transfer Service in Egypt*. Forum for the Future. London.

Granström SC (2009). *The Informal Sector and Formal Competitiveness in Senegal.* Lund University. Lund, Sweden. Available from http://www.nek.lu.se/Publ/mfs/194.pdf.

Griliches Z (1979). Issues in assessing the contribution of research and development to productivity growth. *The Bell Journal of Economics.* 10 (1): 92–116.

GSMA (2008). *Mobile Telephony Contribution to Latin America Caribbean Economies.*

GSMA (2009a). *Asia Pacific Mobile Observatory: The Parallel Development Paths of the Mobile Industry in Asia Pacific.*

GSMA (2009b). *Taxation and the Growth of Mobile in East Africa*.

GSMA and the Cherie Blair Foundation (2010). *Women & Mobile: A Global Opportunity.* Available from http://www.mwomen.org/Files/9479a302.

GTZ (2008). *The Social and Ecological Market Economy – A Model for Asian Development?* Sustainable Economic Development Sector Network. Asia Division 41. Economic Development and Employment. GTZ. Eschborn.

GTZ (2010). *Women's Economic Opportunities in the Formal Private Sector in Latin America and the Caribbean: A Focus on Entrepreneurship*. GTZ. Eschborn. Available from http://idbdocs.iadb.org/wsdocs/getdocument.aspx?docnum=35278574.

Hacibeyoglu C (2009). Azerbaijan: How to create a world-class taxation system from scratch. In: *Celebrating Reform 2009*. World Bank. Washington, D.C. Available from http://www.doingbusiness.org/reforms/case-studies/2009/tax-reform-in-azerbaijan.

Heeks RB and Arun S (2010). Social outsourcing as a development tool: the impact of outsourcing IT services to women's social enterprises in Kerala. *Journal of International Development*. 22:441–454.

Hellström J (2010). The innovative use of mobile applications in East Africa. *Sida Review 2010*:12. Swedish International Development Cooperation Agency. Stockholm.

Humphrey J (2003). Globalization and supply chain networks: the auto industry in Brazil and India. *Global Networks.* 3(2):121–141.

IADB (2011a). Private sector development strategy profile. Washington, D.C. Available from http://idbdocs. iadb.org/wsdocs/getdocument.aspx?docnum=35573660.

IADB (2011b). *Development Connections: Unveiling the Impact of New Information Technologies.* IADB. Washington, D.C.

IADB, Inter-American Investment Corporation & Multilateral Investment Fund (2004). Private sector development strategy. IADB. Washington, D.C.

IFC (2007a). *Designing a Tax System for Micro and Small Businesses: Guide for Practitioners.* World Bank Group. Washington, D.C.

IFC (2007b). *Voices of Women Entrepreneurs – Ghana.* World Bank Group, Washington, D.C. Available from www.ifc.org/ifcext/sustainability.nsf/Content/Publications_Report_VoicesWomen-Ghana.

IFC (2007c). *Reforming the Regulatory Procedures for Import and Export: Guide for Practitioners.* World Bank Group. Washington, D.C.

IFC (2007d). *Creating Opportunities for Small Business.* World Bank Group. Washington, D.C.

IFC (2010). *Economic Opportunities for Women in the Pacific.* Available from www.ifc.org/ifcext/sustainability. nsf/Content/Publications_Report_EconOpWomenPacific.

IFC (2011). IFC's women in business program. Available from http://www.ifc.org/ifcext/sustainability.nsf/ Content/WomeninBusiness.

Ilavarasan P and Levy M (2010). *ICTs and Urban Microenterprises: Identifying and Maximizing Opportunities for Economic Development.* International Development Research Centre. Available from http://www.idrc. ca/uploads/user-S/12802403661ICTs_and_Urban_Microenterprises_104170-001.pdf.

ILO (2007). The promotion of sustainable enterprises. International Labour Conference, Ninety-sixth session, 2007, Report VI. ILO. Geneva.

ILO (2008a). WED: ILO strategy on promoting women's entrepreneurship development. Available from http://www.enterprise-development.org/page/library-item?id=1477.

ILO (2008b). *Women Entrepreneurs in Kenya (A Preliminary Report) & Factors Affecting Women Entrepreneurs in Micro and Small Enterprises in Kenya (A Primary Research Report).* Available from http://www.ilo.org/ empent/Publications/WCMS_107507/lang--en/index.htm.

Infocomm Development Authority (2010). *Realizing the iN2015 Vision: Singapore: An Intelligent Nation, A Global City, Powered by Infocomm.* Available from http://www.ida.gov.sg/images/content/About%20us/ About_Us_level1/_iN2015/pdf/realisingthevisionin2015.pdf.

Instituto Nacional de Estadística e Informática (INEI) (2009). *Encuesta Nacional de Hogares.* INEI. Lima.

Iskenderian M (2011). Banking on women and girls: Key to global poverty alleviation. The conversation blogs, Harvard Business Review. Available from http://blogs.hbr.org/cs/2011/03/banking_on_women_and_girls_key.html.

ITU (2010). *The World in 2010: ICT Facts and Figures.* Available from www.itu.int/ITU-D/ict/material/ FactsFigures2010.pdf.

Japan International Cooperation Agency (undated). *Effective Approaches to the Promotion of Small and Medium Enterprises (SMEs).* Available from www.jica.go.jp/english/publications/reports/study/topical/spd/ pdf/chapter3.pdf.

Junqueira Botelho A and da Silva Alves A (2007). Mobile use/adoption by micro, small and medium enterprises in Latin America and the Caribbean. Background paper. DIRSI (Regional Dialogue on the Information Society). Lima.

Kantor P (2001). Promoting women's entrepreneurship development based on good practice programmes: some experiences from the North to the South. Series on Women's Entrepreneurship Development and Gender in Enterprises – WEDGE. SEED Working Paper No. 9. Geneva.

Kaplinsky R and Morris M (2001). *Handbook on Value Chain Research.* International Development Research Centre. Ottawa. Available from http://www.seepnetwork.org/Resources/2303_file_Handbook_for_Value_ Chain_Research.pdf.

Klapper L and Love I (2011). Entrepreneurship and the financial crisis: An overview of the 2010 Entrepreneurship Snapshots (WBGES).World Bank Group presentation.

Kleine D (2011). "The men never say that they do not know": Telecentres as gendered spaces. In: Steyn J et al., eds. *ICTs for Global Development and Sustainability: Practice and Applications.* Volume 2. IGI Global. New York.

Kumar K et al. (2010). Microfinance and mobile banking: The story so far. Focus Note No. 62. CGAP. Washington, D.C.

Lederman D (2009). Product innovation: The roles of research and development expenditures and the investment climate. In: Fajnyzylber P et al., eds. *Does the Investment Climate Matter? Microeconomic Foundations of Growth in Latin America.* World Bank. Washington, D.C.

Levy M et al. (2010). The economic impact of information and communication technologies (ICTs) on microenterprises in the context of development. ICA Annual Meeting, Singapore, International Communication Association. Unpublished.

Little AD (2010). M-Payments in M-BRIC: How to best leverage the upcoming opportunity. *Telecom & Media Viewpoint.* Available from www.adl.com/m-payments.

Malik P and Mundhe R (2011). *Statistical Compilation of the ICT Sector and Policy Analysis in India.* Orbicom. Montreal.

McCormick D (1999). African enterprise clusters and industrialisation: Theory and reality. *World Development.* 27(9):1531–1551.

McCormick B and Wahba J (2001). Overseas work experience, savings and entrepreneurship amongst return migrants to LDCs. *Scottish Journal of Political Economy.* 48 (2):164–78.

McCormick B and Wahba J (2003). Return international migration and geographical inequality: The case of Egypt. *Journal of African Economies.* 12 (4):500–32.

McKay C and Pickens M (2010). Branchless banking 2010: Who's served? At what price? What's next? Focus Note No. 66. CGAP. Washington, D.C.

Menon R (2011). The emerging world's five most crucial words: "To move money, press pound". In: Dutta S and Mia I, eds. *The Global Information Technology Report 2010–2011: Transformations 2.0.* World Economic Forum. Geneva.

Mexico, Ministry of Finance (2011). Financial inclusion: Mexico experience. Slide presentation, January. Mimeo.

MFA (2008). *Finland's Aid for Trade Action Plan (2008–2011).* Erweko. Helsinki.

Microfund for Women (2011). Microfund for women celebrates one year of helping families to manage risk. Available from http://www.microfund.org.jo/PublicNews/Nws_NewsDetails.aspx?lang=2&site_id=1&page_id=107&NewsID=514&Type=P&M=8.

Miehlbradt AO (1999). How to be demand-led: Lessons for business development service providers from information and communication services in the Philippines. Paper presented at International Conference on Building a Modern Effective Development Services Industry for Small Enterprises, Rio De Janerio, 2–3 March. Committee of Donor Agencies for Small Enterprise Development.

Ministerio de Asuntos Exteriores y de Cooperación (2005). *Plan Director de la Cooperación Española 2005–2008.* Spain. Available from http://www.aecid.pe/publicaciones/store/pub.6.pdf.

Ministry of Foreign Affairs, Netherlands (2007). Private-sector development: Market access and market development. Sustainable Economic Development Department (DDE) Working Paper. Ministry of Foreign Affairs, Netherlands (mimeo).

Mitrovic Z and Bytheway A (2011). Servicing advocacy in e-government: Small business development services in Cape Town. *The African Journal of Information and Communication.* 11:40–54.

Mohini M et al. (2006). *Expanding Access to Finance: Good Practices and Policies for Micro, Small, and Medium Enterprises.* World Bank. Washington, D.C.

Molony T (2007). "I don't trust the phone; it always lies": Trust and information and communication technologies in Tanzanian micro- and small enterprises. *Information Technologies and International Development.* 3(4):67–83. Available from http://itidjournal.org/itid/article/view/238.

Molyneux M (1985). Mobilization without emancipation? Women's interests, the State, and revolution in Nicaragua. *Feminist Studies.* 11:2(1985:summer).

Moyi ED (2003). Networks, information and small enterprises: new technologies and the ambiguity of empowerment. *Information Technology for Development*. 10(4):221–232.

M-PESA (2010). M-PESA key performance statistics. Safaricom. Nairobi.

Munyua A and Mureithi M (2008). Harnessing the power of the cell phone by women entrepreneurs: New frontiers in the gender equation in Kenya. GRACE project research report. Available from http://www.grace-network.net/docs/Research%20Reports/KENYA%20Research%20Report%20-%20AW-MM.pdf.

Murphy JT (2002). Networks, trust and innovation in Tanzania's manufacturing sector. *World Development*. 30 (4)591–619.

Naituli G et al. (2008). Entrepreneurial characteristics among micro and small-scale women owned enterprises in North and Central Meru districts, Kenya. Growing Inclusive Markets Conference. Available from http://cases.growinginclusivemarkets.org/documents/217.

Ndiaye SM et al. (2009). Etat des lieux du secteur informel des TIC au Sénégal. Recherches sur les dynamiques et rôles économiques et sociales du secteur informel des TIC, TIC INFOR AFRIQ. Yam Pukri. Ouagadougou.

NZAID (2008). *Economic Growth and Livelihoods.* NZAID. Wellington.

Nguyen T (2011). Newton International Postdoctoral Fellowship fieldwork finding summary. Royal Holloway, University of London. Unpublished.

Nzépa ON et al. (2011). *Statistical Compilation of the ICT Sector and Policy Analysis in Cameroon*. Orbicom. Montreal.

OECD (1995) *Support of Private Sector Development*. OECD. Paris.

OECD (2002). Reviewing the ICT sector definition: Issues for discussion. Working Party on Indicators for the Information Society. DSTI/ICCP/IIS(2002)2. April. OECD. Paris.

OECD (2004). *The Economic Impact of ICT: Measurement, Evidence and Implications*. OECD. Paris. Available from http://browse.oecdbookshop.org/oecd/pdfs/free/9204051e.pdf.

OECD (2005). *Mobilising Private Investment for Development: Policy Lessons on the Role of ODA*. OECD. Paris.

OECD (2006a). *Promoting Pro-Poor Growth: Private Sector Development.* OECD. Paris. Available from www.oecd.org/dataoecd/43/63/36427804.pdf.

OECD (2006b). Enhancing women's market access and promoting pro-poor growth. In: *Promoting Pro-Poor Growth: Private Sector Development*. OECD. Paris. Available from www.oecd.org/dataoecd/43/63/36427804.pdf.

OECD (2007). Information Economy – Sector definitions based on the International Standards Industry Classification (ISIC 4). Working Party on Indicators for the Information Society. DSTI/ICCP/IIS(2006)2. March. OECD. Paris.

OECD (2009). *Is Informal Normal? Towards More and Better Jobs in Developing Countries*. OECD. Paris.

OECD (2010). Consumer protection in online and mobile payments draft report. DSTI/CCP(2010)22/Rev2. OECD. Paris.

Okello D (2010). E-agriculture for rural women farmers: The WOUGNET experience. Available from http://www.e-agriculture.org/en/blog/e-agriculture-rural-women-farmers-wougnet-experience.

Okello J (forthcoming). ICT-based market information services (MIS) projects, deployment environment and performance: Experiences from KACE and DrumNet projects in Kenya. Forthcoming in: Maumbe B and Patrikakis C, eds. *E-agricuture and Rural Development: Global Innovations and Future Prospects*. IGI Global. New York.

Okello J et al. (2010). Using ICT to integrate smallholder farmers into agricultural value chain: The case of DrumNet project in Kenya. *International Journal of ICT and Research Development*. 1:23–37.

Ovum (2006). *The Economic and Social Benefits of Mobile Services in Bangladesh*. GSMA. London. Available from http://www.dirsi.net/english/files/Ovum%20Bangladesh%20Main%20report1f.pdf.

Oyelaran-Oyeyinka B (2007). Learning in local systems and global links: The Otigba computer hardware cluster in Nigeria. In: Oyelaran-Oyeyinka B and McCormick D, eds. *Industrial Clusters and Innovation Systems in Africa*. United Nations University Press. Tokyo.

Parikh TS et al. (2007). *A Survey of Information Systems Reaching Small Producers in Global Agricultural Value Chains*. School of Information, University of California, Berkley. Available from http://www.stanford.edu/~neilp/pubs/ictd2007.pdf.

Point Topic (2010). World broadband statistics: Short report. Available from http://point-topic.com/dslanalysis.php.

Porcaro RM and Jorge MF (2011). *Statistical Compilation of the ICT Sector and Policy Analysis in Brazil.* Orbicom. Montreal.

Porter ME (1985). *Competitive Advantage: Creating and Sustaining Superior Performance*. Free Press. New York.

Qiang CZW et al. (2006). The role of ICT in doing business. In: *2006 Information and Communications for Development: Global Trends and Policies*. World Bank. Washington, D.C.

Radloff J et al. (2010). *GenARDIS 2002 – 2010: Small Grants that Made Big Changes for Women in Agriculture*. Available from http://www.comminit.com/en/node/330274/38.

Rangaswamy N (2007). ICT for development and commerce: A case study of Internet cafes in India. Available from www.ifipwg94.org.br/fullpapers/R0071-1.pdf .

Rangaswamy N (2009a). ICT for mesh-economy: Case-study of an urban slum. Paper presented at IFIP 2009, Dubai, 26 May. Available from https://research.microsoft.com/en-us/people/nimmir/ifip2009.doc.

Rangaswamy N (2009b). Keywords in communication: Mesh-economy and business channels in an Indian urban slum. Paper presented at ICA 2009, Pre-Conference on India and Communication Studies, Chicago, 21 May. Available from http://research.microsoft.com/en-us/people/nimmir/pre-confica2009.doc.

Ramasamy R and Ponnudurai V (2011). *Statistical Compilation of the ICT Sector and Policy Analysis in Malaysia*. Orbicom. Montreal.

Republic of Ghana (2003). *The Ghana ICT for Accelerated Development (ICT4AD) Policy*. Available from http://img.modernghana.com/images/content/report_content/ICTAD.pdf.

Republic of Korea, Bank of Korea (2006). *Current State and the Way Forward of Knowledge-Based Service Industry in ROK*. Bank of Korea. Seoul.

Research ICT Africa (2006). *SME e-Access and Usage Across 14 African Countries*. Available from www.researchictafrica.net/publications/Research_ICT_Africa_e-Index_Series/SME%20e-Access%20 and%20Usage%20in%2014%20African%20Countries.pdf.

Research ICT Africa (2010). *Comparative Sector performance Review 2009–2010: Towards Evidence-Based ICT Policy and Regulation.* Volume 2, Paper 5. International Development Research Centre.

Richardson D (2003). Agricultural extension transforming ICT: Championing universal access. Paper presented at the ICTs Conference on Transforming Agricultural Extension by CTA. Wageningen, Netherlands.

Sagun R (2011). Case note on ICT for development project: E-governance for municipal development in the Philippines. Available from http://unpan1.un.org/intradoc/groups/public/documents/un-dpadm/unpan037088.pdf.

Schiffer M and Weder B (2001). Firm size and the business environment: Worldwide survey results. Discussion Paper 43. World Bank and IFC. Washington, D.C.

SEWA (2011). Communication for the Information Economy Report 2011. Mimeo.

Sievers M and Vandenburg P (2004). Synergies through linkages: Who benefits from linking finance and business development services? SEED Working Paper No. 64 ILO. Geneva.

Sivapragasam N (2009). The future of the public phone: Findings from a six-country Asian study of telecom use at the BoP. Paper presented at the 4th Communication Policy Research, South Conference, Negombo, Sri Lanka, 7 December. Available from http://papers.ssrn.com/sol3/papers.cfm?abstract_id=1554187.

Souter D et al. (2005). *The Economic Impact of Telecommunications on Rural Livelihoods and Poverty Reduction*. CTO for the United Kingdom Department for International Development. Available from http://www.telafrica.org/R8347/files/pdfs/FinalReport.pdf.

Statistics South Africa (2010). *Survey of Employers and the Self-employed*. Quarter 3, 2009. Available from www.statssa.gov.za.

Stevenson L and St-Onge A (2005). *Support for Growth-oriented Women Entrepreneurs in Tanzania.* ILO. Geneva. Available from www.afdb.org/fileadmin/uploads/afdb/Documents/Policy-Documents/GOWE%20 Tanzania.pdf.

Swiss Agency for Development and Cooperation (2007). Deepening participation and improving aid effectiveness through media and ICTs: A practical manual translating lessons learned into daily practice. Working paper.

Tarazi M and Breloff P (2010). Nonbank e-money issuers: Regulatory approaches to protecting customer funds. Focus Note 63. CGAP. Washington, D.C.

Tarazi M and Breloff P (2011). Regulating banking agents. Focus Note 68. CGAP. Washington, D.C.

TeleGeography (2010). Global Internet geography. Available from http://www.telegeography.com/research-services/global-internet-geography/.

UCC (2007). A review of the postal and telecommunications sector. Presentation, 15 August, Kampala. Available from http://www.ucc.co.ug/reviewofCommunicationSector.pdf [Accessed 18 December 2010].

UNDESA (2010). *The World's Women 2010: Trends and Statistics.* United Nations publication. Sales No. E.10. XVII.11. New York. Available from http://unstats.un.org/unsd/demographic/products/Worldswomen/WW_full%20report_color.pdf.

UNCITRAL (2011). Present and possible future work on electronic commerce. UNCITRAL. A/CN.9/728. 21 March.

UNCTAD (2005a). *Information Economy Report 2005: E-Commerce and Development.* United Nations publication. Sales No. E.05.II.D.19. New York and Geneva.

UNCTAD (2005b). *Improving the Competitiveness of SMEs through Enhancing Productive Capacity: *Proceedings of Four Expert Meetings.* UNCTAD/ITE/TEB/2005/. United Nations. New York and Geneva.

UNCTAD (2006a). *Information Economy Report 2006: The Development Perspective.* United Nations publication. Sales No. E.06.II.D.8. New York and Geneva.

UNCTAD (2006b). *Least Developed Countries Report 2006.* United Nations publication. Sales No. E.06.II.D.9. New York and Geneva.

UNCTAD (2007). *Enhancing the Participation of Developing Countries' SME s in Global Value Chains.* United Nations publication. TD /B/COM.3/EM.31/2. New York and Geneva.

UNCTAD (2008). *Measuring the Impact of ICT Use in Business: The Case of Manufacturing in Thailand.* United Nations publication. Sales no. E.08.II.D.13. New York and Geneva. Available from http://new.unctad.org/Documents/Thai_report_w_cover.pdf.

UNCTAD (2009a). *Information Economy Report 2009: Trends and Outlook in Turbulent Times.* United Nations publication. Sales No. E.09.II.D.18. New York and Geneva.

UNCTAD (2009b). *Study on Prospects for Harmonizing Cyberlegislation in Latin America.* United Nations publication. UNCTAD/DTL/STICT/2009/1. New York and Geneva. In English and Spanish.

UNCTAD (2009c). *Estudio sobre las perspectivas de la harmonización de la ciberlegislación en Centroamérica y el Caribe.* United Nations publication. UNCTAD/DTL/STICT/2009/3. New York and Geneva.

UNCTAD (2010). *Information Economy Report 2010: ICTs, Enterprises and Poverty Alleviation.* United Nations publication. Sales No. E.10.II.D.17. New York and Geneva.

UNCTAD (2011a). *Measuring the Impacts of Information and Communication Technology for Development.* United Nations publication. UNCTAD/DTL/STICT/2011/1. New York and Geneva.

UNCTAD (2011b). *Science, Technology and Innovation Policy Review of Peru.* United Nations publication. UNCTAD/DTL/STICT/2010/2. New York and Geneva.

UNCTAD (2011c). *ICT Policy Review of Egypt.* United Nations publication. New York and Geneva.

UNCTAD (forthcoming). *Applying a Gender Lens to Science, Technology and Innovation* United Nations publication. New York and Geneva.

UNDESA (2010). *United Nations E-Government Survey 2010.* Available from http://www2.unpan.org/egovkb/documents/2010/E_Gov_2010_Complete.pdf.

UNDP (2004). *Unleashing Entrepreneurship: Making Business Work for the Poor.* UNDP. New York.

UNDP (2007). The role of governments in promoting ICT access and use by SMEs, considerations for public policy. APDIP e-Note 12 / 2007. Available from http://www.apdip.net/apdipenote/12.pdf/.

UNDP (2008a). *UNDP and the Private Sector. Fast Facts.* May. UNDP. New York.

UNDP (2008b). *Innovative Approaches to Promoting Women's Economic Empowerment.* Available from http://content.undp.org/go/cms-service/stream/asset/?asset_id=2524504.

UNECA (2009). Enhancing the private sector role and participation in key strategic sectors in Africa. ECA/GPAD/CGPP.1/09/4.

UNECLAC (2010). *ICT for Growth and Equality: Renewing Strategies for the Information Society.* Third Ministerial Conference on the Information Society in Latin America and the Caribbean Lima, 21–23 November, 2010. United Nations. Santiago.

UNESCAP (2005). *Developing Women Entrepreneurs in South Asia: Issues, Initiatives and Experiences.* Available from http://www.unescap.org/tid/publication/indpub2401.pdf.

UNIDO (2009). Programme and Budgets, 2010–2011: Proposals of the Director-General. IDB.36/7–PBC.25/7. 24 March.

United Nations Millennium Project (2005). *Investing in Development. A Practical Plan to Achieve the Millennium Development Goals.* Available from http://www.unmillenniumproject.org/reports/fullreport.htm.

Voice on the Net Coalition (2010). Letter to the Office of the United States Trade Representative. 17 December. Available from www.von.org/filings/year/02_2010/2010_12_17_VON_USTR_Comments.pdf.

Woodruff C and Zenteno R (2001). Remittances and microenterprises in Mexico. Graduate School of International Relations and Pacific Studies Working Paper. University of California San Diego.

World Bank (2003). *Doing Business in 2004: Understanding Regulation.* World Bank, IFC and Oxford University Press. Washington, D.C.

World Bank (2004). *World Development Report: A Better Investment Climate for Everyone.* World Bank. Washington, D.C.

World Bank (2006). *2006 Information and Communications for Development: Global Trends and Policies.* World Bank. Washington, D.C.

World Bank (2009a). *Information and Communication for Development: Extending Reach and Increasing Impact.* World Bank. Washington, D.C.

World Bank (2009b). Information and communication technologies for women's socio-economic empowerment. World Bank Group Working Paper Series. Available from http://siteresources.worldbank. org/EXTINFORMATIONANDCOMMUNICATIONANDTECHNOLOGIES/Resources/2828221208273252769/ ICTs_for_Womens_Socio_Economic_Empowerment.pdf.

World Bank (2010a). *Doing Business 2011: Making a Difference for Entrepreneurs.* World Bank. Washington, D.C.

World Bank (2010b). Kenya economic update. No. 3. December 2010. Available from http://go.worldbank.org/ S743MCDPM0.

World Bank (2011). *Knowledge Map of the Virtual Economy: Converting the Virtual Economy into Development Potential.* World Bank. Washington, D.C.

World Bank (undated). Gender, ICT and entrepreneurship. Available from http://go.worldbank.org/X8T0NPX820.

WTO (2010). *International Trade Statistics 2010.* WTO. Geneva.

Yam Pukri (2010). Dynamiques et rôles économiques et social du secteur informel des TIC en Afrique de l'Ouest et du Centre: Cas du Burkina Faso, du Cameroun et du Sénégal. Rapport final de recherche. September (www.yam-pukri.org).

Yang D (2008). International migration, remittances and household investment: Evidence from Philippine migrants' exchange rate shocks. *Economic Journal.* 118 (528):591–630.

Zain (2009). Economic impact of mobile communications in Sudan. Briefing paper for Ericsson. Available from www.ericsson.com/res/thecompany/docs/sudan_economic_report.pdf.

Zurich Financial Services Group (2011). *Insurance & Technology to Better Serve Emerging Consumers: Learning to Improve Access & Service* available from http://zdownload.zurich.com/main/Insight/ Insurance_and_Technology.pdf.

STATISTICAL ANNEX

Annex table I.1. Donor strategy documents reviewed

PSD documents from multilateral development agencies

Type of agency	Agency	Year of document	Title of document
Multilateral	IFC	2007	Creating Opportunities for Small Business
Multilateral	ILO	2007	The Promotion of Sustainable Enterprises
Multilateral	Inter-American Development Bank	2004	Private Sector Development Strategy
			(The new draft PSD strategy was also considered)
Multilateral	OECD	2006	Promoting Pro-Poor Growth: Private Sector Development
Multilateral	UNDP	2008	UNDP and the Private Sector, Factsheet "Fast Facts"
			(Other UNDP documents reviewed were The MDGs: Everyone's Business; How inclusive business models contribute to development and who supports them; Business and Poverty: Opening Markets to the Poor; Smart Communications: Low-cost Money Transfers for Overseas Filipino Workers; The Role of the Information and Communications Technology Sector in Expanding Economic Opportunity)
Multilateral	UNIDO	2009	Programme and Budgets, 2010–2011, IDB.36/7–PBC.25/7
Multilateral	Asian Development Bank	2006	Private Sector Development: A Revised Strategic Framework
Multilateral	African Development Bank	2000	Strategy Update for the Bank's Private Sector Operations

PSD documents from bilateral development agencies

Country	Agency	Year of document	Title of document
Canada	Canadian International Development Agency	2010	Stimulating Sustainable Economic Growth: CIDA's Sustainable Economic Growth Strategy
Australia	Ausaid	2000	Private Sector Development through Australia's Aid Programme
Denmark	Danida	2011	Strategisk Ramme for Prioritetsområdet Vaekst & Beskaftigelse 2011–2015
Finland	Ministry of Foreign Affairs	2008	Aid for Trade Action Plan 2008–2011
Germany	GTZ	2008	The Social and Ecological Market Economy – A Model for Asian Development?
Netherlands	Ministry of Foreign Affairs	2007–2008	Results in Development: Report 2007–2008
Netherlands	Ministry of Foreign Affairs	2007	Economic Growth and Livelihoods: Towards a Safe and Just World
Netherlands	Ministry of Foreign Affairs	2007	Private Sector Development: Market Access and Market Development
Netherlands	Ministry of Foreign Affairs	2007	Private Sector Development: Legal and Regulatory Framework
Netherlands	Ministry of Foreign Affairs	2007	Private Sector Development: The Key to Economic Growth
Netherlands	Ministry of Foreign Affairs	2007	Private Sector Development: Infrastructure
New Zealand	NZAID	2008	Economic Growth and Livelihoods
Norway/WB	Norwegian Trust Fund for Private Sector and Infrastructure	2009	Annual Report 2009
Spain	Ministry of Foreign Affairs	2005–2008	Sector Strategy Document: Promoting the Economy and Enterprise
Spain	Ministry of Foreign Affairs	2009–2010	Plan Director de la Cooperación Española 2009–2012
Sweden	Ministry of Foreign Affairs	2010	Policy för ekonomisk tillväxt inom svenskt utvecklingssamarbete 2010–2014
Switzerland	Swiss Agency for Development and Cooperation	2007	Deepening Participation and Improving Aid Effectiveness through Media and ICTs: A Practical Manual Translating Lessons Learned into Daily Practice
United States	USAID	2008	Securing the Future: a Strategy For Economic Growth
United States	USAID	2008	Microenterprise Results Reporting
Japan	Japan International Cooperation Agency	Undated	Effective Approaches on the Promotion of Small and Medium Enterprises (SMEs)
Japan	Japan International Cooperation Agency	Undated	Approaches for Systematic Planning of Development Projects / Trade and Investment Promotion

Annex table II.1. Penetration of selected ICTs, 2005 and 2010 or latest year (per 100 inhabitants)

	Fixed telephone lines		Mobile cellular telephone subscriptions		Internet users		Fixed broadband Internet subscriptions	
	2005	2010	2005	2010	2005	2010	2005	2010
Developed economies								
Americas								
Bermuda	81.82	89.00	82.21	135.82	65.45	84.21	28.83	61.75
Canada	56.21	50.04	52.71	70.66	71.66	81.60	21.70	29.81
United States	59.01	48.70	68.63	89.86	67.97	79.00	17.23	26.34
Asia								
Israel	44.46	44.16	117.45	133.11	25.19	67.20	18.62	25.14
Japan	45.93	31.94	76.34	95.39	66.92	80.00	18.44	26.91
Europe								
Andorra	45.51	44.98	82.89	77.18	37.61	81.00	13.28	28.87
Austria	45.42	38.66	105.26	145.84	58.00	72.70	14.26	23.85
Belgium	46.04	43.31	92.23	113.46	59.81	79.26	19.31	31.49
Bulgaria	32.17	29.36	80.69	141.23	19.97	46.23	2.14	14.70
Cyprus	40.68	37.58	75.78	93.70	32.81	52.99	3.09	17.62
Czech Republic	31.48	20.95	115.22	136.58	35.27	68.82	6.94	14.66
Denmark	61.78	47.26	100.55	124.41	82.74	88.72	24.80	37.38
Estonia	32.84	35.96	107.39	123.24	61.45	74.10	13.31	24.34
Faroe Islands	49.37	41.42	87.10	122.05	67.90	75.10	12.16	33.40
Finland	40.42	23.30	100.49	156.40	74.48	86.89	22.39	29.07
France	55.26	56.06	78.84	99.70	42.87	80.10	15.53	33.92
Germany	66.38	55.41	96.04	127.04	68.71	81.85	13.07	31.59
Gibraltar [a]	85.98	82.07	68.79	102.59	39.07	65.07	..	31.80
Greece	56.44	45.81	91.75	108.22	24.00	44.40	1.43	19.83
Greenland	56.22	38.09	81.27	100.09	57.70	63.00	12.46	20.96
Hungary	33.86	29.82	92.40	120.32	38.97	65.27	6.46	19.59
Iceland	65.33	63.72	95.41	108.72	87.00	95.00	26.29	34.65
Ireland	49.35	46.49	102.69	105.18	41.61	69.85	7.76	22.82
Italy	42.69	35.67	121.87	135.42	35.00	53.68	11.63	22.13
Latvia	31.71	23.63	81.18	102.40	46.00	68.42	2.64	19.31
Liechtenstein	57.67	54.40	79.27	98.52	63.37	80.00	24.84	63.83
Lithuania	23.45	22.08	127.45	147.16	36.22	62.12	6.85	20.58
Luxembourg	53.48	53.68	111.55	143.27	70.00	90.62	15.33	32.83
Malta	49.38	59.38	79.16	109.34	41.24	63.00	12.56	27.54
Netherlands	46.61	43.15	97.11	116.23	81.00	90.72	25.14	37.97
Norway	45.61	34.85	102.84	113.15	81.99	93.39	21.44	34.60
Poland	31.01	24.69	76.42	120.18	38.81	62.32	2.48	13.18
Portugal	40.15	42.01	108.57	142.33	34.99	51.10	11.05	19.44
Romania	20.13	20.94	61.34	114.68	21.50	39.93	1.73	13.96
San Marino [a]	68.81	68.81	56.60	76.11	50.26	54.21	4.03	32.03
Slovakia	22.10	20.12	83.84	108.47	55.19	79.42	3.35	16.06
Slovenia	40.78	45.01	87.87	104.55	46.81	70.00	9.82	24.39
Spain	44.85	43.20	98.38	111.75	47.88	66.53	11.60	22.96
Sweden	62.41	53.46	100.83	113.54	84.83	90.00	27.93	31.59

	Fixed telephone lines		Mobile cellular telephone subscriptions		Internet users		Fixed broadband Internet subscriptions	
	2005	2010	2005	2010	2005	2010	2005	2010
Switzerland	69.45	58.56	92.17	123.62	70.10	83.90	22.51	38.16
United Kingdom	56.59	53.71	108.75	130.25	70.00	85.00	16.44	31.38
Oceania								
Australia	49.60	38.89	90.28	101.04	63.00	76.00	9.88	23.19
New Zealand	41.82	42.81	85.39	114.92	62.72	83.00	7.76	24.93
Developing economies								
Africa								
Algeria	7.82	8.24	41.54	92.42	5.84	12.50	0.41	2.54
Angola	0.59	1.59	9.77	46.69	1.14	10.00	0.00	0.10
Benin	1.00	1.51	7.81	79.94	1.27	3.13	0.00	0.29
Botswana	7.28	6.85	30.06	117.76	3.26	6.00	0.09	0.60
Burkina Faso	0.64	0.87	4.46	34.66	0.47	1.40	0.00	0.08
Burundi	0.43	0.39	2.11	13.72	0.54	2.10	0.00	0.00
Cameroon	0.57	2.53	12.83	41.61	1.40	4.00	0.00	0.01
Cape Verde	15.14	14.51	17.28	74.97	6.07	30.00	0.20	3.04
Central African Republic	0.25	0.27	2.49	23.18	0.27	2.30	0.00	..
Chad	0.13	0.46	2.15	23.29	0.40	1.70	0.00	0.00
Comoros	2.63	2.86	2.41	22.49	3.24	5.10	0.00	0.00
Congo	0.45	0.24	15.80	93.96	1.46	5.00	0.00	0.00
Côte d'Ivoire	1.43	1.13	13.04	75.54	1.04	2.60	0.01	0.04
Democratic Republic of the Congo	0.02	0.06	4.78	17.21	0.24	0.72	0.00	0.01
Djibouti	1.31	2.08	5.45	18.64	0.95	6.50	0.01	0.91
Egypt	14.12	11.86	18.37	87.11	11.70	26.74	0.19	1.82
Equatorial Guinea	1.65	1.93	15.94	57.01	1.15	6.00	0.03	0.17
Eritrea	0.84	1.03	0.90	3.53	1.79	5.40	0.00	0.00
Ethiopia	0.02	1.10	0.55	7.86	0.22	0.75	0.00	0.00
Gabon	2.85	2.02	53.74	106.94	4.89	7.23	0.11	0.25
Gambia	2.93	2.82	16.46	85.53	3.80	9.20	0.00	0.02
Ghana	1.49	1.14	13.28	71.49	1.83	8.55	0.01	0.21
Guinea	0.28	0.18	2.09	40.07	0.54	0.96	0.00	0.01
Guinea-Bissau	0.70	0.33	7.23	39.21	1.90	2.45	0.00	..
Kenya	0.81	1.14	12.95	61.63	3.10	20.98	0.02	0.01
Lesotho	2.32	1.79	12.09	32.18	2.58	3.86	0.00	0.02
Liberia	..	0.15	5.03	39.34	..	0.07	..	0.00
Libyan Arab Jamahiriya	14.77	19.33	34.66	171.52	3.92	14.00	..	1.15
Madagascar	0.52	0.83	2.85	39.79	0.57	1.70	0.00	0.02
Malawi	0.80	1.07	3.28	20.38	0.38	2.26	0.00	0.03
Mali	0.58	0.74	5.78	47.66	0.51	2.70	0.00	0.02
Mauritania	1.35	2.07	24.47	79.34	0.67	3.00	0.01	0.19
Mauritius	28.45	29.84	52.26	91.67	15.17	24.90	0.43	6.30
Morocco	4.41	11.73	40.78	100.10	15.08	49.00	0.82	1.56
Mozambique	0.32	0.38	7.24	30.88	0.85	4.17	0.00	0.06
Namibia	6.68	6.66	21.58	67.21	4.01	6.50	0.01	0.42
Niger	0.18	0.54	2.49	24.53	0.22	0.83	0.00	0.02
Nigeria	0.87	0.66	13.29	55.10	3.55	28.43	0.00	0.06

	Fixed telephone lines		Mobile cellular telephone subscriptions		Internet users		Fixed broadband Internet subscriptions	
	2005	2010	2005	2010	2005	2010	2005	2010
Rwanda	0.26	0.37	2.42	33.40	0.56	7.70	0.01	0.02
Sao Tome and Principe	4.66	4.63	7.83	61.97	13.76	18.75	0.00	0.35
Senegal	2.45	2.75	15.91	67.11	4.79	16.00	0.17	0.63
Seychelles	25.63	25.48	70.42	135.91	25.41	41.00	1.14	7.26
Sierra Leone [a]	0.54	0.24	..	34.09	0.22	0.26	0.00	..
Somalia [a]	1.20	1.07	5.98	6.95	1.08	1.16	0.00	..
South Africa	9.89	8.43	71.06	100.48	7.49	12.30	0.35	1.48
Sudan [b]	1.48	0.86	4.76	40.54	1.29	10.16	0.00	0.38
Swaziland	3.17	3.71	18.10	61.78	3.70	8.02	0.00	0.14
Togo	1.16	3.55	8.02	40.69	4.00	5.38	0.00	0.09
Tunisia	12.69	12.30	57.31	106.04	9.66	36.80	0.18	4.60
Uganda	0.31	0.98	4.63	38.38	1.74	12.50	0.00	0.06
United Republic of Tanzania	0.40	0.39	7.63	46.80	4.30	11.00	0.00	0.01
Zambia	0.83	0.69	8.28	37.80	2.85	6.74	0.00	0.08
Zimbabwe	2.61	3.01	5.15	59.66	8.02	11.50	0.08	0.26
Asia								
Afghanistan	0.36	0.45	4.35	41.39	1.22	4.00	0.00	0.00
Bahrain	26.70	18.07	105.84	124.18	21.30	55.00	2.96	12.21
Bangladesh	0.76	0.61	6.40	46.17	0.24	3.70	0.00	0.04
Bhutan	5.01	3.62	5.46	54.32	3.85	13.60	0.00	1.20
Brunei Darussalam	23.10	20.03	64.14	109.07	36.47	50.00	2.24	5.44
Cambodia	0.25	2.54	7.95	57.65	0.32	1.26	0.01	0.25
China	26.80	21.95	30.09	64.04	8.52	34.30	2.86	9.42
China, Hong Kong SAR	55.70	61.61	125.47	190.21	56.90	69.40	24.36	30.16
China, Macao SAR	36.23	30.82	110.67	206.43	34.86	56.80	14.13	24.14
Democratic People's Republic of Korea [ac]	4.21	4.85	0.00	1.77	0.00	0.00	0.00	0.00
India	4.40	2.87	7.91	61.42	2.39	7.50	0.12	0.90
Indonesia	5.94	15.83	20.64	91.72	3.60	9.10	0.05	0.79
Iran (Islamic Republic of)	29.17	36.30	12.20	91.25	8.10	13.00	..	0.68
Iraq	4.08	5.05	5.60	75.78	0.90	5.60	..	0.00
Jordan	11.76	7.84	58.74	106.99	12.93	38.00	0.44	3.18
Kuwait	22.30	20.69	100.57	160.78	25.93	38.25	1.10	1.68
Lao People's Democratic Republic	1.58	1.66	11.43	64.56	0.85	7.00	0.01	0.19
Lebanon	15.66	21.00	24.52	68.00	10.14	31.00	3.21	4.73
Malaysia	16.73	16.10	74.88	121.32	48.63	55.30	1.85	7.32
Maldives	10.94	15.20	68.97	156.50	6.87	28.30	1.10	4.92
Mongolia	6.13	7.01	21.87	91.09	..	10.20	0.07	2.31

	Fixed telephone lines		Mobile cellular telephone subscriptions		Internet users		Fixed broadband Internet subscriptions	
	2005	2010	2005	2010	2005	2010	2005	2010
Myanmar [a]	1.09	1.26	0.28	1.24	0.07	0.22	0.00	0.03
Nepal	1.78	2.81	0.83	30.69	0.83	6.78	0.00	0.38
Occupied Palestinian Territory [de]	9.48	9.37	15.96	45.79	16.01	37.44	0.21	..
Oman	10.92	10.20	54.88	165.54	6.68	62.60	0.54	1.89
Pakistan	3.30	1.97	8.05	59.21	6.33	16.78	0.01	0.31
Philippines	3.94	7.27	40.66	85.67	5.40	25.00	0.14	1.85
Qatar	25.02	16.95	87.31	132.43	24.73	69.00	3.12	9.17
Republic of Korea	50.81	59.24	81.50	105.36	73.50	83.70	25.91	36.63
Saudi Arabia	15.99	15.18	58.92	187.86	12.71	41.00	0.28	5.45
Singapore	43.23	39.00	102.78	143.66	61.00	70.00	15.38	24.72
Sri Lanka	6.27	17.15	16.94	83.22	1.79	12.00	0.11	1.02
Syrian Arab Republic	15.71	19.94	15.96	57.30	5.65	20.70	0.01	0.33
Taiwan Province of China	63.71	70.70	97.55	119.91	50.01	71.50	19.10	22.68
Thailand	10.55	10.14	46.68	100.81	15.03	21.20	0.16	3.87
Timor-Leste	0.23	0.21	3.27	53.42	0.10	0.21	0.00	0.02
Turkey	27.85	22.27	64.00	84.90	15.46	39.82	2.33	9.75
United Arab Emirates	30.39	19.70	111.42	145.45	40.00	78.00	3.18	10.47
Viet Nam [f]	10.19	18.67	11.54	175.30	12.74	27.56	0.25	4.13
Yemen	4.37	4.35	11.03	46.09	1.05	10.85	0.01	0.33
Latin America and the Caribbean								
Antigua and Barbuda	43.47	47.05	102.48	184.72	34.72	80.00	6.82	17.25
Argentina	24.41	24.74	57.28	141.79	17.72	36.00	2.40	9.56
Aruba	37.88	32.60	102.40	122.62	25.40	42.00	12.15	17.88
Bahamas	41.67	37.71	71.32	124.94	25.00	43.00	4.19	7.13
Barbados	49.86	50.30	76.22	128.07	56.07	70.20	11.81	20.56
Belize	12.02	9.72	34.17	62.32	9.21	14.00	1.79	2.86
Bolivia (Plurinational State of)	7.07	8.54	26.47	72.30	5.23	20.00	0.14	0.97
Brazil	21.43	21.62	46.35	104.10	21.02	40.65	1.74	7.23
Cayman Islands	72.70	66.43	154.87	177.65	38.03	66.00	..	33.53
Chile	21.08	20.20	64.84	116.00	31.18	45.00	4.35	10.45
Colombia	17.84	14.71	50.77	93.76	11.01	36.50	0.74	5.66
Costa Rica	32.22	31.80	25.56	65.14	22.07	36.50	1.04	6.19
Cuba	7.61	10.34	1.20	8.91	9.74	15.12	0.00	0.03
Dominica	27.57	22.85	75.44	144.85	38.54	47.45	4.93	47.14
Dominican Republic	9.67	10.17	39.11	89.58	11.48	39.53	0.69	3.64

	Fixed telephone lines		Mobile cellular telephone subscriptions		Internet users		Fixed broadband Internet subscriptions	
	2005	2010	2005	2010	2005	2010	2005	2010
Ecuador	12.51	14.42	46.52	102.18	5.99	24.00	0.20	1.36
El Salvador	16.06	16.16	39.86	124.34	4.20	15.00	0.70	2.83
French Guiana [a]	25.25	19.68	..	..	20.79	25.70	..	..
Grenada	26.70	27.15	45.61	116.71	20.49	33.46	3.14	10.12
Guatemala	9.81	10.41	35.46	125.57	5.70	10.50	0.21	1.80
Guyana	14.76	19.86	37.71	73.61	..	29.90	0.27	1.59
Haiti	1.55	0.50	5.35	40.03	6.38	8.37	0.00	x..
Honduras	7.18	8.81	18.63	125.06	6.50	11.09	0.00	1.00
Jamaica	11.90	9.60	73.89	113.22	12.80	26.10	1.68	4.26
Mexico	18.32	17.54	44.26	80.55	17.21	31.00	1.81	9.98
Netherlands Antilles	45.71	44.85	..	..	..	..	..	..
Nicaragua	4.07	4.46	20.64	65.14	2.57	10.00	0.19	0.82
Panama	14.53	15.73	54.00	184.72	11.48	42.75	0.54	7.84
Paraguay	5.43	6.27	31.99	91.64	7.91	23.60	0.09	0.61
Peru	8.72	10.87	20.26	100.13	17.10	34.30	1.28	3.14
Puerto Rico	27.44	23.79	52.71	78.26	23.40	45.30	3.13	14.72
Saint Kitts and Nevis [a]	41.28	39.31	103.72	161.44	26.46	32.87	13.22	25.00
Saint Lucia [a]	23.60	23.58	63.93	102.89	21.57	36.00	4.24	10.67
Saint Vincent and the Grenadines [a]	20.69	19.85	64.93	120.54	9.20	69.59	3.35	11.43
Suriname	16.23	16.19	46.62	169.64	6.40	31.59	0.22	2.99
Trinidad and Tobago	24.50	21.87	70.25	141.21	28.98	48.50	0.82	10.81
Uruguay	30.28	28.56	34.76	131.71	20.09	43.35	1.46	11.37
Venezuela (Bolivarian Republic of)	13.69	24.44	46.86	96.20	12.55	35.63	1.34	5.37
Virgin Islands (U.S.) [a]	65.56	69.51	73.43	..	27.34	27.40	2.71	8.34
Oceania								
American Samoa	16.52	15.20	..	..	..	..	..	..
Fiji	13.68	15.92	24.92	116.19	8.45	14.82	0.85	1.86
French Polynesia	20.95	20.29	47.08	79.73	21.54	49.00	4.32	11.91
Guam [a]	38.86	36.41	..	..	38.56	50.64	..	1.67
Kiribati	4.57	4.12	0.71	10.05	4.00	9.00	..	0.90
Marshall Islands [a]	8.46	8.14	1.27	7.03	3.88	3.55	0.00	..
Micronesia, (Federated States of)	11.38	7.61	12.88	24.78	11.88	20.00	0.04	0.90
Nauru	17.80	0.00	..	60.46	..	6.00	..	3.90
New Caledonia [a]	23.94	28.78	58.10	88.02	32.36	33.99	4.15	15.23
Northern Mariana Islands	34.58	41.86	..	..	..	..	0.00	..

	Fixed telephone lines		Mobile cellular telephone subscriptions		Internet users		Fixed broadband Internet subscriptions	
	2005	2010	2005	2010	2005	2010	2005	2010
Palau	40.07	34.08	30.40	70.89	..	..	0.50	1.14
Papua New Guinea	1.05	1.77	1.23	27.84	1.72	1.28	0.00	0.09
Samoa	10.82	19.28	13.32	91.43	3.35	7.00	0.04	0.11
Solomon Islands	1.58	1.56	1.28	5.57	0.84	5.00	0.10	0.37
Tonga	13.62	29.79	29.60	52.18	4.91	12.00	0.64	0.96
Tuvalu	9.18	16.49	13.41	25.44	..	25.00	1.55	3.26
Vanuatu	3.30	2.09	6.01	119.05	5.08	8.00	0.03	0.13
Transition economies								
Albania	8.88	10.35	48.71	141.93	6.04	45.00	0.01	3.43
Armenia	19.39	19.08	10.37	125.01	5.25	37.00	0.06	2.69
Azerbaijan	12.74	16.33	26.11	99.04	8.03	35.99	0.03	5.44
Belarus [g]	33.43	43.13	41.72	107.69	16.20	31.70	0.02	17.36
Bosnia and Herzegovina	25.82	26.58	42.17	80.15	21.33	52.00	0.30	10.40
Croatia	42.38	42.37	82.16	144.48	33.14	60.32	2.62	18.25
Georgia	12.74	13.72	26.23	73.36	6.08	27.00	0.05	5.09
Kazakhstan	17.85	25.03	35.58	123.35	2.96	34.00	0.02	5.28
Kyrgyzstan	8.73	9.41	10.74	91.86	10.53	20.00	0.05	0.29
Montenegro	27.27	26.84	86.67	185.28	28.82	52.00	1.22	8.30
Republic of Moldova	24.67	32.50	28.93	88.59	14.63	40.00	0.28	7.53
Russian Federation	27.88	31.45	83.42	166.26	15.23	43.00	1.10	10.98
Serbia	32.93	40.52	71.80	129.19	26.30	40.90	0.44	8.50
Tajikistan	4.34	5.35	4.11	86.37	0.30	11.55	0.00	0.07
The former Yugoslav Republic of Macedonia	26.18	20.05	55.49	104.51	26.45	51.90	0.61	12.47
Turkmenistan	8.38	10.31	2.21	63.42	1.00	2.20	..	0.01
Ukraine	24.86	28.47	63.96	118.66	3.75	23.00	0.28	8.06
Uzbekistan	6.91	6.79	2.77	76.34	3.34	20.00	0.03	0.32

Notes:

[a]   Number of Internet users in 2010 column refers to the year 2009.
[b]   Number of Internet users in 2010 column refers to the year 2008.
[c]   Number of fixed broadband subscriptions in 2010 column refers to the year 2009.
[d]   Number of fixed telephone lines in 2010 column refers to the year 2009.
[e]   Number of Mobile telephone subscriptions in 2010 column refers to the year 2009.
[f]   Number of fixed telephone lines in 2005 column refers to the year 2006.
[g]   Number of Internet users in 2005 column refers to the year 2006.

Annex table II.2.   Use of computers by enterprise size, latest available reference year (%)
B1 - Proportion of businesses using computers

Economy	Reference year	All enterprises	Enterprises with more than 10 employees	0–9 persons employed	10–49 persons employed	50–249 persons employed	250+ persons employed
Developed economies							
Australia [a]	2006	89	98	87	97	100	100
Austria [b]	2010	..	98	..	98	100	100
Belgium [b]	2010	..	99	..	98	100	100
Bermuda [c]	2006	82	82	82	82	82	..
Bulgaria [b]	2010	..	90	..	88	98	99
Croatia [b]	2010	..	97	..	96	99	100
Cyprus [b]	2010	..	92	..	91	99	100
Czech Republic [b]	2010	..	96	..	95	99	100
Denmark [b]	2010	..	98	..	98	99	99
Estonia [b]	2010	..	97	..	96	99	100
Finland [b]	2010	..	100	..	100	100	100
France [b]	2010	..	98	..	98	100	100
Germany [b]	2010	..	98	83	98	99	99
Greece [b]	2010	..	92	..	91	100	100
Hungary [b]	2010	..	91	..	90	97	98
Iceland [b]	2010	..	98	88	98	100	100
Ireland [b]	2010	..	93	..	92	100	100
Israel [i]	2008	96	96	91	95	100	100
Italy [b]	2010	..	95	..	95	99	100
Latvia [b]	2010	..	95	..	94	99	100
Lithuania [b]	2010	..	97	..	96	100	100
Luxembourg [b]	2010	..	98	..	98	100	100
Malta [b]	2010	..	96	..	95	100	100
Netherlands [b]	2010	..	100	..	100	100	100
New Zealand	2008	96	98	93	97	99	99
Norway [b]	2010	..	98	..	98	99	99
Poland [b]	2010	..	97	..	97	99	100
Portugal [b]	2010	..	97	62	97	100	100
Romania [b]	2010	..	82	..	79	92	97
Slovakia [b]	2010	..	98	82	98	99	99
Slovenia [b]	2010	..	98	..	97	100	100
Spain [b]	2010	..	98	..	98	100	100
Sweden [b]	2010	..	97	..	96	99	100
Switzerland	2008	100	..	..	..	..	..
United Kingdom [b]	2010	..	92	..	91	99	99
Developing economies							
Argentina	2006	100	100	100	100	100	100
Brazil [d]	2009	97	97	..	96	100	100
Chile	2007	43	..	..	..	..	..
China, Hong Kong SAR [f]	2009	64	92	60	90	99	100
China, Macao SAR	2007	44	80	39	74	97	100
Colombia [e]	2006	89	92	69	87	97	97

Economy	Reference year	All enterprises	Enterprises with more than 10 employees	0–9 persons employed	10–49 persons employed	50–249 persons employed	250+ persons employed
Cuba	2007	94	95	86	93	93	96
Egypt	2009	64	64	..	56	79	92
Jordan	2008	18	86	14	79	97	100
Lesotho	2008	34	76	19	71	89	96
Mauritius	2009	98	98	85	97	100	100
Mongolia	2006	37	..	..	..	..	..
Occupied Palestinian Territory	2009	30	87	28	87	..	..
Panama [g]	2006	79	90	65	87	98	97
Philippines	2008	..	..	..	..	..	..
Qatar	2008	67	98	60	98	100	100
Republic of Korea	2008	50	98	46	98	100	100
Senegal	2008	92	96	88	94	98	100
Singapore	2009	78	94	74	92	98	100
Thailand	2008	23	81	22	75	93	99
Tunisia [h]	2009	83	83	..	79	98	99
Turkey [b]	2010	..	92	..	91	97	98
United Arab Emirates	2008	97	97	..	92	100	100
Uruguay	2007	92	..	..	..	..	..
Transition economies							
Azerbaijan	2009	25	43	15	35	54	75
Kazakhstan	2008	76	76	..	74	98	100
Kyrgyzstan	2009	97	98	94	98	99	100
Russian Federation [i]	2008	92	92	..	84	99	100
Serbia [b]	2007	92	92	..	90	98	100
The former Yugoslav Republic of Macedonia	2009	63	95	60	94	96	100

Notes:
[a]   Data refer to all businesses during the year ending 30 June 2006.
[b]   Data refer to NACE rev. 2 excluding sector K (financial and insurance activities).
[c]   Enterprises with 250+ persons employed are included in 50–249.
       The total includes public administration numbers.
[d]   Estimates.
[e]   The category 0–9 corresponds to establishments with 1 to 10 persons employed.
[f]   Data refer to "establishments" rather than "enterprises".
[g]   Preliminary figures.
[h]   The breakdown by enterprise size is 6–49, 50–199, and 200+. This breakdown does not concern public enterprises, and the total includes public enterprises.
[i]   The category 10–49 corresponds to establishments with 1 to 50 persons employed.
[j]   The category 0–9 only includes ISIC Rev 3.1 sector K72 and K73.

Annex table II.3. Use of Internet by enterprise size, latest available reference year (%)
B3 - Proportion of businesses using the Internet

Economy	Reference Year	All enterprises	Enterprises with more than 10 employees	0–9 persons employed	10–49 persons employed	50–249 persons employed	250+ persons employed
Developed economies							
Australia [a]	2007	87	96	84	96	99	99
Austria [b]	2010	..	97	..	97	100	100
Belgium [b]	2010	..	97	..	97	99	100
Bermuda [c]	2006	71	71	71	71	71	..
Bulgaria [b]	2010	..	85	..	83	96	99
Canada [d]	2007	95	95	..	94	99	100
Croatia [b]	2010	..	95	..	95	98	100
Cyprus [b]	2010	..	88	..	86	98	100
Czech Republic [b]	2010	..	95	..	94	98	100
Denmark [b]	2010	..	97	..	97	98	98
Estonia [b]	2010	..	96	..	95	99	100
Finland [b]	2010	..	100	..	100	100	100
France [b]	2010	..	97	..	96	99	100
Germany [b]	2010	..	97	80	97	99	99
Greece [b]	2010	..	90	..	89	99	100
Hungary [b]	2010	..	90	..	88	97	98
Iceland [b]	2010	..	98	87	97	100	100
Ireland [b]	2010	..	92	..	91	99	100
Israel [i]	2008	93	93	90	91	100	100
Italy [b]	2010	..	94	..	93	99	99
Japan [e]	2009	100	100	..	..	99	100
Latvia [b]	2010	..	91	..	89	98	99
Lithuania [b]	2010	..	96	..	95	100	100
Luxembourg [b]	2010	..	96	..	96	99	100
Malta [b]	2010	..	94	..	93	98	100
Netherlands [b]	2010	..	98	..	98	99	100
New Zealand	2008	93	95	90	95	98	99
Norway [b]	2010	..	97	..	96	99	99
Poland [b]	2010	..	96	..	95	99	100
Portugal [b]	2010	..	94	53	93	100	100
Romania [b]	2010	..	79	..	76	90	97
Slovakia [b]	2010	..	98	78	98	99	99
Slovenia [b]	2010	..	97	..	96	100	100
Spain [b]	2010	..	97	..	96	99	100
Sweden [b]	2010	..	96	..	95	98	100
Switzerland	2008	100	..	..	..	..	..
United Kingdom [b]	2010	..	91	..	89	99	99
Developing economies							
Brazil [f]	2009	93	93	..	91	100	100
Chile	2007	39	..	..	..	..	..
China, Hong Kong SAR [h]	2009	61	87	57	86	95	99
China, Macao SAR	2007	36	66	31	60	88	96

Economy	Reference Year	All enterprises	Enterprises with more than 10 employees	0–9 persons employed	10–49 persons employed	50–249 persons employed	250+ persons employed
Colombia [g]	2006	86	89	58	82	96	97
Cuba	2007	70	70	86	80	65	71
Egypt	2009	35	35	..	26	51	72
Jordan	2008	10	76	6	68	90	98
Lesotho	2008	17	46	7	37	89	72
Mauritius	2009	92	92	72	89	98	100
Occupied Palestinian Territory	2009	20	71	19	71	..	..
Panama [i]	2006	68	80	52	75	95	97
Philippines	2008	73	..	..	..	..	..
Qatar	2008	50	95	40	93	100	99
Republic of Korea	2008	49	97	45	97	99	100
Senegal	2008	84	91	73	88	96	97
Singapore	2009	75	92	70	91	98	100
Suriname	2006	16	59	12	55	77	74
Thailand	2008	16	68	14	59	85	95
Tunisia [j]	2009	71	70	..	65	91	95
Turkey [b]	2010	..	91	..	90	97	98
United Arab Emirates	2008	92	..	..	..	..	..
Uruguay	2007	84	..	..	..	..	..
Transition economies							
Azerbaijan	2009	17	30	9	22	38	68
Kazakhstan	2008	56	56	..	53	94	95
Kyrgyzstan	2009	38	40	33	37	41	54
Russian Federation [k]	2008	76	76	..	59	91	96
Serbia [b]	2007	87	87	..	86	86	94
The former Yugoslav Republic of Macedonia	2009	46	86	42	85	91	100

Notes:

[a] Data refer to proportion of all businesses during the year ending 30 June 2007.
[b] Data refer to NACE rev. 2 excluding sector K (financial and insurance activities).
[c] Enterprises with 250+ persons employed are included in 50-249. The total includes public administration numbers.
[d] Enterprise size categories are: 10–49; 50–299; 300+.
[e] Data refer to the sample and have not been extrapolated to the target population. Enterprise sizes 0–9 and 10–49 persons employed are not surveyed. "50–249" refers to "100–299", and "250+" refers to "300+".
[f] Estimates.
[g] The classification 0–9 corresponds to establishments with 1–10 persons employed.
[h] Data refer to "establishments" rather than "enterprises".
[i] Preliminary figures.
[j] The breakdown by enterprise size is 6–49, 50–199, and 200+. This breakdown does not concern public enterprises, and the total includes public enterprises.
[k] The category 10–49 corresponds to establishments with 1 to 50 persons employed.
[l] The category 0–9 only includes ISIC Rev 3.1 sector K72 and K73.

Annex table II.4. Type of enterprise connection to the Internet, by enterprise size (%)
B9 - Proportion of businesses using the Internet by type of access
(fixed broadband and mobile broadband)

Economy	Reference year	Fixed broadband				Mobile broadband			
		0–9 persons employed	10–49 persons employed	50–249 persons employed	250+ persons employed	0–9 persons employed	10–49 persons employed	50–249 persons employed	250+ persons employed
Developed economies									
Australia [a]	2007	93	97	94	100	..	..	..	..
Austria [b]	2010	..	72	90	96	..	42	65	91
Belgium [b]	2010	..	88	96	99	..	24	49	70
Bulgaria [b]	2010	..	57	75	88	..	7	14	34
Canada [c]	2007	..	93	98	99	..	..	..	..
Croatia [b]	2010	..	73	86	97	..	29	41	71
Cyprus [b]	2010	..	82	97	100	..	9	19	39
Czech Republic [b]	2010	..	83	94	99	..	13	35	51
Denmark [b]	2010	..	82	93	95	..	39	63	81
Estonia [b]	2010	..	86	92	99	..	7	13	36
Finland [b]	2010	..	92	97	98	..	64	88	95
France [b]	2010	..	92	98	99	..	23	46	68
Germany [b]	2010	67	86	95	96	7	16	38	63
Greece [b]	2010	..	78	94	99	..	5	14	20
Hungary [b]	2010	..	76	90	97	..	18	36	57
Iceland [b]	2010	82	94	100	100	20	36	74	78
Ireland [b]	2010	..	81	95	97	..	31	52	73
Italy [b]	2010	..	82	93	98	..	16	38	66
Japan [d]	2009	..	..	82	71	..	..	..	..
Latvia [b]	2010	..	63	82	92	..	10	19	41
Lithuania [b]	2010	..	76	85	94	..	16	32	62
Luxembourg [b]	2010	..	85	93	94	..	17	26	57
Malta [b]	2010	..	90	96	97	..	24	41	62
Netherlands [b]	2010	..	89	96	99	..	23	47	68
New Zealand [e]	2008	86	91	96	97	6	10	27	42
Norway [b]	2010	..	83	93	97	..	35	61	84
Poland [b]	2010	..	61	82	96	..	16	32	64
Portugal [b]	2010	40	82	90	98	9	20	48	75
Romania [b]	2010	..	45	63	84	..	6	14	33
Slovakia [b]	2010	51	68	81	94	21	32	46	67
Slovenia [b]	2010	..	83	93	100	..	26	47	73
Spain [b]	2010	..	94	98	99	..	31	57	75
Sweden [b]	2010	..	87	96	99	..	50	76	91
United Kingdom [b]	2010	..	85	96	98	..	30	58	79
Developing economies									
Argentina [f]	2006	17	16	23	42	0	6	10	7
Brazil [g]	2009	..	59	78	87	..	7	20	30
China, Hong Kong SAR [h]	2009	57	85	95	99	0	0	1	6
Colombia [i]	2006	35	60	81	90	..	..	..	..
Egypt	2009	..	24	49	67	..	..	..	..
Lesotho	2008	2	11	39	47	..	..	..	..

Economy	Reference year	Fixed broadband				Mobile broadband			
		0–9 persons employed	10–49 persons employed	50–249 persons employed	250+ persons employed	0–9 persons employed	10–49 persons employed	50–249 persons employed	250+ persons employed
Occupied Palestinian Territory	2009	12	63	..	..	..	..	..	..
Qatar	2008	28	81	95	95	..	..	..	..
Republic of Korea ʲ	2008	45	97	99	100	..	..	..	..
Senegal	2008	72	86	96	97	5	8	9	82
Singapore	2009	56	75	85	83	8	9	11	8
Thailand ᵏ	2008	10	42	67	83	..	..	..	..
Tunisiaˡ	2009	..	29	45	58	..	..	..	..
Turkey ᵇ	2010	..	87	96	98	..	13	25	41
United Arab Emirates	2008	..	76	83	76	..	..	..	..
Uruguay ᵍ	2005	23	53	68	84	..	..	..	..
Transition economies									
Azerbaijan	2009	0	4	12	17	0	2	3	8
Kazakhstan	2008	..	2	11	16	..	2	6	13
Kyrgyzstan ᵐ	2009	12	34	41	53	..	..	..	..
Russian Federation ⁿ	2008	..	28	52	70	..	..		
Serbia	2007	..	36	36	46	..	..	..	..
The former Yugoslav Republic of Macedonia ⁿ	2009	34	77	81	88	6	20	17	29

Notes:

a   Data refer to total broadband connection with year ending 30 June 2007.

b   Mobile broadband connection refers to the connection to the Internet via portable computer using 3G modem or via 3G handset, e.g. smartphone.

c   Enterprise size categories: 10–49; 50–299; 300+. Data refer to all broadband connections and include ADSL, Cable, other fixed and wireless broadband; they exclude ISDN.

d   Data refer to the sample and have not been extrapolated to the target population. Enterprise size "50–249" refers to "100–299", and "250+" refers to "300+". Fixed broadband refers to access by CATV, FTTH, FWA, BWA and DSL.

e   Estimates; answers include "don't know" responses.

f   Mobile broadband includes mobile wireless and fixed wireless.

g   Estimates.

h   Enterprise size "0–9" refers to establishmentes with 1–10 persons employed. Data refer to enterprises connecting by ADSL, dedicated channels, wireless, Frame Relay and EDGE.

i   Data refer to "establishments" rather than "enterprises".

j   Includes mobile broadband (HSDPA etc).

k   Data refer to total broadband, i.e. both fixed and mobile.

l   Breakdown by enterprise size is "6–49", "50–199", and "200+".

m   Data refer to fixed broadband with 256 kbit or more, ADSL, xDSL.

n   Mobile broadband includes narrowband and broadband (no distinction was made in the questionnaire between these two types of mobile connections).

o   The category 10–49 corresponds to establishments with 1 to 50 persons employed. Access to internet with 256kbit and higher.

Annex table II.5. Use of computers by economic activity (ISIC Rev 3.1), latest available reference year (%) B1 - Proportion of businesses using computers

Economy	Reference year	A	B	C	D	E	F	G	G50	G51	G52	H	I	I60	I61	I62	I63	I64	J	K70	K71	K72	K73	K74	M	N	O
Developed economies																											
Australia [a]	2006	:	:	89	89	96	88	:	:	97	83	76	:	79	:	:	:	83	94	:	:	:	:	:	:	97	:
Austria [b]	2010	:	:	:	98	100	99	99	:	:	:	100	98	:	:	:	:	:	100	93	97	100	99	:	:	:	:
Belgium [b]	2010	:	:	:	98	:	100	98	82	:	:	100	98	:	:	:	:	:	83	:	99	99	99	:	:	:	:
Bermuda [c]	2006	82	:	:	82	83	82	82	82	:	:	82	82	:	:	:	:	:	83	85	83	94	:	:	82	82	82
Bulgaria [b]	2010	:	:	:	89	91	92	91	:	:	:	100	92	:	:	:	:	:	95	:	:	:	98	:	:	:	:
Croatia [b]	2010	:	:	:	96	:	94	99	99	99	99	92	99	86	:	:	:	100	100	92	:	100	99	:	:	:	100
Cyprus [b]	2010	:	:	:	95	95	86	98	97	99	95	96	93	96	:	:	:	99	95	99	97	:	98	:	:	:	98
Czech Republic [b]	2010	:	:	:	96	97	98	97	96	97	98	95	94	93	:	:	:	100	96	100	95	98	99	:	:	:	:
Denmark [b]	2010	:	:	:	99	:	99	99	99	99	:	:	98	98	:	:	:	99	:	99	96	98	98	:	:	:	:
Estonia [b]	2010	:	:	:	97	97	95	99	99	100	98	96	97	98	:	:	:	100	96	100	98	100	100	:	:	:	:
Finland [b]	2010	:	:	:	100	100	100	100	100	100	100	100	99	98	:	:	:	100	100	99	100	100	100	:	:	:	:
France [b]	2010	:	:	:	98	99	99	99	98	98	99	99	98	97	:	:	:	95	98	100	97	100	:	:	:	:	:
Germany [b]	2010	:	:	:	98	99	99	99	96	99	93	93	97	95	:	:	:	87	100	88	98	98	99	:	:	:	:
Greece [b]	2010	:	:	:	95	100	92	96	95	98	88	100	93	94	:	:	:	100	100	100	99	100	100	:	:	:	:
Hungary [b]	2010	:	:	:	92	100	92	92	92	95	87	93	89	90	:	:	:	88	99	90	87	99	95	:	:	:	:
Iceland [b]	2010	:	:	:	99	93	98	99	98	99	97	100	100	100	:	:	:	100	100	100	100	100	100	:	:	:	:
Ireland [b]	2010	:	:	:	99	99	97	97	98	99	97	100	93	98	:	:	:	100	100	94	97	100	97	:	:	:	:
Israel [i]	2008	:	:	100	96	100	87	100	97	100	100	83	98	95	:	:	100	100	100	98	100	100	100	99	:	:	:
Italy [b]	2010	:	:	:	97	99	95	98	97	100	92	99	94	895	:	:	:	95	100	98	92	99	99	:	:	:	:
Latvia [b]	2010	:	:	:	95	99	96	96	90	99	90	97	95	96	:	:	:	100	100	97	98	99	97	:	:	:	:
Lithuania [b]	2010	:	:	:	98	100	98	97	96	98	95	97	93	92	:	:	:	100	98	100	96	100	100	:	:	:	:

Column headings (ISIC Rev 3.1):
A — Agriculture, hunting and forestry; B — Fishing; C — Mining and quarrying; D — Manufacturing; E — Electricity, gas and water supply; F — Construction; G — Wholesale and retail trade; repair of motor vehicles, motorcycles, etc.; G50 — Sale, maintenance and repair of motor vehicles and motorcycles, etc.; G51 — Wholesale trade and commission trade, except of motor vehicles and motorcycles; G52 — Retail trade, except of motor vehicles and motorcycles, etc.; H — Hotels and restaurants; I — Transport, storage and communications; I60 — Land transport; transport via pipelines; I61 — Water transport; I62 — Air transport; I63 — Supporting and auxiliary transport activities; activities of travel agencies; I64 — Post and telecommunications; J — Financial intermediation; K70 — Real estate activities; K71 — Renting of machinery and equipment; K72 — Computer and related activities; K73 — Research and development; K74 — Other business activities; M — Education; N — Health and social work; O — Other community, social and personal service activities

Economy	Reference year	A Agriculture, hunting and forestry	B Fishing	C Mining and quarrying	D Manufacturing	E Electricity, gas and water supply	F Construction	G Wholesale and retail trade; repair of motor vehicles, motorcycles, etc.	G50 Sale, maintenance and repair of motor vehicles and motorcycles; etc.	G51 Wholesale trade and commission trade, except of motor vehicles and motorcycles	G52 Retail trade, except of motor vehicles and motorcycles; etc.	H Hotels and restaurants	I Transport, storage and communications	I60 Land transport; transport via pipelines	I61 Water transport	I62 Air transport	I63 Supporting and auxiliary transport activities; activities of travel agencies	I64 Post and telecommunications	J Financial intermediation	K70 Real estate activities	K71 Renting of machinery and equipment	K72 Computer and related activities	K73 Research and development	K74 Other business activities	M Education	N Health and social work	O Other community, social and personal service activities
Luxembourg [b]	2010	..	..	..	96	100	99	99	97	98	95	99	98	95	..	..	..	97	100	..	99	99	100	..	..	..	..
Malta [b]	2010	..	..	..	96	..	88	99	88	91	82	95	98	98	..	..	..	100	100	100	95	100	99	..	..	..	..
Netherlands [b]	2010	..	..	..	100	100	100	100	100	100	100	100	100	100	100	100	100	100	100	100	100	100	100	..	..	..	..
New Zealand	2008	84	92	94	98	100	98	97	97	99	94	91	99	98	100	100	100	98	99	91	99	99	100	98	100	98	96
Norway [b]	2010	..	..	..	98	100	100	99	96	100	93	100	95	96	..	..	..	100	100	100	95	99	99	..	..	..	..
Poland [b]	2010	..	..	..	97	100	97	98	95	93	91	95	98	95	..	..	..	98	98	99	95	99	98	..	..	..	..
Portugal [b]	2010	..	..	..	98	100	94	99	98	93	100	97	100	100	..	..	..	96	100	88	100	100	100	..	..	..	..
Romania [b]	2010	..	..	..	82	89	80	83	82	82	82	97	81	80	..	..	..	100	..	100	70	93	90	..	..	..	..
Slovakia [b]	2010	..	..	..	98	100	99	99	98	100	97	100	98	99	..	..	..	100	99	100	97	100	98	..	..	..	..
Slovenia [b]	2010	..	..	..	99	100	90	99	99	100	98	100	100	100	..	..	..	100	100	100	98	100	100	..	..	..	..
Spain [b]	2010	..	..	..	99	100	98	99	99	100	97	100	99	97	..	..	..	100	100	100	97	100	100	..	..	..	..
Sweden [b]	2010	..	..	..	99	100	96	98	98	99	96	97	93	90	..	..	..	95	100	100	97	99	97	..	..	..	..
United Kingdom [b]	2010	..	..	..	98	99	95	93	93	97	86	100	94	94	..	..	76	95	96	91	96	96	95	..	..	..	..
Developing economies																											
Argentina	2006	..	..	..	100	..	..	..	..	..	..	..	..	..	..	..	..	..	..	..	..	..	..	..	..	..	..
Brazil [d]	2009	..	..	..	98	..	98	98	98	..	..	88	98	..	..	..	..	..	..	..	..	..	..	..	..	..	96
Chile	2007	35	..	46	56	66	67	29	29	..	..	32	49	39	..	..	..	..	72	..	..	..	..	..	..	..	39
China, Hong Kong SAR [e]	2009	..	..	..	69	..	55	..	..	..	..	..	..	..	..	..	−	..	82	..	..	..	..	..	57	..	..
China, Macao SAR	2007	..	..	..	63	..	64	36	36	46	27	27	70	42	69	100	76	73	..	73	..	..	..	81	..	..	100
Colombia	2006	..	..	..	82	..	..	97	97	98	95	..	..	..	..	..	..	..	..	..	..	..	..	..	..	..	65
Cuba	2007	89	95	100	98	100	99	100	100	99	81	94	90	96	100	100	100	100	100	100	100	100	100	99	99	97	..
Egypt	2009	..	..	..	53	..	94	76	76	..	..	78	74	..	..	..	..	..	100	..	..	..	..	..	..	..	..

Column codes:
- A — Agriculture, hunting and forestry
- B — Fishing
- C — Mining and quarrying
- D — Manufacturing
- E — Electricity, gas and water supply
- F — Construction
- G — Wholesale and retail trade; repair of motor vehicles, motorcycles, etc.
- G50 — Sale, maintenance and repair of motor vehicles and motorcycles; etc.
- G51 — Wholesale trade and commission trade, except of motor vehicles and motorcycles
- G52 — Retail trade, except of motor vehicles and motorcycles; etc.
- H — Hotels and restaurants
- I — Transport, storage and communications
- I60 — Land transport; transport via pipelines
- I61 — Water transport
- I62 — Air transport
- I63 — Supporting and auxiliary transport activities; activities of travel agencies
- I64 — Post and telecommunications
- J — Financial intermediation
- K70 — Real estate activities
- K71 — Renting of machinery and equipment
- K72 — Computer and related activities
- K73 — Research and development
- K74 — Other business activities
- M — Education
- N — Health and social work
- O — Other community, social and personal service activities

Economy	Reference year	A	B	C	D	E	F	G	G50	G51	G52	H	I	I60	I61	I62	I63	I64	J	K70	K71	K72	K73	K74	M	N	O
Jordan	2008	:	:	55	12	100	47	12	12	29	12	14	72	16	100	100	83	100	99	47	16	99	100	71	:	40	12
Lesotho	2008	:	0	:	69	:	:	25	25	:	:	56	:	:	:	:	:	:	:	:	:	:	:	:	:	:	:
Mongolia	2006	14	:	50	39	53	53	23	23	26	18	34	51	42	50	91	51	64	32	31	32	71	75	54	74	42	43
Occupied Palestinian Territory	2009	:	:	:	23	:	67	21	21	:	:	:	65	:	:	:	:	:	84	:	:	:	:	:	:	:	52
Panama [g]	2006	78	:	100	74	92	92	81	81	77	87	55	85	65	90	96	93	97	100	67	91	100	100	94	88	90	87
Philippines	2008	66	55	88	89	97	99	82	82	91	74	86	90	84	82	100	90	92	96	100	93	100	100	96	97	91	84
Republic of Korea [f]	2008	64	:	:	64	:	78	:	:	70	43	24	20	:	:	:	:	:	97	:	:	:	:	:	62	:	:
Singapore	2009	100	:	:	82	75	76	75	75	:	:	51	75	17	:	:	:	:	86	76	:	97	98	92	85	88	56
Thailand	2008	:	:	:	14	:	39	26	26	45	23	22	22	:	:	:	79	:	:	35	34	90	:	76	:	100	13
Tunisia [h]	2009	86	:	97	76	100	89	89	89	:	:	62	96	:	:	:	:	:	99	:	:	:	99	:	100	91	97
Turkey [b]	2010	:	:	:	92	98	89	95	93	:	:	96	94	97	100	90	94	100	98	91	87	99	100	89	80	87	:
Uruguay	2007	:	:	:	91	100	:	95	95	94	94	87	96	:	:	:	:	:	:	:	100	100	100	:	:	:	:
Transition economies																											
Azerbaijan	2009	:	:	19	26	75	21	46	46	63	32	32	34	18	69	56	31	67	88	4	:	27	42	28	59	27	10
Kazakhstan	2008	:	:	94	77	96	75	76	76	98	94	82	82	93	:	100	94	98	87	90	100	94	97	99	98	95	95
Kyrgyzstan [i]	2009	86	50	96	95	90	96	97	97	93	92	98	96	94	96	99	93	99	100	78	77	98	97	93	98	100	91
Russian Federation [j]	2008	95	89	:	96	:	96	92	92	82	90	90	95	100	:	:	:	100	96	100	:	100	:	:	:	98	81
Serbia [k]	2007	:	:	:	94	:	90	85	85	:	:	96	100	:	:	:	:	:	:	:	:	:	:	:	:	:	100
The former Yugoslav Republic of Macedonia	2009	:	:	:	75	:	76	53	53	:	:	100	63	:	:	:	:	:	95	:	:	:	:	:	:	:	100

Notes:

a   Data refer to the year ending 30 June 2006. As industry division data cannot be split by ISIC 60-63, a total is included for Transport and Storage in ISIC 60. No totals are available for ISIC G and I. No data are available for O as they are collected under two separate divisions: Cultural and recreational services and Personal and other services.

b   Data refer to NACE Rev 2 sectors C, D, E, F, G, I J, K64-66, L, N, J, M.

c   Sector A includes fishing. Sector K includes real estate and rent, business services, other business activities, and international businesses. Public administration is not included.

d   Estimates. Data refer to national projection for enterprises with more than 9 employees.

e   Data refer to "establishments" rather than "enterprises".

f   Sector A includes sectors A, B and C. Sector M includes sectors L, M, N, O and E.

g   Preliminary figures.

h   Enterprise totals also include public enterprises.

i   Data include sector L75, Public administration.

j   Sector A refers to 'Forestry and provision of services in this area' (NACE code 02); sector M refers to 'Higher education' (code 803); sector O refers to 'Entertainment, Recreation, Arts and Sports' (code 92).

k   sector H includes NACE-Rev.1 Groups 55.1 and 55.2 - 'Hotels' and 'Camping sites and other provision of short stay accomodation'; sector I60 includes I60-63; sector K70 includes K70, 71, 73, 74; sector O includes O92.1 and 92.2 - Motion picture and Video activities' and 'Radio and Television activities'

l   The category 0-9 only includes ISIC Rev 3.1 sector K72 and K73.

Annex table II.6. Use of Internet by economic activity (ISIC Rev 3.1), latest available reference year (%) B3- Proportion of businesses using the Internet

Economy	Reference year	Agriculture, hunting and forestry A	Fishing B	Mining and quarrying C	Manufacturing D	Electricity, gas and water supply E	Construction F	Wholesale and retail trade; repair of motor vehicles, motorcycles, etc. G	Sale, maintenance and repair of motor vehicles and motorcycles; etc. G50	Wholesale trade and commission trade, except of motor vehicles and motorcycles G51	Retail trade, except of motor vehicles and motorcycles; etc. G52	Hotels and restaurants H	Transport, storage and communications I	Land transport; transport via pipelines I60	Water transport I61	Air transport I62	Supporting and auxiliary transport activities; activities of travel agencies I63	Post and telecommunications I64	Financial intermediation J	Real estate activities K70	Renting of machinery and equipment K71	Computer and related activities K72	Research and development K73	Other business activities K74	Education M	Health and social work N	Other community, social and personal service activities O
Developed economies																											
Australia [a]	2006	..	..	89	89	96	88	..	..	97	83	76	..	79	..	..	..	83	94	..	..	..	..	..	..	97	..
Austria [b]	2010	..	..	..	98	100	99	99	..	..	..	100	98	..	..	..	..	..	100	93	97	100	99	..	..	..	..
Belgium [b]	2010	..	..	..	98	..	100	98	..	..	..	100	98	..	..	..	..	..	..	..	99	99	99	..	..	..	..
Bermuda [c]	2006	82	..	..	82	83	82	82	82	..	..	82	82	..	..	..	..	..	83	85	83	94	98	..	82	82	82
Bulgaria [b]	2010	..	..	..	89	91	92	91	..	..	..	100	92	..	..	..	..	..	95	..	..	94	98	..	..	..	..
Croatia [b]	2010	..	..	..	96	..	94	99	99	99	99	92	99	86	..	..	..	..	..	..	..	100	99	..	..	..	..
Cyprus [b]	2010	..	..	..	95	95	86	98	97	99	96	96	93	96	..	..	..	100	100	92	97	100	98	..	..	..	100
Czech Republic [b]	2010	..	..	..	96	97	98	97	96	97	95	95	94	96	..	..	..	99	95	99	98	100	99	..	..	..	..
Denmark [b]	2010	..	..	..	99	..	99	99	99	99	98	..	98	93	..	..	..	99	..	88	95	90	98	..	..	..	98
Estonia [b]	2010	..	..	..	97	97	95	96	99	100	98	96	97	98	..	..	..	100	96	100	96	98	98	..	..	..	..
Finland [b]	2010	..	..	..	100	100	100	100	100	100	100	100	99	98	..	..	..	100	100	99	100	100	100	..	..	..	..
France [b]	2010	..	..	..	98	100	99	99	98	99	95	99	98	97	..	..	..	95	98	100	97	100	100	..	..	..	..
Germany [b]	2010	..	..	..	98	99	99	99	96	98	93	100	97	95	..	..	..	87	100	88	98	100	99	..	..	..	..
Greece [b]	2010	..	..	..	95	100	92	96	95	98	88	100	93	94	..	..	..	100	100	90	99	100	100	..	..	..	..
Hungary [b]	2010	..	..	..	92	100	92	92	92	95	87	93	89	90	..	..	..	88	99	90	87	99	95	..	..	..	..
Iceland [b]	2010	..	..	..	99	93	98	99	100	100	100	100	100	100	..	..	..	100	100	100	100	100	100	..	..	..	..
Ireland [b]	2010	..	..	..	99	99	97	96	95	99	97	100	93	98	..	..	..	100	100	94	97	100	97	..	..	..	..
Israel	2008	..	..	100	95	100	87	93	95	97	85	78	96	93	..	..	100	95	100	96	95	100	..	99	..	..	..
Italy [b]	2010	..	..	..	97	99	95	98	97	100	92	99	94	895	..	..	..	95	100	98	92	99	100	..	..	..	..
Latvia [b]	2010	..	..	..	95	99	96	96	94	99	90	97	95	96	..	..	..	100	100	97	98	99	97	..	..	..	..

Economy	Reference year	A Agriculture, hunting and forestry	B Fishing	C Mining and quarrying	D Manufacturing	E Electricity, gas and water supply	F Construction	G Wholesale and retail trade; repair of motor vehicles, motorcycles, etc.	G50 Sale, maintenance and repair of motor vehicles and motorcycles; etc.	G51 Wholesale trade and commission trade, except of motor vehicles and motorcycles	G52 Retail trade, except of motor vehicles and motorcycles; etc.	H Hotels and restaurants	I Transport, storage and communications	I60 Land transport; transport via pipelines	I61 Water transport	I62 Air transport	I63 Supporting and auxiliary transport activities; activities of travel agencies	I64 Post and telecommunications	J Financial intermediation	K70 Real estate activities	K71 Renting of machinery and equipment	K72 Computer and related activities	K73 Research and development	K74 Other business activities	M Education	N Health and social work	O Other community, social and personal service activities
Lithuania [b]	2010	:	:	:	98	100	98	97	96	98	95	97	93	92	:	:	-	100	98	100	96	100	100	:	:	:	:
Luxembourg [b]	2010	:	:	:	96	100	99	99	97	98	95	99	98	95	:	:	-	97	100	:	99	99	100	:	:	:	:
Malta [b]	2010	:	:	:	96	:	88	99	88	91	82	95	98	98	100	100	100	100	:	100	95	100	99	:	:	:	:
Netherlands [b]	2010	:	:	:	100	100	100	100	100	100	100	100	100	100	100	100	100	100	100	100	100	100	100	:	:	:	:
New Zealand	2008	84	92	94	98	100	98	97	97	99	94	91	99	98	:	:	:	98	99	91	99	99	100	98	100	98	96
Norway [b]	2010	:	:	:	98	100	100	99	96	100	93	100	95	96	:	:	:	100	100	100	95	99	99	:	:	:	:
Poland [b]	2010	:	:	:	97	100	97	98	95	98	91	95	98	95	:	:	:	98	100	100	95	99	98	:	:	:	:
Portugal [b]	2010	:	:	:	98	100	94	99	98	98	100	97	100	100	:	:	:	98	100	99	100	100	100	:	:	:	:
Romania [b]	2010	:	:	:	82	89	80	83	82	82	82	97	81	80	:	:	:	96	:	88	70	93	90	:	:	:	:
Slovakia [b]	2010	:	:	:	98	100	99	98	98	99	97	100	98	99	:	:	:	100	99	100	97	100	98	:	:	:	:
Slovenia [b]	2010	:	:	:	99	100	90	99	98	100	98	100	100	100	:	:	:	100	100	100	98	100	100	:	:	:	:
Spain [b]	2010	:	:	:	99	100	98	99	98	100	97	100	99	97	:	:	:	100	100	100	97	99	97	:	:	:	:
Sweden [b]	2010	:	:	:	99	100	96	98	96	99	96	97	93	90	:	:	:	95	100	100	97	99	97	:	:	:	:
United Kingdom [b]	2010	:	:	:	98	99	95	93	93	97	86	100	94	94	:	:	:	95	96	91	96	96	95	:	:	:	:
Developing economies																											
Brazil [d]	2009	:	:	:	98	:	98	98	98	:	:	88	98	:	:	:	:	:	:	:	:	:	:	:	:	:	96
Chile	2007	35	:	46	56	66	67	29	29	:	:	32	49	39	:	:	:	:	72	:	:	:	:	:	:	:	39
China, Hong Kong SAR [e]	2009	:	:	:	69	:	55	:	:	:	:	:	:	39	:	:	:	:	82	:	:	:	:	:	57	:	:
China, Macao SAR	2007	:	:	:	63	:	64	36	36	46	27	27	70	42	69	100	75	73	:	73	:	:	:	81	:	:	:
Colombia	2006	:	95	100	82	:	:	97	97	98	95	94	90	96	:	:	:	:	:	:	:	:	:	:	:	:	:
Cuba	2007	89	:	:	98	100	99	100	100	99	81	:	:	100	100	100	100	100	100	100	100	100	100	99	99	97	65
Egypt	2009	:	:	:	53	:	94	76	76	:	:	78	74	:	:	:	:	:	100	:	:	:	:	:	:	:	:

Column legend:
- A — Agriculture, hunting and forestry
- B — Fishing
- C — Mining and quarrying
- D — Manufacturing
- E — Electricity, gas and water supply
- F — Construction
- G — Wholesale and retail trade; repair of motor vehicles, motorcycles, etc.
- G50 — Sale, maintenance and repair of motor vehicles and motorcycles; etc.
- G51 — Wholesale trade and commission trade, except of motor vehicles and motorcycles
- G52 — Retail trade, except of motor vehicles and motorcycles; etc.
- H — Hotels and restaurants
- I — Transport, storage and communications
- I60 — Land transport; transport via pipelines
- I61 — Water transport
- I62 — Air transport
- I63 — Supporting and auxiliary transport activities; activities of travel agencies
- I64 — Post and telecommunications
- J — Financial intermediation
- K70 — Real estate activities
- K71 — Renting of machinery and equipment
- K72 — Computer and related activities
- K73 — Research and development
- K74 — Other business activities
- M — Education
- N — Health and social work
- O — Other community, social and personal service activities

Economy	Reference year	A	B	C	D	E	F	G	G50	G51	G52	H	I	I60	I61	I62	I63	I64	J	K70	K71	K72	K73	K74	M	N	O
Jordan	2008	14	:	55	12	100	47	12	12	29	12	14	72	16	100	100	83	100	99	47	16	99	100	71	:	40	12
Lesotho	2008	:	:	:	69	:	:	25	25	:	:	56	:	:	:	:	:	:	:	:	:	:	:	:	:	:	:
Mongolia	2006	:	0	50	39	53	53	23	23	26	18	34	51	42	50	91	51	64	32	31	32	71	75	54	74	42	43
Occupied Palestinian Territory	2009	:	:	:	23	:	67	21	21	:	:	:	65	:	:	:	:	:	84	:	:	:	:	:	:	:	52
Panama [g]	2006	78	:	100	74	92	92	81	81	77	87	55	85	65	90	96	93	97	100	67	91	100	100	94	88	90	87
Philippines	2008	66	55	88	89	97	99	82	82	91	74	86	90	84	82	100	90	92	96	100	93	100	100	96	97	91	84
Republic of Korea [f]	2008	64	:	:	64	:	78	:	:	70	43	24	20	:	:	:	:	:	97	:	:	:	:	:	62	:	:
Singapore	2009	100	:	:	82	75	76	75	75	:	:	51	75	:	:	:	:	:	86	76	34	97	98	92	85	88	56
Thailand	2008	:	:	:	14	:	39	26	26	45	23	22	22	17	:	:	79	:	:	35	:	90	:	76	:	100	13
Tunisia [h]	2009	:	:	97	76	100	89	89	89	:	:	62	96	:	:	:	:	:	99	91	87	:	99	:	100	91	97
Turkey [b]	2010	:	:	:	92	98	89	95	97	98	94	96	94	:	:	:	:	:	98	:	100	99	100	89	80	87	:
Uruguay	2007	:	:	:	91	100	:	95	95	94	94	87	96	97	100	90	94	100	:	:	:	100	100	:	:	:	:
Transition economies																											
Azerbaijan	2009	:	:	19	26	75	21	46	46	63	32	32	34	18	69	56	31	67	88	4	:	27	42	28	59	27	10
Kazakhstan	2008	:	:	:	77	:	75	76	76	:	:	82	82	:	:	:	:	:	87	:	:	:	:	:	:	:	95
Kyrgyzstan [i]	2009	86	50	94	95	96	96	97	97	98	94	98	96	93	:	100	94	98	100	90	100	94	97	99	98	100	91
Russian Federation [j]	2008	95	89	96	96	90	96	92	92	82	92	90	95	94	96	99	93	99	96	78	77	98	97	93	98	98	81
Serbia [k]	2007	:	:	:	94	:	90	85	85	:	90	96	100	100	:	:	:	100	:	100	:	100	:	:	:	:	100
The former Yugoslav Republic of Macedonia	2009	:	:	:	75	:	76	53	53	:	:	100	63	:	:	:	:	:	95	:	:	:	:	:	:	:	100

Notes:

a Data refer to the year ending 30 June 2006. As industry division data cannot be split by ISIC 60-63 a total is included for Transport and Storage in ISIC 60. No totals are available for ISIC G and I. No data are available for O as they are collected under two separate divisions Cultural and recreational services and Personal and other services.

b Data refer to NACE Rev 2 sectors C, D, E, F, G, I J, K64-66, L, N, J, M.

c Sector A includes fishing. Sector K includes real estate and rent, business services, other business activities, and international businesses. Public administration is not included.

d Estimates. Data refer to national projection for enterprises with more than 9 employees.

e Data refer to "establishments" rather than "enterprises".

f Sector A includes sectors A, B and C. Sector M includes sectors L, M, N, O and E.

g Preliminary figures.

h Enterprise totals also include public enterprises.

i Data include sector L75, Public administration.

j Sector A refers to 'Forestry and provision of services in this area' (NACE code 02); the sector M refers to 'Higher education' (code 803);   the sector O refers to 'Entertainment, Recreation, Arts and Sports' (code 92).

k Sector H includes NACE-Rev.1 Groups 55.1 and 55.2 - 'Hotels' and 'Camping sites and other provision of short stay accomodation'; sector I60 includes I60-63; sector K70 includes K70, 71, 73, 74; sector O includes O92.1 and 92.2 - 'Motion picture and Video activities' and 'Radio and television activities'.

Annex table II.7. Use of the Internet by type of activity, latest available reference year
Enterprises with 10 or more persons employed

Economy	Reference year	With a website	Receiving orders over the Internet	Placing orders over the Internet	Sending and receiving e-mail	Information about goods or services	Information from public authorities	Information searches or research	Internet banking or financial services	Internet banking	Accessing other financial services	Interacting with general government organizations	Providing customer services	Delivering products online	Other types of activity	Telephoning via the Internet/VoIP, or using videoconferencing	Instant messaging and bulletin boards	Staff training	Internal or external recruitment
		B5	B7	B8	B12a	B12 b i	B12 b ii	B12 b iii	B12 c	B12 c i	B12 c ii	B12 d	B12 e	B12 f	B12 g	B12 h	B12 i	B12 j	B12 k
Developed economies																			
Australia [a]	2007	61	31	56	:	:	:	:	:	89	:	81	:	:	:	:	:	35	:
Austria [b]	2008	80	14	33	:	:	71	:	:	85	:	81	5	:	:	:	:	30	:
Belgium [c]	2008	76	16	7	:	:	:	:	:	86	:	:	3	:	:	:	:	24	:
Bermuda	2006	43	6	24	:	:	:	:	:	:	:	:	:	:	:	:	:	:	:
Bulgaria [b]	2008	33	2	4	:	:	53	:	:	52	:	58	6	:	:	:	:	17	:
Canada	2007	70	13	65	:	:	:	:	:	:	:	59	:	:	:	:	:	:	:
Croatia	2009	57	23	31	:	:	56	:	:	84	:	66	:	:	:	:	:	29	:
Cyprus [b]	2008	49	7	14	:	:	63	:	:	55	:	73	2	:	:	:	:	35	:
Czech Republic [b]	2008	74	15	27	:	:	70	:	:	88	:	90	6	:	:	:	:	29	:
Denmark [b]	2008	87	20	38	:	:	86	:	:	94	:	77	8	:	:	:	:	28	:
Estonia [b]	2008	66	11	18	:	:	75	:	:	94	:	95	5	:	:	:	:	37	:
Finland [b]	2008	82	:	25	:	:	90	:	:	92	:	74	7	:	:	:	:	41	:
France [b]	2008	54	13	18	:	:	67	:	:	77	:	56	3	:	:	:	:	23	:
Germany [d]	2008	77	:	:	:	:	47	:	:	75	:	78	5	:	:	:	:	14	:
Greece [b]	2008	57	6	9	:	:	64	:	:	62	:	60	7	:	:	:	:	45	:
Hungary [b]	2008	48	4	7	:	:	56	:	:	70	:	91	2	:	:	:	:	16	:
Iceland [b]	2008	63	21	35	:	:	89	:	:	99	:	91	1	:	:	:	:	20	:
Ireland [b]	2008	65	26	54	:	:	84	:	:	85	:	41	3	:	:	:	:	37	:
Israel	2008	61	47	43	89	79	77	:	:	86	56	82	33	:	:	26	27	16	44
Italy [b]	2008	58	3	12	:	:	74	:	:	86	:	:	12	:	:	:	:	17	:

Economy	Reference year	Proportion of enterprises:			Proportion of enterprises using the Internet for:														
		With a website (B5)	Receiving orders over the Internet (B7)	Placing orders over the Internet (B8)	Sending and receiving e-mail (B12a)	Information about goods or services (B12bi)	Information from public authorities (B12bii)	Information searches or research (B12biii)	Internet banking or financial services (B12c)	Internet banking (B12ci)	Acquiring other financial services (B12cii)	Interacting with general government organizations (B12d)	Providing customer services (B12e)	Delivering products online (B12f)	Other types of activity (B12g)	Telephoning via the Internet/VoIP, or using videoconferencing (B12h)	Instant messaging and bulletin boards (B12i)	Staff training (B12j)	Internal or external recruitment (B12k)
Japan e	2009	92	23	40	:	:	:	:	:	:	:	:	:	:	:	:	:	:	:
Latvia b	2008	42	6	9	:	:	51	:	:	83	:	55	5	:	:	:	:	30	:
Lithuania b	2008	55	22	25	:	:	83	:	:	91	:	86	15	:	:	:	:	54	:
Luxembourg b	2008	65	10	23	:	:	82	:	:	76	:	90	10	:	:	:	:	23	:
Malta b	2008	58	13	13	:	:	72	:	:	74	:	74	4	:	:	:	:	26	:
Netherlands b	2008	85	27	40	:	:	77	:	:	88	:	85	4	:	:	:	:	16	:
New Zealand	2008	64	42	66	:	:	69	:	:	86	:	80	65	:	:	:	:	24	44
Norway b	2008	73	30	44	:	:	70	:	:	85	:	76	6	:	:	:	:	36	:
Poland b	2008	57	8	11	:	:	56	:	:	75	:	68	5	:	:	:	:	14	:
Portugal b	2008	46	19	20	:	:	67	:	:	75	:	75	13	:	:	:	:	33	:
Romania b	2008	27	4	4	:	:	37	:	:	48	:	39	3	:	:	:	:	41	:
Slovakia b	2008	73	5	9	:	:	82	:	:	91	:	88	9	:	:	:	:	48	:
Slovenia b	2008	71	8	15	:	:	85	:	:	92	:	88	11	:	:	:	:	41	:
Spain b	2008	55	10	19	:	:	59	:	:	82	:	64	5	:	:	:	:	33	:
Sweden b	2008	86	19	50	:	:	76	:	:	90	:	78	7	:	:	:	:	26	:
United Kingdom b	2008	76	32	47	:	:	60	:	:	75	:	64	2	:	:	:	:	24	:
Developing economies																			
Brazil f	2009	53	41	51	91	86	60	:	:	72	:	31	44	10	:	19	50	29	:
China, Hong Kong SAR h	2009	51	6	25	86	85	77	:	:	34	22	:	15	50	:	7	:	:	:
China, Macao SAR	2007	:	19	24	:	56	:	:	73	:	:	:	19	:	:	:	:	:	:
Colombia g	2006	44	39	37	86	60	49	54	10	:	:	51	45	10	:	:	:	:	:
Cuba i	2007	26	2	3	70	70	70	70	:	:	:	:	39	2	70	:	:	:	:
Egypt	2009	22	2	2	29	24	13	:	:	8	:	6	16	6	:	:	:	:	:
Jordan	2008	50	5	7	67	72	25	:	:	:	:	:	26	5	:	26	:	:	:

Economy	Reference year	Proportion of enterprises:			Proportion of enterprises using the Internet for:														
		With a website	Receiving orders over the Internet	Placing orders over the Internet	Sending and receiving e-mail	Information about goods or services	Information from public authorities	Information searches or research	Internet banking or financial services	Internet banking	Accessing other financial services	Interacting with general government organizations	Providing customer services	Delivering products online	Other types of activity	Telephoning via the Internet/VoIP or using videoconferencing	Instant messaging and bulletin boards	Staff training	Internal or external recruitment
		B5	B7	B8	B12a	B12 b i	B12 b ii	B12 b iii	B12 c	B12 c i	B12 c ii	B12 d	B12 e	B12 f	B12 g	B12 h	B12 i	B12 j	B12 k
Lesotho	2008	22	:	:	44	44	:	:	56	:	14	:	:	:	:	:	:	:	:
Mauritius	2008	44	35	34	:	:	:	:	:	:	:	:	:	:	:	:	:	:	:
Occupied Palestinian Territory	2009	38	19	:	47	15	:	:	:	3	:	:	7	:	:	:	:	:	:
Panama [j]	2006	:	31	35	78	65	54	49	56	:	:	29	31	:	56	:	:	:	:
Qatar	2008	64	61	47	84	76	76	:	:	48	:	57	49	:	:	:	:	:	:
Republic of Korea	2008	55	6	42	91	73	73	:	:	75	20	69	29	15	:	14	:	20	26
Senegal	2008	35	3	12	89	78	57	:	:	52	:	:	49	:	:	:	:	:	:
Singapore [k]	2009	60	41	42	88	85	79	:	:	62	:	85	:	36	:	29	33	18	41
Suriname	2006	17	:	:	:	:	:	:	:	:	:	:	:	:	:	:	:	:	:
Thailand [l]	2008	38	10	11	57	64	:	:	:	14	:	18	29	4	:	:	:	:	:
Tunisia [m]	2009	30	10	11	63	59	48	:	:	29	:	30	3	5	:	19	:	5	5
Turkey	2009	52	9	15	:	:	56	:	:	68	:	5	:	:	:	:	:	:	:
United Arab Emirates	2008	:	:	:	86	83	71	:	:	54	:	62	48	25	:	:	:	:	:
Transition economies																			
Azerbaijan	2009	6	1	1	22	10	12	:	:	13	:	22	4	2	:	1	4	1	1
Kazakhstan	2008	7	14	15	49	27	24	:	:	20	:	20	39	2	:	:	:	:	8
Kyrgyzstan	2009	12	:	:	33	:	2	:	:	2	:	2	:	3	:	:	:	:	:
Russian Federation [o]	2008	25	12	18	73	49	39	:	:	20	:	53	:	4	:	13	:	22	19
Serbia [p]	2007	53	15	17	:	:	44	47	56	:	:	52	:	:	:	:	:	:	:
The former Yugoslav Republic of Macedonia [n]	2009	48	4	7	:	:	63	:	:	61	:	65	:	:	:	:	:	33	:

Notes:

a   Data refer to year ending 30 June 2007.

b   Data refer to the enterprises using the Internet, EDI or other networks for: 1- sales or purchases (at least 1% of electronic sales or purchases); 2 - banking and financial services; 3 - electronically sharing information with customers (info on demand forecasts, inventories, production plans, progress of deliveries, etc.). B12b.ii - Including getting information from government.

c   Data refer to the enterprises using the Internet, EDI or other networks for: 1- sales or purchases (at least 1% of electronic sales or purchases);
2 - banking and financial services; 3 - electronically sharing information with customers (info on demand forecasts, inventories, production plans, progress of deliveries, etc.).

d   Data refer to the enterprises using the Internet, EDI or other networks for: 1- sales or purchases (at least 1% of electronic sales or purchases); 2 - banking and financial services. B12b.ii - Including getting information from government.

e   Data refer to the sample and have not been extrapolated to the target population. Data refer to 100+ employees.

f   Estimates. Data refer to national projection for enterprises with more than 9 employees. They include enterprises using the Internet for accessing other financial services.

g   Use of the Internet for staff training refers to training and education.

    Includes search for information of all kinds.

h   Data refer to "establishments" rather than "enterprises". B12b.i refers using the Internet for: 1 - Sourcing of general information; 2 - Receipt of goods, services or information; and 3 - Making enquiries to business partners. Includes transactions with Government organizations/public authorities. B12h refers to video conference only.

i   Estimates.

j   Preliminary figures.

k   B12c.i - No distinction between Internet banking and accessing other financial services. Data refer to enterprises which have "used the Internet for banking and financial services". B12j - refers to enterprises that have "used the Internet for formal education or training activities". B12k - refers to enterprises that have "used the Internet for finding information about employment opportunities (recruitment and search)".

l   B12b - includes b.i and b.ii; and B12c -Includes c.i and c.ii.

m   Data refer to public administration and/or enterprises. Enterprises using banking or financial services online.

n   Includes enterprises that used the Internet for Internet banking or other financial services.

o   Data refer to enterprises using the Internet for payments.

p   Data refer to enterprises using the Internet for market monitoring (e.g. prices). B12b.ii - Including getting information from government.

LIST OF SELECTED PUBLICATIONS
IN THE AREA OF SCIENCE, TECHNOLOGY,
AND ICT FOR DEVELOPMENT

A. Flagship reports

Information Economy Report 2011: ICTs as an Enabler for Private Sector Development. United Nations publication.
Sales no. E.11.II.D.6. New York and Geneva.

Technology and Innovation Report 2010: Enhancing Food Security in Africa through Science, Technology and Innovation. United Nations publication. UNCTAD/TIR/2009. New York and Geneva.

Information Economy Report 2010: ICTs, Enterprises and Poverty Alleviation. United Nations publication.
Sales no. E.10.II.D.17. New York and Geneva. October.

Information Economy Report 2009: Trends and Outlook in Turbulent Times. United Nations publication.
Sales no. E.09.II.D.18. New York and Geneva. October.

Information Economy Report 2007–2008: Science and Technology for Development – The New Paradigm of ICT.
United Nations publication. Sales no. E.07.II.D.13. New York and Geneva.

Information Economy Report 2006: The Development Perspective. United Nations publication.
Sales no. E.06.II.D.8. New York and Geneva.

Information Economy Report 2005: E-commerce and Development. United Nations publication.
Sales no. E.05.II.D.19. New York and Geneva.

E-Commerce and Development Report 2004. United Nations publication. New York and Geneva.

E-Commerce and Development Report 2003. United Nations publication. Sales no. E.03.II.D.30.
New York and Geneva.

E-Commerce and Development Report 2002. United Nations publication. New York and Geneva.

E-Commerce and Development Report 2001. United Nations publication. Sales no. E.01.II.D.30.
New York and Geneva.

B. ICT Policy Reviews

ICT Policy Review of Egypt. United Nations publication (2011). New York and Geneva.

C. Science, Technology and Innovation Policy Reviews

Science, Technology and Innovation Policy Review of Peru. United Nations publication.
UNCTAD/DTL/STICT/2010/2. New York and Geneva.

Science, Technology and Innovation Policy Review of Ghana. United Nations publication.
UNCTAD/DTL/STICT/2009/8. New York and Geneva.

Science, Technology and Innovation Policy Review of Lesotho. United Nations publication.
UNCTAD/DTL/STICT/2009/7. New York and Geneva.

Science, Technology and Innovation Policy Review of Mauritania. United Nations publication.
UNCTAD/DTL/STICT/2009/6. New York and Geneva.

Science, Technology and Innovation Policy Review of Angola. United Nations publication.
UNCTAD/SDTE/STICT/2008/1. New York and Geneva.

Science, Technology and Innovation Policy Review: the Islamic Republic of Iran.
United Nations publication. UNCTAD/ITE/IPC/2005/7. New York and Geneva.

Investment and Innovation Policy Review of Ethiopia. United Nations publication.
UNCTAD/ITE/IPC/Misc.4. New York and Geneva.

Science, Technology and Innovation Policy Review: Colombia. United Nations publication.
Sales no. E.99.II.D.13. New York and Geneva.

Science, Technology and Innovation Policy Review: Jamaica. United Nations publication.
Sales no. E.98.II.D.7. New York and Geneva.

D. Other publications

Implementing WSIS Outcomes: Experience to Date and Prospects for the Future. United Nations Commission on Science and Technology for Development. United Nations publication. UNCTAD/DTL/STICT/2011/3. New York and Geneva.

Water for Food: Innovative Water Management Technologies for Food Security and Poverty Alleviation. UNCTAD Current Studies on Science, Technology and Innovation. United Nations publication. UNCTAD/DTL/STICT/2011/2. New York and Geneva.

Measuring the Impacts of Information and Communication Technology for Development. UNCTAD Current Studies on Science, Technology and Innovation. United Nations publication. UNCTAD/DTL/STICT/2011/1. New York and Geneva.

Estudio sobre las Perspectivas de la Harmonización de la Ciberlegislación en Centroamérica y el Caribe. United Nations publication. UNCTAD/DTL/STICT/2009/3. New York and Geneva. (Spanish only).

Study on Prospects for Harmonizing Cyberlegislation in Latin America. UNCTAD publication. UNCTAD/DTL/STICT/2009/1. New York and Geneva. (In English and Spanish.)

Financing Mechanisms for Information and Communication Technologies for Development. UNCTAD Current Studies on Science, Technology and Innovation. United Nations publication. UNCTAD/DTL/STICT/2009/5. New York and Geneva.

Renewable Energy Technologies for Rural Development. UNCTAD Current Studies on Science, Technology and Innovation. United Nations publication. UNCTAD/DTL/STICT/2009/4. New York and Geneva.

Manual for the Production of Statistics on the Information Economy 2009 Revised Edition. United Nations publication. UNCTAD/SDTE/ECB/2007/2/REV.1. New York and Geneva.

WSIS Follow-up Report 2008. United Nations publication. UNCTAD/DTL/STICT/2008/1. New York and Geneva.

Measuring the Impact of ICT Use in Business: the Case of Manufacturing in Thailand. United Nations publication. Sales no. E.08.II.D.13. New York and Geneva.

World Information Society Report 2007: Beyond WSIS. Joint United Nations and ITU publication. Geneva.

World Information Society Report 2006. Joint United Nations and ITU publication. Geneva.

The Digital Divide: ICT Diffusion Index 2005. United Nations publication. New York and Geneva.

The Digital Divide: ICT Development Indices 2004. United Nations publication. New York and Geneva.

Africa's Technology Gap: Case Studies on Kenya, Ghana, Tanzania and Uganda. United Nations publication. UNCTAD/ITE/IPC/Misc.13. New York and Geneva.

The Biotechnology Promise: Capacity-Building for Participation of Developing Countries in the Bioeconomy. United Nations publication. UNCTAD/ITE/IPC/2004/2. New York and Geneva.

Information and Communication Technology Development Indices. United Nations publication. Sales no. E.03.II.D.14. New York and Geneva.

Investment and Technology Policies for Competitiveness: Review of Successful Country Experiences. United Nations publication. UNCTAD/ITE/IPC/2003/2. New York and Geneva.

Electronic Commerce and Music Business Development in Jamaica: A Portal to the New Economy? United Nations publication. Sales no. E.02.II.D.17. New York and Geneva.

Changing Dynamics of Global Computer Software and Services Industry: Implications for Developing Countries. United Nations publication. Sales no. E.02.II.D.3. New York and Geneva.

Partnerships and Networking in Science and Technology for Development. United Nations publication. Sales no. E.02.II.D.5. New York and Geneva.

Transfer of Technology for Successful Integration into the Global Economy: A Case Study of Embraer in Brazil. United Nations publication. UNCTAD/ITE/IPC/Misc.20. New York and Geneva.

Transfer of Technology for Successful Integration into the Global Economy: A Case Study of the South African Automotive Industry. United Nations publication. UNCTAD/ITE/IPC/Misc.21. New York and Geneva.

Transfer of Technology for the Successful Integration into the Global Economy: A Case Study of the Pharmaceutical Industry in India. United Nations publication. UNCTAD/ITE/IPC/Misc.22. New York and Geneva.

Coalition of Resources for Information and Communication Technologies. United Nations publication. UNCTAD/ITE/TEB/13. New York and Geneva.

Key Issues in Biotechnology. United Nations publication. UNCTAD/ITE/TEB/10. New York and Geneva.

An Assault on Poverty: Basic Human Needs, Science and Technology. Joint publication with IDRC. ISBN 0-88936-800-7.

Compendium of International Arrangements on Transfer of Technology: Selected Instruments. United Nations publication. Sales no. E.01.II.D.28. New York and Geneva.

E. Publications by the Partnership on Measuring ICT for Development

Core ICT Indicators 2010. ITU. Geneva.

The Global Information Society: A Statistical View 2008. United Nations publication. Santiago.

Measuring ICT: The Global Status of ICT Indicators. Partnership on Measuring ICT for Development. United Nations ICT Task Force. New York.

F. Issues in Brief

Measuring the information economy: How ICT contributes to development. Issues in Brief No. 7: UNCTAD/IAOS/MISC/2005/13.

E-Tourism in developing countries: More links, fewer leaks. Issues in Brief No. 6. UNCTAD/IAOS/MISC/2005/11.

ICT and e-commerce: An opportunity for developing countries. Issues in Brief No. 1. UNCTAD/ISS/MISC/2003/6.

READERSHIP SURVEY

Information Economy Report 2011: ICTs as an Enabler for Private Sector Development

In order to improve the quality of this report and other publications of the Science, Technology and ICT Branch of UNCTAD, we welcome the views of our readers on this publication. It would be greatly appreciated if you would complete the following questionnaire and return it to:

ICT Analysis Section, Office E-7075
Science, Technology and ICT Branch
Division on Technology and Logistics
United Nations
Palais des Nations,
CH-1211, Geneva, Switzerland
Fax: 41 22 917 00 50
ICT4D@unctad.org

1. Name and address of respondent (optional)

....

....

....

2. Which of the following best describes your area of work?

Government ministry (please specify)	☐	Not-for-profit organization	☐
National statistics office	☐	Public enterprise	☐
Telecommunication regulatory authority	☐	Academic or research institution	☐
Private enterprise	☐	Media	☐
International organization	☐	Other (please specify)	☐

3. In which country do you work? ....

4. What is your assessment of the contents of this publication?

Excellent ☐
Good ☐
Adequate ☐
Poor ☐

5. How useful is this publication to your work?

Very useful	☐
Somewhat useful	☐
Irrelevant	☐

6. Please indicate the three things you liked best about this publication.

a) ....

b) ....

c) ....

7. Please indicate the three things you liked least about this publication.

a) ....

b) ....

c) ....

8. What additional aspects would you like future editions of this report to cover:

....

....

....

9. Other comments:

....

....

....

READERSHIP SURVEY

Information Economy Report 2011: ICTs as an Enabler for Private Sector Development

In order to improve the quality of this report and other publications of the Science, Technology and ICT Branch of UNCTAD, we welcome the views of our readers on this publication. It would be greatly appreciated if you would complete the following questionnaire and return it to:

ICT Analysis Section, Office E-7075
Science, Technology and ICT Branch
Division on Technology and Logistics
United Nations
Palais des Nations,
CH-1211, Geneva, Switzerland
Fax: 41 22 917 00 50
ICT4D@unctad.org

1. Name and address of respondent (optional)

....
....
....

2. Which of the following best describes your area of work?

Government ministry (please specify)	☐	Not-for-profit organization	☐
National statistics office	☐	Public enterprise	☐
Telecommunication regulatory authority	☐	Academic or research institution	☐
Private enterprise	☐	Media	☐
International organization	☐	Other (please specify)	☐

3. In which country do you work? ....

4. What is your assessment of the contents of this publication?

Excellent	☐
Good	☐
Adequate	☐
Poor	☐

5. How useful is this publication to your work?

           Very useful   ☐

  Somewhat useful   ☐

           Irrelevant   ☐

6. Please indicate the three things you liked best about this publication.

a) ....

b) ....

c) ....

7. Please indicate the three things you liked least about this publication.

a) ....

b) ....

c) ....

8. What additional aspects would you like future editions of this report to cover:

....

....

....

9. Other comments:

....

....

....

READERSHIP SURVEY

Information Economy Report 2011: ICTs as an Enabler for Private Sector Development

In order to improve the quality of this report and other publications of the Science, Technology and ICT Branch of UNCTAD, we welcome the views of our readers on this publication. It would be greatly appreciated if you would complete the following questionnaire and return it to:

ICT Analysis Section, Office E-7075
Science, Technology and ICT Branch
Division on Technology and Logistics
United Nations
Palais des Nations,
CH-1211, Geneva, Switzerland
Fax: 41 22 917 00 50
ICT4D@unctad.org

1. Name and address of respondent (optional)

....

....

....

2. Which of the following best describes your area of work?

Government ministry (please specify)	☐	Not-for-profit organization	☐
National statistics office	☐	Public enterprise	☐
Telecommunication regulatory authority	☐	Academic or research institution	☐
Private enterprise	☐	Media	☐
International organization	☐	Other (please specify)	☐

3. In which country do you work? ....

4. What is your assessment of the contents of this publication?

Excellent ☐
Good ☐
Adequate ☐
Poor ☐

5. How useful is this publication to your work?

Very useful   □
Somewhat useful   □
Irrelevant   □

6. Please indicate the three things you liked best about this publication.

a) ....

b) ....

c) ....

7. Please indicate the three things you liked least about this publication.

a) ....

b) ....

c) ....

8. What additional aspects would you like future editions of this report to cover:

....

....

....

9. Other comments:

....

....

....